Approaches to Teaching Shakespeare's *Romeo and Juliet*

SECOND EDITION

Approaches to Teaching Shakespeare's *Romeo and Juliet*

SECOND EDITION

Edited by

Joseph M. Ortiz

The Modern Language Association of America
New York   2024

The MLA office is located on the island known as Mannahatta (Manhattan) in Lenapehoking, the homeland of the Lenape people. The MLA pays respect to the original stewards of this land and to the diverse and vibrant Native communities that continue to thrive in New York City.

Approaches to Teaching World Literature 174
ISSN 1059-1133

Library of Congress Cataloging-in-Publication Data

Names: Ortiz, Joseph M., 1972- editor.
Title: Approaches to teaching Shakespeare's Romeo and Juliet / edited by Joseph M. Ortiz.
Description: Second edition. | New York : The Modern Language Association of America, 2024. | Series: Approaches to teaching world literature, 10591133 ; 174 | Includes bibliographical references.
Identifiers: LCCN 2023052606 (print) | LCCN 2023052607 (ebook) | ISBN 9781603296472 (hardcover) | ISBN 9781603296489 (paperback) | ISBN 9781603296496 (EPUB)
Subjects: LCSH: Shakespeare, William, 1564-1616. Romeo and Juliet. | Shakespeare, William, 1564-1616—Study and teaching.
Classification: LCC PR2831 .A89 2024 (print) | LCC PR2831 (ebook) | DDC 822.3/3—dc23/eng/20231129
LC record available at https://lccn.loc.gov/2023052606
LC ebook record available at https://lccn.loc.gov/2023052607

CONTENTS

Acknowledgments   ix

Preface   xi

PART ONE: MATERIALS

Editions   3

Contextual Readings   6

Film and Text Adaptations   8

Critical Readings   11

Pedagogical Resources   16

PART TWO: APPROACHES

Introduction   21
  Joseph M. Ortiz

Age, Authority, Marriage

"Get Her Heart": Reading *Romeo and Juliet* through Early Modern
    Ideas of Marriage   29
  Robert Matz

Juliet's Age and Questioning Authority in *Romeo and Juliet*   37
  Peter C. Herman

Individualism and the Character Turn in *Romeo and Juliet*   43
  Meghan C. Andrews

Gender and Sexuality

An Intersectional Approach to Girls and Girlhoods in Shakespeare's
    Verona   50
  Ariane M. Balizet

Juliet and Girl Power   58
  Natalie K. Eschenbaum

Queering *Romeo and Juliet* with Film Adaptations   65
  Anthony Guy Patricia

Considering Genre

Rediscovering the Familiar: Comedy in *Romeo and Juliet*   72
   Stephanie Pietros

"Love at First Sonnet": Romeo and Juliet's Collaborative Sonnet
   in Context   78
   Joshua Reid

Textual and Performance Histories

Editing *Romeo and Juliet* in the General Education
   Shakespeare Course   86
   Rebecca Olson

Benvolio Must Die: Q1's "Conceited" *Romeo and Juliet*   93
   Sarah Neville

Teaching *Romeo and Juliet* with Cue Scripts   102
   Marguerite A. Tassi

The High School Classroom

Scene Variations: *Romeo and Juliet* in the High School Classroom   111
   Abbey Bachmann

So You Already "Know" *Romeo and Juliet*? How to Capitalize
   on Students' Familiarity with the Play   119
   Mary T. Christel

Intersections with Race Studies

Romeo and Juliet in a Course on Shakespeare and Race   128
   Maya Mathur

Dancing with the Queen of Sheba: *Romeo and Juliet*, Ballet,
   and Race Studies   135
   Jehbreal Muhammad Jackson and Julia Reinhard Lupton

Shakespeare and Latinidades

Not-So-Ancient Grudges: Grounding *Romeo and Juliet* in
   the Histories of the US-Mexico Borderlands   144
   Kathryn Vomero Santos

Erasing for Inclusion: *Romeo and Juliet* at Hispanic-Serving
   Institutions   151
   Jonathan Burton

Diversifying Fair Verona: Shakespeare in Multilingual Classrooms   161
   Robin Alfriend Kello and Rhonda Sharrah

Notes on Contributors   169

Survey Participants   173

Works Cited   175

ACKNOWLEDGMENTS

I would like to thank James Hatch, MLA senior acquisitions editor, for his unflagging support and encouragement of this project from its inception. I also want to thank the MLA Publications Committee and the anonymous readers who gave their thoughtful responses to the book proposal and completed manuscript. Their keen insights and suggestions offered helpful guidance throughout the various stages of the project. Erika Suffern expertly shepherded this book during the final stages of publication. I also want to thank my colleagues and students at the State University of New York, Brockport, and at the University of Texas, El Paso. They made the experience of teaching Shakespeare an enjoyable and rewarding one, and together they all made me a better teacher. Finally, I want to thank my husband, Paul Hinkle, whose love and support have made me a better person.

PREFACE

In one of its popular *YouTube* videos, the renowned Second City theater group features a short, punchy satire of Shakespeare's *Romeo and Juliet*. The video is part of the group's "Sassy Gay Friend" series, in which the writer and comedian Brian Gallivan, a sassy gay man, appears in front of famous women in literature and history and curtly instructs them to take a different course of action. As might be expected, his take on *Romeo and Juliet* focuses on the scene of Juliet's suicide at the end of the play. Gallivan's character appears in the middle of Juliet's "O happy dagger" speech and grabs her arm as she is about to kill herself. He proceeds to give her a snippy lecture on the stupidity of her response to Romeo's death: "You love him? You met him Sunday. *It's barely Thursday morning.* Slow down, crazy!" He also points out some of the other bad decisions she has already made during the week, such as taking "a roofie from a priest."

As a satirical sketch, the video is very entertaining, but more striking are the thousands of comments posted in response. The vast majority are from high school and college students, some who are preparing to read the play and some who have already read it. It is clear that Gallivan's satire is fully intelligible to students regardless of grade level and regardless of whether they have read the play. The comments on the *YouTube* page repeatedly express gleeful amusement at the sensicalness of Gallivan's observations, which mirror the commenters' own instinctive reactions to the events of the play. They are happy to see their ideas validated by a professional actor whose theatrical knowledge is greater than their own, and this sense of affirmation makes them feel a little more comfortable with bringing their ideas into the classroom. One student commenter reported that while writing an essay in class on the true cause of Romeo's and Juliet's deaths, a classmate gave as his answer "severe lack of a sassy gay friend."

The Second City video and its reception on *YouTube* encapsulate an important fact about the experience of reading and teaching *Romeo and Juliet*. While no work of literature exists in a vacuum, this particular play is an extreme case. A student who reads *Romeo and Juliet* in the twenty-first century inhabits a culture that is saturated with citations and adaptations of the play, making it nearly impossible to study the work without coming across various analogues and commentaries, some more insightful than others. The contributors to this volume are well attuned to this fact, and they devise approaches to the play cognizant of the media landscape that their students navigate on a daily basis. Moreover, the contributors not only acknowledge this reality but in many cases take advantage of it to find pedagogical value in the anachronisms and appropriations that shape their students' experience of the play. For example, while an earlier generation of students might have needed some guidance to see Shakespeare as critiquing religious authority through the figure of the friar, students today are more likely to take a perspective that sees Juliet "taking a roofie from a priest."

Other modern takes can also lead to critical insights about the play and about the social problems that literature classes are increasingly expected to address.

Most of the essays in this volume were written during the height of the COVID-19 pandemic in the United States, though they were planned beforehand. While the essays do not (with a couple of exceptions) specifically address the challenges of teaching during the pandemic, they reflect in many ways the experience of teaching virtually during challenging circumstances. For example, the Materials section does not contain a separate Digital Resources section, in large part because the vast majority of the texts discussed are available in digital form—a trend that was accelerated by the pandemic and that is expected to continue. Many of the other sections and essays also move comfortably between print, web-based, and other media resources. It is my hope that the approaches to teaching Shakespeare's *Romeo and Juliet* described in this volume generate further strategies for developing the kind of adaptability and responsiveness required for the twenty-first-century classroom.

Part One

MATERIALS

Editions

Unlike most other Shakespeare plays, *Romeo and Juliet* is regularly taught in high school, college, and graduate literature classes. The choice of an edition is thus highly dependent on the education level of the students and the objectives of the course. High school teachers and college instructors of introductory literature courses and courses for non–English majors typically prefer single editions that incorporate helpful reading aids, such as modernized spelling and easily readable glosses. Instructors of advanced undergraduate and graduate Shakespeare courses are more likely to favor complete editions that include information about the play's textual history as well as introductions or essays that cover the play's historical context and performance history. Notably, in the survey of instructors of *Romeo and Juliet* conducted by the MLA for this volume, the most frequently cited reason for choosing a specific edition—regardless of the type of course—was cost. This likely reflects an awareness of the economic challenges students face as well as the growing need to make Shakespeare more accessible to students from underrepresented groups.

As expected, the survey found that instructors of Shakespeare classes for English majors and graduate Shakespeare classes often encourage their students to buy a complete edition, even if they are only assigning a few of the plays, on the grounds that students will likely need it in the future. Instructors who use a complete edition most often cited *The Norton Shakespeare*, which has been significantly revised for the third edition (Greenblatt et al.). Whereas the first two editions use what is generally known as the Oxford Shakespeare (edited by Stanley Wells and Gary Taylor) for the text of the plays, the new edition features a newly edited text overseen by Suzanne Gossett and Gordon McMullan. Most instructors will not be concerned with the minor differences in the new *Romeo and Juliet* text (most glosses and footnotes have been retained, as has the introduction to the play by Stephen Greenblatt), and they may appreciate the expanded discussion of the play's textual history and the added section on relevant films (which, to its credit, includes a number of films outside the American mainstream, such as the Chinese film *Qing ren jie* [*A Time to Love*]). Instructors who teach online or who use digital editions—a practice that was vastly accelerated by the COVID-19 pandemic—may be especially interested in Norton's accompanying digital edition of the plays. The digital edition includes the same text and paratextual material as the print edition along with several additional features such as the first and second quarto versions of the play (the print edition uses only Q1) and a pop-up window option that allows readers to view a facsimile image of the corresponding page in the original quarto text. The print edition has the option of being purchased as two volumes (early and late plays) or four volumes (comedies, tragedies, histories, romances, and poems).

Another complete edition used by survey respondents is *The Bedford Shakespeare*, edited by Russ McDonald and Lena Cowen Orlin. In addition to a readable text with useful and unobtrusive glosses, this edition features short essays on various topics (e.g., "Empire," "Law," "Race") and pithy notes and illustrations interspersed within the playtext. For example, act 2, scene 4 of *Romeo and Juliet* is illustrated with a photograph of David Tennant as Romeo in a 2000 Royal Shakespeare Company (RSC) production; the image is used to emblematize the "homosocial realm that Romeo relinquishes in giving himself to Juliet" (McDonald and Orlin 300). Such features made the edition especially attractive to respondents who regularly teach the play to education majors. *The Complete Pelican Shakespeare*, edited by Stephen Orgel and A. R. Braunmuller, offers a good compromise between affordability and convenience for college-level courses. It includes a moderately (though somewhat awkwardly) glossed text of the plays and introductions that are appropriately tailored to college students. Peter Holland's introduction to *Romeo and Juliet* in this edition approaches the well-trodden topic of adaptation and revision through an entertaining discussion of David Garrick's eighteenth-century changes to the play.

Other editions used by respondents are now either out of print or difficult to find. *The Riverside Shakespeare*, edited by G. Blakemore Evans, was the most popular complete edition when the MLA first published a teaching volume on *Romeo and Juliet*, but it is no longer available. Not surprisingly, no respondents reported using *The New Oxford Shakespeare*, edited by Gary Taylor and colleagues—a work that has been widely criticized for its delicate paper and weighty bulkiness, which make it impractical for student use—despite its much publicized appearance in 2016. An online edition is available as part of *Oxford Scholarly Editions Online*, but this requires an expensive institutional subscription. Although the second edition of *The RSC Shakespeare: Complete Works*, edited by Jonathan Bate and Eric Rasmussen, appeared too late to be included in the survey, it is likely to be a popular choice in the future, especially for instructors interested in theatrical approaches to the plays.

Many instructors favor a stand-alone edition of the play, even in Shakespeare courses, in large part because of their inexpensiveness and portability. Among these, the most popular is the Folger Shakespeare Library edition edited by Barbara A. Mowat and Paul Werstine (Shakespeare, *Romeo* [Mowat and Werstine]). This edition boasts a number of features that make it attractive to non–English majors and students with little experience reading Shakespeare, such as short summaries of each scene and ample explanations of words and phrases on facing pages. For those wishing to venture into criticism of the play, the updated edition includes an essay by Gail Kern Paster, entitled "A Modern Perspective," that discusses the play's historical originality in "privileging" individual desire and identity. The edition also includes a generously annotated bibliography of nineteen essays and books covering topics from early modern English theater history to the play's construction of masculinity.

Several instructors cited the Arden Shakespeare (Bloomsbury) edition of *Romeo and Juliet* edited by René Weis, which boasts an unusually copious amount of paratextual material, even for Arden's standards (Shakespeare, *Romeo* [Weis]). Instructors interested in performance and textual history will find much to learn from the 116-page introduction, which includes a substantial discussion of Shakespeare's primary source for the play, Arthur Brooke's 1562 poem "The Tragical History of Romeus and Juliet." Additionally, one of the edition's four appendices offers a facsimile of the entire first quarto of *Romeo and Juliet*.

The Norton Critical Edition edited by Gordon McMullan likely appeared too late to be reflected in the survey responses, but it also features a generous amount of paratextual reading aids (Shakespeare, *Romeo* [McMullan]). In addition to a three-hundred-line excerpt from Brooke's "Romeus and Juliet" (roughly a tenth of the poem), excerpts from six other early modern versions of the story are included. Like other Norton single-work editions, a good part of the volume is taken up by a representative set of critical essays. A few of the usual suspects are here—Susan Snyder's foundational essay on genre in *Romeo and Juliet*, Gayle Whittier's essay on the play's rehearsal of Petrarchan lyric—but also included are reflective essays by the actors Niamh Cusack and David Tennant as well as an excerpt from Baz Luhrmann and Craig Pearce's script for the 1996 film version. An up-to-date bibliography further makes the Norton edition an attractive option for graduate courses or advanced undergraduate courses with a research component.

Instructors who teach the play in high school or general education courses are typically less concerned with the amount of introductory or critical material in editions of the play, according to the survey. They highly value a readable text with practical glosses and annotations, and they also often cited portability and cost as factors in their selection of a text. By far the most popular edition in this category was the Pelican Shakespeare volume edited by Peter Holland (Shakespeare, *Romeo* [Holland]). This edition offers a concise introduction that discusses the theatrical conditions of the play's earliest performances and a short essay on the challenges of editing Shakespeare's plays. Holland's introduction is clear, if somewhat conventional, insofar as it interprets the play as a representation of the conflict between individual desire and social structures. Some respondents also reported using the similarly readable yet old-fashioned Signet Classic edition, now distributed by Penguin Random House (Shakespeare, *Romeo* [Bryant]). Despite the longtime popularity of the Signet Classic Shakespeare titles, their future is in question since Penguin now only carries a handful of titles in the series and is promoting the Pelican editions, which it also owns, much more strongly.

Only a few respondents cited the use of free, online-only versions of the play. The *Open Source Shakespeare* website makes available for free the nineteenth-century Globe Shakespeare edition of the plays. It provides no textual glosses or other reading aids, though it has a useful concordance and search engine; users can also access a collated list of all speeches by an individual character. Not surprisingly, a few instructors acknowledged the possibility that some of their students rely on No Fear Shakespeare (i.e., *SparkNotes*), which provides a translation of the play into modern, idiomatic English ("*Romeo and Juliet*: No Fear Translation"). More surprising was the fact that a couple of respondents reported using the No Fear Shakespeare version as an assigned text for high school students. The benefits and disadvantages of this resource will not be rehearsed here.

Contextual Readings

Instructors interested in teaching some of the historical contexts of *Romeo and Juliet* may find helpful Lawrence Stone's *The Family, Sex and Marriage in England 1500–1800*. Although now over forty-five years old, Stone's hefty book offers much useful information about early modern perspectives on family and marriage that can provide entry points for discussion of certain aspects of the play. For example, the section on wet nurses (in a long chapter on parent-child relationships) explains how the practice of wet-nursing could elucidate differences in social class. Instructors who assign excerpts from Stone should take care not to present his arguments—which were already criticized as too sweeping and generalizing when the book was published—as settled fact; the study is more useful as a way of denaturalizing supposedly universal ideas about childhood and marriage.

A much more recent resource is Susan D. Amussen and David E. Underdown's *Gender, Culture and Politics in England, 1560–1640*, which uses a case-study approach to explore the social history of gender relations in early modern England. The book's chapters "Unruly Women" and "Failed Patriarchs" may provide especially fruitful contexts for discussions of patriarchy and marriage in *Romeo and Juliet*. Two important books by the legal and social historian Laura Gowing also shed light on the construction of gender in early modern England: *Common Bodies: Women, Touch and Power in Seventeenth-Century England*, which explores early modern womanhood through the lens of reproduction (a topic that is especially relevant in light of the United States Supreme Court's *Dobbs* decision), and *Gender Relations in Early Modern England*, which includes over seventy easily assignable excerpts from primary sources. Those who wish to put the topic of gender relations, particularly father-daughter relations, in a global context may find useful Marianna G. Muravyeva, Phillip Shon, and Raisa Maria Toivo's *Parricide and Violence against Parents*.

Another recent resource that addresses both Shakespeare and the history of gender relations is B. J. Sokol and Mary Sokol's *Shakespeare, Law, and Marriage*. This book discusses the legal conditions of marriage in early modern England in clearly organized chapters that each focus on a specific aspect of marriage. The book considers how Shakespeare's plays simultaneously refer to and ignore the pertinent legal factors in each of these aspects. For example, in the chapter

"Arranging Marriages," Sokol and Sokol discuss Juliet's refusal to marry Paris, her parents' choice, as an instance of "rebellious disobedience" that could have been seen by some early modern legal theorists as a form of "household treason" (37). Of course, marriage law represents only certain views of the purpose of marriage. Other views may be gleaned from reading early modern marriage sermons, some of which can be accessed through *Early English Books Online* and *HathiTrust Digital Library*. Robert Matz's *Two Early Modern Marriage Sermons* offers a modern edition of two of the most relevant sermons, including helpful annotations of the text and a long introduction that discusses in detail competing views of marriage in early modern England (see also the essay by Matz in this volume).

An important recent development in Shakespeare studies in the last several years has been the examination of race in relation to the plays, in terms of both early modern histories of race and the plays' applicability to contemporary discussions of race. Although *Romeo and Juliet* has typically not figured prominently in these studies (as opposed to plays like *Othello* and *The Tempest*), instructors who wish to understand better the early modern history of race have a number of useful books to choose from. Kim F. Hall's landmark study *Things of Darkness: Economies of Race and Gender in Early Modern England* remains one of the authoritative texts in the field, as does Ian Smith's *Race and Rhetoric in the Renaissance*. Recent work has built on these and other studies, such as Patricia Akhimie's *Shakespeare and the Cultivation of Difference*, whose opening chapter offers a clear explanation of the ways that constructions of race in early modern Europe were intertwined with definitions of class and social conduct. In the same vein, two exciting edited collections that were still in press at the time of this writing are Noémie Ndiaye and Lia Markey's *Seeing Race before Race* and Matthieu Chapman and Anna Wainwright's *Teaching Race in the European Renaissance: A Classroom Guide*. Instructors who wish to assign an introductory piece on the topic—particularly in response to the viewpoint that race "did not exist" in the Renaissance—will want to consider Ayanna Thompson's introduction to *The Cambridge Companion to Shakespeare and Race*, appropriately titled "Did the Concept of Race Exist for Shakespeare and His Contemporaries?"

Instructors who use *Romeo and Juliet* to teach the history of Renaissance sonnets have many practical options for sonnet texts. Robert Durling's *Petrarch's Lyric Poems* remains the best edition of Petrarch's sonnets in English. In addition to Durling's elegant translations, the edition includes the Italian text of the poems on facing pages and helpful glosses. While editions of Shakespeare's sonnets are ubiquitous, an attractive option is Paul Edmondson and Stanley Wells's *All the Sonnets of Shakespeare*. Unlike most editions, which present the sonnets in the same order as the 1609 *Shakespeare's Sonnets*, Edmondson and Wells group the sonnets based on their (conjectured) date of composition and intersperse them with sonnets from the plays; the embedded sonnet in *Romeo and Juliet* thus appears next to sonnets 61–77. Other English Renaissance sonnets that provide useful models for the play's Petrarchan language can be taken from Sir Philip Sidney's *Astrophil and Stella*, Edmund Spenser's *Amoretti*, Lady Mary Wroth's *Pamphilia to Amphilanthus*, and Samuel Daniel's *Delia*. All of these are conveniently excerpted in the excellent *Penguin Book of Renaissance Verse*, edited by David Norbrook and H. R. Woudhuysen. (See also the essay by Joshua Reid in this volume for other useful suggestions.) Scholars interested in exploring the homoerotic dimensions of *Romeo and Juliet* and English Petrarchan poetry will likely want to look at—in addition to Shakespeare's sonnets—Richard Barnfield's *Affectionate Shepherd* and *Cynthia* sonnets. English Petrarchism is also heavily invested in the poetry of Ovid, and a particularly interesting analogue to *Romeo and Juliet* is Ovid's account of Pyramus and Thisbe in book 4 of his *Metamorphoses*.

Instructors who wish to explore more than one kind of contextual approach to the play can do little better than Bedford/St. Martin's Romeo and Juliet: *Texts and Contexts*, edited by Dympna Callaghan (Shakespeare, Romeo and Juliet: *Texts*). In addition to providing excerpts from early modern marriage treatises and Petrarchan sonnet sequences (like those described above), the volume contains several excerpts from primary sources that elucidate a number of topics: the perception of Italy in Renaissance England, Elizabethan statutes regarding duels and fighting, early modern treatises on pharmacology, and a series of letters between members of the Bagot family that present a more complicated picture of early modern attitudes toward marriage and family relationships than that usually assumed by modern readers. The edition also contains an extensive bibliography of additional primary sources that can be fruitfully consulted for more extensive research.

Film and Text Adaptations

There is no question that the most widely used supplementary materials in high school and college classes on *Romeo and Juliet* are film versions and adaptations. The works that fall into this category are legion, but by far the most popular choice among survey respondents is Baz Luhrmann's *William Shakespeare's Romeo + Juliet*, starring Leonardo DiCaprio and Claire Danes. The film's appeal as a classroom teaching aid is easy to see: the kinds of translation that Luhrmann performs on the Shakespearean text—transposing the setting to contemporary Los Angeles while retaining much of the play's language, for example—makes it an ideal vehicle through which to discuss theories of adaptation. It also features a kaleidoscopic, MTV-inspired visual aesthetic, a hits-laden soundtrack, and attractive actors. In terms of popularity, Franco Zeffirelli's *Romeo and Juliet*, starring Leonard Whiting and Olivia Hussey, was a distant but solid second choice among instructors. The film is frequently used as an example of a traditional version of Shakespeare, especially when shown alongside adaptations by Luhrmann and others. Other relatively straightforward film versions include George Cukor's 1936 film starring Leslie Howard and Norma Shearer, which frequently generates discussion about the importance of the characters' ages (Howard and Shearer were forty-three and thirty-four years old, respectively, when the film was made); Renato Castellani's sumptuous 1954 version starring Laurence Harvey and Susan Shentall; and the filmed version of the 2013 Broadway stage production directed by Don Roy King and starring Orlando Bloom and Condola Rashad. Instructors who have a penchant for postmodernist, self-reflexive productions may want to find the 2021 PBS *Great Performances* film of the National Theatre production directed by Simon Godwin and starring Josh O'Connor and Jessie Buckley. This unexpected version, which was filmed during the COVID-19 pandemic lockdown (having been originally intended as a regular theatrical run), places the action of the play in the actual spaces of a working theater. As such, it provokes questions about theatricality itself and about the conditions of performance.

The possibilities become even more cornucopian and variegated when we consider works that are more loosely based on, or "inspired by," Shakespeare's play. By far the most popular film in this genre is the 1961 *West Side Story* directed by Robert Wise and Jerome Robbins, well known for its music by Leonard Bernstein and lyrics by Stephen Sondheim. The film is a cinematic version of the original Broadway stage production, which was recently used as the basis for a new *West Side Story* film directed by Steven Spielberg and written by Tony Kushner (the Pulitzer Prize–winning writer of *Angels in America*). The Spielberg-Kushner film was highly praised by critics and audiences, in large part for its success in taking a more complex view of ethnic conflict and for avoiding the earlier film's problematic representation of Puerto Rican communities. I expect that this version of *West Side Story* will become the preferred option for Shakespeare teachers in the future.

Despite the more nuanced representation of ethnicity in Spielberg's film, an increasing number of Shakespeare instructors are uncomfortable with the film's "*West Side Story* effect," which Carla Della Gatta defines as "the re-inscribing of Shakespearean representations of difference of various kinds—class, locale, familial—as a cultural-linguistic difference" ("From *West Side Story*" 152). Instructors wanting to explore other film adaptations have a number of interesting options: Andrzej Bartkowiak's *Romeo Must Die*, a martial arts action film starring Jet Li and Aaliyah; Carlo Carlei's *Romeo and Juliet*, a lavish, chivalric melodrama that boasts a screenplay by Julian Fellowes (who created and cowrote *Downton Abbey*); Jonathan Levine's *Warm Bodies*, a combination of romantic comedy and postapocalyptic zombie film; and Alan Brown's *Private Romeo*, which reimagines Shakespeare's play as a romance between two male cadets at a high school military academy. Kelly Asbury's *Gnomeo and Juliet* is a lighthearted computer-animated film about garden gnomes that boasts a glittering cast of voice actors (Maggie Smith, Michael Caine, Dolly Parton, et al.) and a song ("Hello Hello") by Elton John and Lady Gaga. For discussions of the use of these films in the Shakespeare classroom, see the essays by Maya Mathur, Anthony Guy Patricia, and Mary Christel in this volume.

The range of adaptations of *Romeo and Juliet* in global cinema and television is remarkably rich, though some of these titles may be more difficult to access than others (and not all are readily available with English subtitles). Given the constantly evolving landscape of video discs and streaming services, I have not attempted to provide suggestions for accessing these films. Not surprisingly, many of the most recent cinematic adaptations of *Romeo and Juliet* draw on the play's representation of civic violence to explore themes of ethnic, racial, and class difference. Anno Saul's *Kebab Connection* uses *Romeo and Juliet* as a backdrop and intertext for its slapstick, comedic rendition of Turkish-German relations in Hamburg. Fernando Sariñana's *Amar te duele* (*Loving Hurts You*) sets the story in modern-day Mexico City and casts it as an adolescent romance between Ulises, the poor son of a street merchant, and Renata, a wealthy, lighter-skinned girl. The film deftly borrows tropes from Mexican telenovelas (soap operas), and Ulises's talent as a graffiti artist is used for a remarkable visual sequence that frames the film as a graphic novel. Ekta Kapoor's *Romil and Jugal* is a Hindi web film series that uses the setting of an Indian gay dating show to dramatize the romance between two young men. Yves Desgagnés's *Roméo et Juliette* is a French-language Canadian film that also thematizes class divides while addressing the issues of governmental and judicial corruption. Lúcia Murat's *Maré, nossa historia de amore* (*Maré, Another Love Story*), a film about rival drug gangs in Rio de Janeiro, is at times brilliantly self-reflexive regarding its own status as an adaptation of Shakespeare and its relation to other adaptations. For an excellent introduction to several global adaptations of *Romeo and Juliet* (and of other Shakespeare plays), see Mark Thornton Burnett's *Shakespeare and World Cinema*.

Of course, not all Shakespeare adaptations are in film. Young adult novels that use *Romeo and Juliet* as source material may be especially useful in courses for English education majors. Alana Quintana Albertson's *Ramón and Julieta* translates the play to modern-day San Diego and focuses on the romance between Ramón Montez, an Ivy League–educated mariachi singer, and Julieta Campos, a celebrity chef who runs a sea-to-table taqueria. In a different vein, Chloe Gong's *These Violent Delights* melds the genres of young adult fiction and science fiction, imaging the story in the gang warfare of 1920s Shanghai. In my view, the most exciting new resource for Shakespeare adaptations is a series being produced by the Arizona Center for Medieval and Renaissance Studies, *The Bard in the Borderlands: An Anthology of Shakespeare Appropriations en La Frontera*. The first volume in the series, edited by Katherine Gillen, Adrianna M. Santos, and Kathryn Vomero Santos, includes six plays that translate Shakespeare to the US–Mexico borderlands. Four of these are adaptations of *Romeo and Juliet*: Edit Villareal's *The Language of Flowers*, James Lujan's *Kino and Teresa*, Seres Jaime Magaña's *The Tragic Corrido of Romeo and Lupe*, and Olga Sanchez Saltveit's *¡O Romeo!*. Together the plays creatively use Shakespeare to explore themes of migration, linguistic difference, civil rights, environmental justice, and Indigenous histories, among others. In doing so they show how adaptations can be used productively to understand and interpret Shakespeare—and also how Shakespeare can be used to explore and understand important contemporary issues.

Critical Readings

As one would expect, the amount of scholarship on Shakespeare's *Romeo and Juliet* is vast. I have attempted here only to suggest a sampling of useful books and essays on the most currently relevant topics in the play. I have especially tried to include studies that can be reasonably assigned to advanced undergraduate and graduate students, who may not have an extensive background in Renaissance studies or literary theory. For a historical overview of criticism of the play, a good place to start is Naomi Conn Liebler's "The Critical Backstory," which is part of Julia Reinhard Lupton's excellent new collection of essays on *Romeo and Juliet* published as part of Bloomsbury's Arden Early Modern Drama Guides. Other edited collections of essays on the play include the *Romeo and Juliet* entry in the Bloom's Modern Critical Interpretations series, edited by Harold Bloom. The volume includes nine previously published essays, all of high quality and all relatively recent, together covering a diverse (if somewhat eclectic) set of topics. The fifteen modern essays and excerpts included in the Norton Critical Edition of *Romeo and Juliet* (discussed above) likewise constitute a useful collection of essays on the play; the volume's selected bibliography is also considerably ample and up to date.

Much scholarship on *Romeo and Juliet* takes a historicist approach to the play. This is especially true of studies that examine Shakespeare's representation of marriage as a civic, social, and religious institution that is usually (but not always) seen as inimical to individual desire. In addition to the book by Sokol and Sokol discussed above, instructors may wish to consult Zdravko Planinc's essay "Politics, Religion, and Love's Transgression: The Political Philosophy of *Romeo and Juliet.*" Planinc argues that the play functions as a critique of religious and political authorities, who are ultimately revealed to be woefully inadequate governors of individual spirituality and human emotions. In "Defying the Stars: Tragic Love as the Struggle for Freedom in *Romeo and Juliet*," Paul A. Kottman refers to the conventional reading of this conflict between civic institutions and individual desire as the condition of modernity itself, as "the so-called 'world alienation' experienced by human beings in the wake of scientific, economic, and philosophical modernity" (3). He then revises this model, arguing that modern subjectivity exists outside of this conflict, in a process of individuation that Romeo and Juliet undergo through their relationship. Gerry Brenner's "Shakespeare's Politically Ambitious Friar" reads the play's civic broils and marital squabbles as revealing a conflict between the church and the state. In a particularly insightful article, "Tragedy and the Crisis of Authority in Shakespeare's *Romeo and Juliet*," Peter C. Herman takes a new-historicist approach to argue that the play's putatively personal and interfamilial conflicts are actually representative of a crisis of authority that was acutely felt by English subjects in the 1590s.

Another important strand of historicist scholarship considers the play's participation in early modern constructions of gender. Robert Appelbaum's article "'Standing to the Wall': The Pressures of Masculinity in *Romeo and Juliet*" argues that, from its opening scene, the play engages a fundamental contradiction in definitions of masculinity that associates it with aggressive violence on the one hand and with the stability of social position on the other. In "'Draw, If You Be Men': Saviolo's Significance for *Romeo and Juliet*," Joan Ozark Holmer focuses on the play's dueling scenes to argue that the play ambiguously locates masculinity between aggressive violence and "courageous wisdom." Holmer traces the gendered language of the play's duels to Elizabethan fencing manuals that frame the activity as an exercise in disciplined reason. Studies that analyze the construction of femininity in *Romeo and Juliet* tend to focus on the play's language of reproduction and nursing. Gail Kern Paster's foundational book *The Body Embarrassed: Drama and the Disciplines of Shame in Early Modern England*, for example, includes a substantial discussion of *Romeo and Juliet* in its chapter on breastfeeding (220–33). Paster shows how the prevalence of wet-nursing in early modern England points to a subtly complex relationship between gender and social class that the play evokes in the Nurse's recollections of Juliet's weaning. Ariane M. Balizet's "Breastfeeding, Grief, and the Fluid Economy of Healthy Children in Shakespeare's Plays" further develops this line of inquiry, showing how early modern debates over wet-nursing reflect an unstable identification of motherhood and the lactating body. Balizet further shows how a subsequent association between breastfeeding and grief over the loss of a child is mobilized in *Romeo and Juliet* and other Shakespeare plays. (See the essay by Balizet in this volume for strategies for incorporating this material in the classroom.)

The play's fixation on Juliet's age—she is weaned at the relatively late age of three and prepared for marriage at the relatively early age of thirteen—has made *Romeo and Juliet* a natural object of scrutiny for the growing field of girlhood studies. The central study in this area is Deanne Williams's *Shakespeare and the Performance of Girlhood*, which discusses the play's representation of Juliet as "wayward," a designation that refers both to her social status as a girl and to her identity as an independent, thinking subject (43–51). Although Jennifer Higginbotham makes only a few comments about *Romeo and Juliet* in her book *The Girlhood of Shakespeare's Sisters: Gender, Transgression, Adolescence*, her chapter on early modern definitions of girlhood usefully traces the evolution of girlhood as a socially defined category in England over the course of the sixteenth century. Ursula Potter's "Navigating the Dangers of Female Puberty in Renaissance Drama," published around the same time as the books by Williams and Higginbotham, takes a similarly historicist approach to the representation of girlhood in English Renaissance drama. In the article, Potter shows how the growing availability of medical knowledge about female puberty in early modern England (particularly on the topic of menstruation) was reflected by the increasingly consistent representation of female puberty—placed at the age of fourteen—in English Renaissance plays, including *Romeo and Juliet*. An exciting and substantial new contribution to the field is Caroline Bicks's *Cognition and Girlhood in Shakespeare's World*, whose first main chapter compares Shakespeare's Juliet with Mary Glover, an actual fourteen-year-old London girl whose 1602 trial over an alleged bewitchment reveals much about early modern perspectives on girlhood.

For obvious reasons, scholarship on gender and girlhood in *Romeo and Juliet* intersects in many ways with studies of maturity and adolescence in the play. Coppélia Kahn's frequently cited essay "Coming of Age in Verona" was one of the first to make the case that the management (or mismanagement) of adolescence is the main driver of the play's tragedy. For Kahn, the feud is both a *"rite-de-passage"* that prescribes adolescent behavior and a "symbol of the patriarchy's destructive power over its children" (5–6). Victoria Sparey's "Performing Puberty: Fertile Complexions in Shakespeare's Plays" offers a challenging response to Kahn, arguing that Kahn and others focus too much on adolescence as a category defined by discrete bodily changes—and thus accept too uncritically the notion of adolescence as a negative, "self-destructive" life stage in constant need of regulation. Sparey points instead to sources that suggest a more gradual process of maturation in both boys and girls, a mode of development that is registered as more "positive" in Shakespeare's plays. In "Youth and Privacy in *Romeo and Juliet*," Rachel Prusko takes a productively modern approach to the issue of adolescence in the play, arguing that Shakespeare's play anticipates and helps to produce modern ideas about adolescence. As she suggests, the idea that adolescence is a life stage shaped by "guarded interiority" and the felt need for privacy is one that resonates strongly with young people today.

The topic of romantic desire continues to be a perennial issue of concern for Shakespeare scholars, though modern criticism has productively taken the discussion in new and important directions. Instructors wishing to complicate the play's cultural status as a "monument" to heterosexual desire should begin with Jonathan Goldberg's essay *"Romeo and Juliet*'s Open Rs," which opens by discussing the play's final vision of Romeo and Juliet as monuments. Originally published in the groundbreaking collection *Queering the Renaissance* (edited by Goldberg), the essay draws attention to the play's language of romance—which, Goldberg argues, renders ambiguous, or even inconsequential, the object of affection. Building on Goldberg's essay, Carla Freccero's "Romeo and Juliet Love Death" (in another edited collection of early modern queer studies) reads Romeo and Juliet's romance as remarkably nonheteronormative in its "deconstruct[ion] of reproductive futurism" (306). For more general discussions of queerness in

Shakespeare, two excellent resources are Anthony Guy Patricia's essay "Queer Studies" in *The Arden Research Handbook of Contemporary Shakespeare Criticism* and Melissa Sanchez's book *Shakespeare and Queer Theory*.

Other models of romantic desire are considered by studies that address the play's incorporation of Petrarchan poetic conventions. In "Neo-Petrarchan Kitsch in *Romeo and Juliet*," Robin Headlam Wells suggests that Shakespeare's rehearsal of Petrarchan language is fundamentally ironic, a satirical response to Petrarchan poetry as sentimental and unrealistic. Gayle Whittier's provocative essay "The Sonnet's Body and the Body Sonnetized in *Romeo and Juliet*" sees the play's Petrarchism as a more serious exploration of the conflicts between different modes of language. Employing a Barthesian notion of textuality, Whittier teases out the many disjunctions between the Petrarchan sonnet as an abstract lyric form and as a form that Romeo attempts to use as a referential language in the "real" world. David Schalkwyk also draws on the theory of referentiality in his discussion of the topic in *Speech and Performance in Shakespeare's Sonnets and Plays*, arguing that, by activating Petrarchan language in a theatrical context, Shakespeare exposes and intensifies the futility of the desire for transcendence that the sonnet form promises to satisfy. The other genre that Shakespeare incorporates into *Romeo and Juliet* is comedy, and instructors interested in this aspect of generic mixing should read the relevant chapter in Susan Snyder's foundational book *The Comic Matrix of Shakespeare's Tragedies*. Another useful piece on the topic is Mary Bly's essay "Bawdy Puns and Lustful Virgins," which argues that generic turns in Shakespeare have implications for the plays' representations of gender as well.

Since the pioneering work by Leah Marcus and David Scott Kastan on the textual history and editing practices of Shakespearean texts, there has been considerable scholarly interest in the early editions of *Romeo and Juliet*. Traditionally dubbed the "bad quarto," the 1597 Q1 *Romeo and Juliet* (the earliest published text of the play) has received serious reconsideration in the last twenty years. The most extensive study of Q1 is Lukas Erne's *The First Quarto of* Romeo and Juliet, which argues that the much-maligned text is actually a theatrical version of the play—and thus tells us a lot about the "dramatic specificities" of Shakespearean performance practices (25). (On the attempt to test this theory through modern-day performance, see the essay by Sarah Neville in this volume.) In *Shakespeare, Court Dramatist*, Richard Dutton challenges part of Erne's argument by suggesting that the Q2 text was an expansion of Q1, which Shakespeare deliberately revised for a court performance. Other important contributions to the debate include Lynette Hunter's "Adaptation and/or Revision in Early Quartos of *Romeo and Juliet*" and David Farley-Hills's "The 'Bad' Quarto of *Romeo and Juliet*." A fascinating interjection in the debate is Heather James's "The Ovidian Girlhood of Shakespeare's Boy Actors," which argues that, contrary to the general consensus, the Q2 text is a very "theatrical" text—one that shows Shakespeare's increasing investment in a theatrical Ovid in the 1590s. Instructors who pair the play with *A Midsummer Night's Dream* or Ovid's "Pyramus and Thisbe" may be particularly interested in James's essay.

Those interested in learning more about the early performance history and theatrical conditions of *Romeo and Juliet* may reasonably start with Simon Palfrey and Tiffany Stern's "What Does the Cued Part Cue? Parts and Cues in *Romeo and Juliet*." The essay is closely related to their book-length study (*Shakespeare in Parts*) on the early modern theatrical practice of giving actors only their individual parts rather than the full playtext, meaning that actors relied heavily on the "cues" included in their scripts. (For a discussion of using this method in the classroom, see the essay by Marguerite Tassi in this volume.) A more general, student-friendly introduction to the conditions of Shakespeare's theater is Arthur F. Kinney's *Shakespeare by Stages*. Although not a peer-reviewed source, Farah Karim-Cooper's engaging blog post on the *Shakespeare's Globe* website, "*Romeo and Juliet*: A Tale of Heaven to Hell," explains how the architecture of Shakespeare's theater encouraged a notion of verticality and how *Romeo and Juliet* repeatedly refers to this vertical structure in its language.

As I mentioned above, an important and rapidly growing field in Shakespeare studies is scholarship on the construction of race in the plays. While most of this criticism has focused on plays other than *Romeo and Juliet*, a notable exception is Kyle Grady's insightful essay "'Envy Pale of Hew': Whiteness and Division in 'Fair Verona,'" in *White People in Shakespeare*, a collection edited by Arthur L. Little, Jr. As Grady shows, although the play's Verona is racially homogeneous (and phenotypically white), Romeo and other characters make use of a "racializing language of blackness" to make hierarchical distinctions among Verona's citizens (92). In doing so, they both inaugurate and perpetuate a discourse of "racial hierarchization" that is readily exportable to other, less homogeneous contexts. More typical of studies that put *Romeo and Juliet* in dialogue with race studies are those that examine modern productions of Shakespeare plays. Among the most important of these is Ayanna Thompson's edited collection *Colorblind Shakespeare: New Perspectives on Race and Performance*; the essays by Antonio Ocampo-Guzman ("My Own Private Shakespeare; or, Am I Deluding Myself?" 125–36) and Margo Hendricks ("Gestures of Performance: Rethinking Race in Contemporary Shakespeare," 187–203) in this collection include particularly rich discussions of *Romeo and Juliet*. Another important recent work in this vein is Carla Della Gatta's groundbreaking book *Latinx Shakespeares: Staging U.S. Intracultural Theater*, which traces the extraordinarily rich tradition of Shakespeare performance in Latine theatrical traditions in the United States in the twentieth and twenty-first centuries.

Other critical studies that focus on adaptation and performance of *Romeo and Juliet* include Joyce Green MacDonald's chapter (47–76) on *Mississippi Masala*, Mira Nair's 1991 film about a romance between an Indian woman and African American man; the chapter shows how the film develops a racializing logic already nascent in Shakespeare's play. In a similar vein, Laura B. Turchi and Ann C. Christensen's "When the 'House' (of Montague) Is a Color, Not a Clan" discusses the powerful cultural and pedagogical effects that are produced by performances and adaptations of *Romeo and Juliet* that structure the central feud along lines of racial or ethnic difference. In *Shakespeare in America*, Alden T. Vaughan and Virginia Mason Vaughan examine this performance trend by discussing the proliferation of "multicultural" productions of *Romeo and Juliet* in recent years. Taking a broader view of history, Marjorie Garber's *Shakespeare and Modern Culture* suggests that it is precisely the play's amenability to such adaptations—its "availability . . . as a transposable love story"—that partly accounts for the play's "modern ubiquity" (46, 37). A very recent collection of essays on global Shakespearean afterlives—and one that is sure to become a cornerstone in the field—is *The Routledge Handbook of Shakespeare and Global Appropriation*, edited by Christy Desmet, Sujata Iyengar, and Miriam Jacobson. The forty essays in the volume address film adaptations of the plays as well as appropriations of Shakespeare in modern novels, poems, stage plays, visual media, and manga (graphic novels).

Pedagogical Resources

In addition to this volume, there are a number of useful online and print resources that are specifically targeted to the Shakespeare classroom. The Shakespeare's Globe website offers a rich assortment of teaching materials for both secondary- and college-level courses on Shakespeare, all of which can be accessed from the site's "Teaching Resources" page. Of particular interest also are the many (over a hundred) blog posts and podcast episodes on various topics related to Shakespeare, including entries on early modern history and current Shakespeare productions. For example, Will Tosh's blog post "Was Shakespeare Gay?," originally created for LGBTQ+ History Month, takes up the knotty issue of early modern sexuality in a remarkably lucid and engaging manner; the post (and others in the series) could easily be assigned to high school or college students. The Folger Shakespeare Library's website also provides a plethora of teaching resources, though these are generally geared more toward high school courses. The website's "Resources" section offers a large number of play-specific modules, including three (at the time of writing) on *Romeo and Juliet*. For example, one of these modules outlines a detailed lesson plan for reading and rereading the play's prologue to acclimate students to the play's language, style, and themes.

An especially welcome development in recent years has been the publication of teaching volumes that show how Shakespeare can be used to engage students with the topics of race, class, gender, sexuality, and social justice. Although not all of these volumes have an essay or chapter specifically devoted to *Romeo and Juliet*, they suggest several ways of thinking *through* Shakespeare about complex, contemporary problems. Relevant titles include Hillary Eklund and Wendy Beth

Hyman's *Teaching Social Justice through Shakespeare: Why Renaissance Literature Matters Now*; Ayanna Thompson and Laura Turchi's *Teaching Shakespeare with Purpose: A Student-Centered Approach*; a special issue of *Early Modern Culture* entitled *First-Generation Shakespeare*, edited by Rebecca Olson and Stephanie Pietros; and David Ruiter's *Arden Research Handbook of Shakespeare and Social Justice*. Although not technically a teaching volume, Ruben Espinosa's highly original *Shakespeare on the Shades of Racism* offers a series of demonstrations of how to open up the plays to contemporary issues of racism, nationalism, and politics. Many student-friendly writings on Shakespeare and social justice are public-facing works that can be quickly read and used to generate classroom discussion. Some of the best examples of short, provocative writing in this rapidly growing genre are Espinosa's "Your Mountainish Inhumanity," Karim-Cooper's "Anti-Racist Shakespeare," and Katherine Gillen and Lisa Jennings's "Decolonizing Shakespeare? Toward an Antiracist, Culturally Sustaining Praxis." While Shakespeare may remain a staple in the American classroom, such writing shows that the plays offer many opportunities for teaching that extend beyond matters of conventional literary form.

Part Two

APPROACHES

Introduction

Joseph M. Ortiz

Does anyone actually introduce students to *Romeo and Juliet*? Given the ubiquity of Shakespeare's play in both popular culture and secondary school curricula, the experience of teaching *Romeo and Juliet* can often seem like a process of undoing rather than building upon previous instruction. At other times it can seem like a therapy session. The first time I taught a Shakespeare class as a newly minted PhD, my students were split between those who thought they hated Shakespeare (because of traumatic memories of parsing passages from *Romeo and Juliet* in high school) and those who thought they loved Shakespeare (because of Leonardo DiCaprio). While DiCaprio may not have the same currency with young adults now as he did in the 1990s, there is little question that, when compared with other Shakespeare plays, *Romeo and Juliet* comes into the classroom with a considerable amount of baggage.

The essays in this volume acknowledge the various and sometimes incongruous manifestations of Shakespeare's *Romeo and Juliet* in twenty-first-century American culture. At the same time, the contributors to this book see this multiplicity as an opportunity for innovative teaching approaches rather than as an impediment to be overcome. This attitude is especially evident in moments where instructors turn to performances and adaptations to generate discussion about the play and the many questions it provokes. The large number of available film versions and recorded theatrical performances of *Romeo and Juliet* makes possible a rich investigation of the ways in which performance can suggest possibilities for interpretation. Many respondents to the MLA's survey of instructors for this volume reported using the popular film versions by Franco Zeffirelli and Baz Luhrmann, along with other video recordings produced by the BBC (directed by Alvin Rakoff) and the Royal Shakespeare Company (directed by Erica Whyman). Even more plentiful are freer adaptations of *Romeo and Juliet*—works that are clearly inspired by the play but that use it to tell a different story. Examples of works in this genre range widely, from the immensely popular 1961 film *West Side Story* (which will now likely be superseded by the 2021 film by Steven Spielberg); to Alan Brown's film *Private Romeo*, a reenvisioning of the play as a gay love story in an American high school military academy; to Guadalupe García McCall's young adult novel *Shame the Stars*, which translates the interfamilial feud in Shakespeare's play to the US–Mexico border conflicts during the Mexican Revolution.

For many instructors, film and book adaptations of *Romeo and Juliet* provide a very effective set of models for students to create their own reimaginings of Shakespeare's play. A number of the essays in this collection come from high school and college instructors who have developed innovative classroom exercises built upon creative response. These are projects that might require students to recontextualize a scene and then produce a performance of it in some medium—an endeavor that is often facilitated by the availability of media-technology resources such as *YouTube*, video-editing software, web-editing tools, and so on. The benefits of such creative assignments are manifold. In addition to promoting active learning and spurring student interest in Shakespeare, they offer another powerful way of linking adaptation to interpretation. They also allow instructors and students to make a powerful case for the contemporary relevance of Shakespeare, an issue that has become even more pressing for high school and college teachers in the last few years. The recent collection by Hillary Eklund and Wendy Beth Hyman, *Teaching Social Justice through Shakespeare: Why Renaissance Literature Matters Now*, makes the point forcefully: "historical literatures [like Shakespeare] *can* speak to the demands of our current moment, and . . . as specialists in older fields, we share responsibility with our colleagues in newer fields for doing that work" (5). Other collections on Shakespearean pedagogy have made a strong case for orienting literature classes, especially those on Shakespeare, to address contemporary political and social concerns.[1]

Interestingly, this presentist turn in teaching approaches—a term I use without derision—has been a catalyst for more nuanced historicist readings of the play. The rise of girlhood studies beginning in the 1990s has had a particularly profound effect on both criticism and performances of the play. For example, Deanne Williams's *Shakespeare and the Performance of Girlhood*, which examines how Shakespeare's plays reflect and critique the cultural construction of girlhood in early modern England, uncovers a Juliet who is more autonomous and resistant than the reductive version typically promulgated in popular culture. In an interview given to the Folger Shakespeare Library, Williams describes the revelatory experience of reading *Romeo and Juliet* through the lens of girlhood studies: "When I was writing this book I was astonished, really, how different the Juliet that appeared before me . . . it was so different from my own recollection of Juliet as this kind of twee figure, simpering, sort of tiptoeing across the stage . . . a cultural memory of Juliet, which was very different from what I encountered on Shakespeare's pages" (Williams, "Shakespeare"). This discrepancy between the early modern playtext and modern uses of the play points to a historical constructedness—not only of girlhood but of marriage and sexuality as well. Accordingly, a number of survey respondents and contributors use the play as an opportunity to investigate early modern ideas about marriage and sexuality, often with the aim of showing that such ideas were as much contested in the sixteenth century as they are in the twenty-first century. According to one survey respondent, the play can function as a critique of both early modern and modern institutions: "Shakespeare constructs the play as an interrogation into the various forms of authority (parental, religious, secular) that were supposed to be unquestionable. All the institutions that were supposed to protect the young failed Romeo and Juliet."

This invigorated historical approach to the play extends to matters of literary history and theater history as well. While Shakespeare's use (some would call it a send-up) of Petrarchism in *Romeo and Juliet* has long been recognized, the recent spate of critical studies of Petrarchan lyric and its influence has made this aspect of the play more interesting and urgent. Lynn Enterline's *The Rhetoric of the Body from Ovid to Shakespeare* and William J. Kennedy's *Petrarchism at Work: Contextual Economies in the Age of Shakespeare*—to name only two recent studies of Petrarchan poetry—show how the imitation of Petrarchan poetry in Renaissance Europe is embroiled in a wide range of cultural and social formations. The ideological dimensions of Renaissance Petrarchism have affected how some instructors frame the lyrical passages in *Romeo and Juliet*, which can be seen as exposing the ideological work performed by Petrarchan language. As one survey respondent puts it, "I emphasize the constructedness of romantic (Petrarchan) language—its artificiality and theatricality." A number of respondents described a similar approach, while some reported pairing Petrarch with Shakespeare's other favorite poet, Ovid. Instructors who assign Ovid's "Pyramus and Thisbe" episode from the *Metamorphoses* (often in a unit that includes *A Midsummer Night's Dream*) are able to show how Shakespeare took his own classroom texts and experimented with them, crossing genres and changing endings.

And, often, one approach leads to another. In a recent essay on the first two quarto versions of *Romeo and Juliet*, Heather James shows how Shakespeare revised Juliet by giving her more Ovidian language, a change that James argues was part of Shakespeare's deliberate attempt to advance the cultural status of London's professional theaters in the 1590s. James's essay intervenes in a long-standing debate over the history of the early published editions of *Romeo and Juliet*. In the last thirty years, this debate has been shaped by (and has helped to shape) exciting developments in the fields of history of the book and of early modern theater. The goal of this research is no longer to establish a singular authentic literary text—precisely because the notion of an authentic text has been dismantled as a Romantic fantasy. Instead, the new scholarship has shown how different published versions of a play can reveal much about Renaissance theatrical practices, about the evolving relationship between print and the stage, and about Shakespeare's own changing ideas about his theater. Indeed, one sign of the impact of book history and performance studies on *Romeo and Juliet* scholarship is the fact that virtually no one refers to the 1597 quarto version of *Romeo and Juliet* (Q1) as a "bad quarto" without irony or qualification. Equally refreshing is the extent to which the textual history of the play has become a fruitful object of investigation in the classroom. A number of survey respondents described teaching approaches that draw on these scholarly developments in book history and theater history, whether directly or indirectly. As some of the essays in this volume show, such academic exploration can itself be used as the impetus for other pedagogical activities, including close reading and classroom performance.

The eighteen essays in this volume chart this range of approaches to teaching *Romeo and Juliet* at different levels of instruction: high school students, undergraduate English majors and non–English majors, and graduate students. Many of the essays also address the changing and diverse student demographic that typically composes the Shakespeare classroom in the twenty-first century. In this respect, these essays extend and update the excellent Approaches to Teaching World Literature volume edited by Maurice Hunt and published in 2000. While Hunt's edition remains extremely useful, overall it reflects an approach to the play that is focused more on formal concerns, often privileging character and form as the central objects of study. This is not to say that formalism in the Shakespeare classroom is dead. Some respondents described a strictly text-based approach to the play, sometimes including the examination of universal themes or archetypes of romantic love. These tend to be in the minority, however, as more respondents cited the wealth of newly available materials, in multiple media, as an incentive for exploring different aspects of the play and its reception. Interestingly, the final two essays in the earlier Approaches volume— on film adaptations and musical-balletic adaptations, respectively—look ahead to the direction that *Romeo and Juliet* teaching has taken in the last twenty years. The current volume charts the fruitful pedagogical possibilities that have developed since these earlier forays.

At the end of Q1 *Romeo and Juliet*, Lord Montague vows to erect a golden statue of Juliet that will serve as a monument to Romeo's love for her: "There shall no statue of such price be set, / As that of *Romeos* loued *Iuliet*" (Shakespeare, *Excellent Conceited Tragedie*, sig. 2K3r). Q2's Montague, however, describes the statue as a representation of Juliet's love: "There shall no figure at such rate be set / As that of true and faithful Juliet" (act 5, scene 3, lines 301–02).[2] In contrast to both versions of Montague, most instructors of *Romeo and Juliet* do not present the play as a monument to romantic love, instead framing it in terms of a conflict between the individual and society. The first three essays in this collection take up this approach, each with close attention to the complex social pressures and cultural scripts that work to both curb and define the individual subject. Robert Matz uses early modern marriage sermons to give students a nuanced, historically informed understanding of the ways in which ideas about marriage were themselves contested in Renaissance England. As Matz shows, the relationship between marriage and romantic love was ambiguous and subject to debate, making it impossible to read Romeo and Juliet's marriage as simply either a rebellious action or a capitulation to orthodoxy. Peter C. Herman tackles head-on what is perhaps the most common misperception of the play held by students—that Juliet's marriage at the age of thirteen or fourteen was perfectly normal in Renaissance England and therefore unremarkable. To address this, Herman introduces his students to primary sources that show that at least some people in Shakespeare's audience would have reacted differently. His method is a deeply historicist approach that sees the play as highly critical of authorities—familial, religious, and civic. Meghan Andrews also focuses on the challenges that authority imposes on Romeo and Juliet, but she frames the characters' ability to think outside of social norms as constitutive of individual character. Her approach uses a carefully designed set of exercises that prompt students to practice close reading and thereby notice the subtle but powerful "evolution" that Romeo and Juliet experience in terms of individual thought and psychological agency.

The next group of essays in the volume show how *Romeo and Juliet* can be used to think through the important topics of gender and sexuality—as they were constructed in early modern England and as they are constructed in contemporary American culture. Ariane M. Balizet and Natalie K. Eschenbaum devise productive approaches to the play that draw on recent work in girlhood studies, though they do this in very different ways. Balizet engages her students with rigorously historicist and philological inquiries that show that the category of "girl" is profoundly unstable—both in early modern England and in the play. Like Herman, Balizet also dismantles the notion that Juliet's age is unremarkable, and she performs an intersectional reading of the play to show how profoundly the idea of girlhood is inextricable from categories of class and race. Eschenbaum approaches the topic of girlhood through modern borrowings and adaptations of *Romeo and Juliet,* from Taylor Swift's hit song "Love Story" to the 2021 film *R#J.* For Eschenbaum, the goal is to demonstrate how Shakespeare's play can be used to reveal her students' notions of girlhood as much as it does early modern notions of girlhood. Anthony Guy Patricia also turns to modern adaptations to engage students on issues of gender and sexuality. Patricia shows "how *Romeo and Juliet* can be queered in the classroom" through a viewing of *Private Romeo,* Alan Brown's 2011 film that adapts the play to dramatize a same-sex romance at an all-male high school military academy. Patricia deftly guides his students through earlier film versions (by Cukor, Zeffirelli, and Luhrmann) before screening *Private Romeo,* showing them how heterosexuality is constructed and then deconstructed.

The next section, "Considering Genre," attests to the fact that *Romeo and Juliet* has remained a core text in high school and college curricula in part for its usefulness in teaching basic literary concepts. The two essays in this section deal with the well-worn terrain of genre, though they do so with innovative and relevant approaches. Stephanie Pietros pairs the play with *A Midsummer Night's Dream* and Ovid's "Pyramus and Thisbe" to put into relief the way in which Shakespeare incorporates conventions of comedy in *Romeo and Juliet.* While this generic mixing in the play has long been observed by critics, Pietros goes further by prompting her students to consider the possible affiliations between generic distinction and class distinctions. She points out, for example, that the play's opening comic scene takes place among working-class figures rather than aristocratic ones. Joshua Reid works with the other well-known example of generic mixing in the play: its rehearsal of Petrarchan sonnets. His essay details strategies for using a sampling of English Renaissance sonnets (by Shakespeare, Philip Sidney, Edmund Spenser, Michael Drayton, Barnabe Barnes) to teach fundamental poetic forms and concepts—an important component of many high school and college curricula—and to prompt students to discover how the conventions of Renaissance sonnets could be "co-opted" on the stage to generate audience expectations.

The importance of audience, whether on the stage or page, is a central issue in the essay on textual editing practices by Rebecca Olson that opens the next section, "Textual and Performance Histories." From the start, Olson dispels the notion that editing Shakespeare's texts is the domain of advanced specialists, instead making it a key component in her general education course on Shakespeare. Taking advantage of online Shakespeare resources (in particular, Oregon State University's Open Educational Resources edition of *Romeo and Juliet*, which Olson and her students developed), Olson's students become editors of Shakespeare themselves, making decisions as they prepare a version of the text and then later explaining the reasons for their decisions. The point here is not to establish a definitive "right" text but to understand how any text is the result of individual editors who have specific audiences in mind. In the section's next essay, Sarah Neville likewise dispenses with a "right-answerism" approach to textual editing and prompts her students to consider the effects of different versions of a text by examining the differences between Q1 and Q2 *Romeo and Juliet*. She then gives several examples that demonstrate how performance, both in the classroom and on the professional stage, can enliven these textual differences and show what is at stake when choosing which version of the text to use. In the last essay in this section, Marguerite Tassi also anchors the teaching of textual history in performance by focusing on cue scripts, the individual parts by which actors in London's early modern professional theaters learned their roles (without access to the rest of the play). Tassi's creative approach calls on students to become cue-script actors themselves, an exciting process that defamiliarizes the conditions of Shakespeare's theater and highlights the meaningful effects of physical actions and spontaneous choices on stage.

One of the aims of this new volume on *Romeo and Juliet* is to give more attention to the importance of teaching approaches in high school courses, partly because the play remains a standard text in high school English literature courses (and on many standardized-test reading lists) and partly because a significant job for many university English instructors is training future and current high school English teachers. The essays by Abbey Bachmann and Mary T. Christel, in the section of this volume dedicated to the high school classroom, both emanate from their experiences working directly with high school students and teachers. They acknowledge the challenges faced by many high school teachers of the play (difficulties that often extend to the college classroom) and suggest creative strategies for turning these challenges into opportunities for active learning. Bachmann has her students assume the role of film critics whose observations of specific details in a film can then be linked to close reading moments in the text. Christel takes the play's hyperfamiliarity—a factor that many survey respondents cited as a perennial challenge—and uses it as an asset, devising exercises that prompt students to think critically about narrative structures and dramatic choices.

The final two sections in this volume showcase what has arguably been the most important development in Shakespeare studies in the last few years. The impetus to decolonize Shakespeare has recently become something of a disciplinary imperative, a project that has been fueled by groundbreaking work on the ideology of race in the plays. Accordingly, several leading Shakespeare scholars have advocated for the need to practice Shakespeare scholarship in a manner that "enkindles provocative understandings of present-day issues surrounding social and racial inequities" (Espinosa, *Shakespeare* 4). This project has been particularly urgent for teachers of Shakespeare, who increasingly feel the responsibility to make Shakespeare more relevant to their students' lives and help them address the real challenges posed by racial and economic inequalities. Maya Mathur's essay details strategies for incorporating *Romeo and Juliet* into a course on Shakespeare and race. Her approach uses the model of popular culture adaptations of *Romeo and Juliet* to prompt students to "speak back to the text" and assess the construction of race in the play and in its adaptations. Jehbreal Muhammad Jackson and Julia Reinhard Lupton come at the play from a wonderfully interdisciplinary angle, incorporating into their teaching a rigorously historicist understanding of the racial underpinnings of dance conventions. Their fascinating exposition of the racial texture of dance shows how the study of Shakespeare in the arts can be used to engage with issues of race and history. While the essays in this collection do not discuss the many operatic adaptations of *Romeo and Juliet*, Jackson and Lupton's essay demonstrates how a careful triangulation of Shakespearean text, art history, and visual adaptation can help to foster culturally aware performances.

The final section in this volume features teaching approaches that take advantage of the remarkable confluence between *Romeo and Juliet* and Hispanic culture—a rich tradition of Shakespearean appropriation that extends far beyond *West Side Story* and that falls into the category of what is now referred to as Borderlands Shakespeare. Kathryn Vomero Santos uses two contemporary adaptations of the play that thematize the colonial history of the US–Mexico borderlands: James Lujan's play *Kino and Teresa* and Guadalupe García McCall's young adult novel *Shame the Stars*. Her teaching of these works shows that the feud in *Romeo and Juliet* has many analogues in borderlands history and that Shakespeare's works can be fruitfully conscripted to examine and critique this history. Jonathan Burton uses another adaptation, Valeria Luiselli's short story "Shakespeare, New Mexico," as a preparatory reading for *Romeo and Juliet* at his college, a Hispanic-serving institution. His approach, which is deeply informed by recent research on the experiences of Hispanic students in high schools and universities in the United States, encourages students to treat the Shakespearean text *as* textual matter, always ready to be deconstructed and reconfigured to express ideas and issues "relevant to their own lives." The final essay in this volume, by Robin Alfriend Kello and Rhonda Sharrah, introduces an exciting new resource for teachers of *Romeo and Juliet*. This public-facing resource places Shakespeare's play alongside early modern Spanish versions of

Romeo and Juliet, creating myriad opportunities to connect the play to culturally diverse writers and traditions. Like the essays in this volume, the project is deliberately designed to help teachers "empower students of all backgrounds to 'talk back' to Shakespeare."

NOTES

1. See, for example, Thompson and Turchi, *Teaching*; Olson and Pietros; Ruiter; O'Dair and Francisco.

2. In this volume, all citations of Shakespeare plays and poems come from the third edition of *The Norton Shakespeare* (Greenblatt et al.), and citations of *Romeo and Juliet* are from the text of the second quarto (Q2) in this edition unless otherwise indicated (Shakespeare, *Most Lamentable Tragedy* [Greenblatt et al.]). For the original edition of Q2, see Shakespeare, *Most Excellent and Lamentable Tragedie*.

"Get Her Heart": Reading *Romeo and Juliet* through Early Modern Ideas of Marriage

Robert Matz

Students often read *Romeo and Juliet* as if it were documentary evidence of how marriage worked in Shakespeare's England or as a universal expression of love. Teaching the play in relation to early modern views of marriage offers a more informed understanding of these issues and adds new perspective to a commonly read play. More broadly, this approach helps students think more deeply about the idea of historical context in reading literature, and the ways in which literary texts relate to that context.

This essay suggests ways to provide students with historical context for the play through selected passages from early modern marriage sermons as well as suggestions for further reading in this genre. Through this juxtaposition, students will discover that the deep affection depicted by the play—"their loves . . . exceed that of children to parents" (Matz 136)—was also celebrated by Protestant orthodoxy. For all their seeming rebelliousness, when Romeo and Juliet marry, they invest their love and themselves in a key social institution. But the play also suggests ambivalence about basing marriage in romantic love, an ambivalence likewise found in early modern English marriage sermons. This love threatened the authority of parents, kin, and friends as well as that of the potentially uxorious husband. Students can see how the play celebrates marriage for love but also seeks to control this ideal through its tragic ending. They also learn how literary plots do not merely reflect a static historical context but help to negotiate historically dynamic cultural change.

At first, *Romeo and Juliet* seems to lend itself to the view that the historical context of Shakespeare's plays is mere backdrop—a particular and limited set of situations or beliefs that Shakespeare's universality transcends. The feuding families and arranged marriages seem like historical relics, while Romeo and Juliet's love appears as a private, passionate emotion that exists out of history altogether.

As the *SparkNotes* analysis puts it, "It is possible to see *Romeo and Juliet* as a battle between the responsibilities and actions demanded by social institutions and those demanded by the private desires of the individual" ("Literary Devices"). Students might be asked in this respect how much they believe that their own private desires exist within or are opposed to current social institutions or expectations. More broadly, do their experiences of romantic love exist outside of contemporary frameworks or assumptions? Romeo, of course, first appears in the play as a conventional courtly lover. When Juliet demands that if Romeo loves her, he should marry her, readers sometimes see a demand that he give up the pose of a lover and become a real one. Yet marriage provides another, more orthodox social and public framework for desire. In following the path from courtly love to marriage, Romeo and Juliet are participating in what C. S. Lewis identifies as "the final defeat of courtly love by the romantic conception of marriage" (298).

Students may acknowledge the social role of marriage in the play but have a hard time recognizing its centrality to the play's conflicts and, ultimately, tragedy. For the conflicts around marriage to come into view, we need to shift our focus away from the feud. It can be useful for many approaches to the play to have students consider how much of a dead letter the feud is in *Romeo and Juliet*. The only characters who keep it alive are comic servants, condemned by their masters, and Tybalt, whose uncle condemns him for his hostility to Romeo. The prince forbids the feud, the townspeople condemn it, years have gone by without an eruption of fighting, and the Capulet and Montague patriarchs believe it should be easy to keep the peace.

Putting the feud at the play's narrative center obscures the role of marriage as driver of the play's conflict. It also obscures the changed social and political world of *Romeo and Juliet*, in which marriage takes on new importance. It may be, in the words of the first chorus, "Verona, where we lay our scene" (prologue, line 2), but Verona also serves as a space for Shakespeare to represent an English polity and culture that is no longer the warrior world of his history plays but rather "civil" (prologue, line 4). The prince rules civil Verona. His role in the play points to the struggle for supreme authority by the monarch against a fractious nobility, the great subject of Shakespeare's histories. A cultural effect of the centralization of royal power was what Norbert Elias calls "the courtization of warriors" (258–70), which sublimated warrior violence into habits of courtesy. Another effect was what Lawrence Stone argues was a new emphasis on the nuclear family against extended kin networks, an emphasis that in social terms complemented the Protestant religious celebration of marriage (132–45). Aside from Tybalt, the main characters in the play are courtiers, children, fathers, and mothers. In this civil society, the prince has the sole right to punish, warriors have become courtly lovers, and courtly lovers have become husbands.

In the readings that follow, I detail some conflicts that this transformation to the domestic creates, through comparison of the play to advice given in English sermons on marriage. I focus on three areas: the role of parental consent in marriage, the role and value of sexual desire and even love within the marriage, and the husband's role in marriage in relation to his wife. In a class on *Romeo and Juliet*, one could assign all or part of one or more of these sermons, which set out the English Protestant ideal of a good marriage and are thus interesting both in themselves and in relation to the play. In the appendix, I outline some possible sources for these marriage sermons to use in a class on *Romeo and Juliet* and sermons for further reading.

In describing a new "romantic conception of marriage," Lewis follows a long historical tradition that associates the Protestant break from the Catholic Church with the elevation of married love. Some historians have challenged the idea that marriage for love was an invention of Protestantism. I believe that Lewis's broad outlines of a new Protestant idealization of married love are correct but also that no cultural attitudes change completely.[1] In *Romeo and Juliet* I think we can find another continuity between earlier and later ideas of marriage. Not the continuity of marriage for love from the Catholic past, but rather the opposite: a continuing view of married love as a source of potential danger and sin. The play reflects a new, Protestant celebration of married love. But *The Tragedy of Romeo and Juliet* also reflects deep uncertainty about married love in Protestant England.

As Lewis argues, for marriage to be elevated beyond its role in securing the legitimacy of heirs and binding families together, it had to become the home of love as well. And for that to happen, the man and woman had to enter into the relationship freely and because they loved each other. We see this shift from marriage for alliance to marriage for love in *Romeo and Juliet*. A marriage between Paris and Juliet would be a good match in Lord Capulet's eyes—Paris is, after all, kin to the prince. But when Paris asks Capulet—not Juliet—for permission to wed Juliet, Capulet redirects him toward winning Juliet's love:

> But woo her, gentle Paris; get her heart—
> My will to her consent is but a part—
> And, she agreed, within her scope of choice
> Lies my consent and fair according voice.
> (act 1, scene 2, lines 16–19)

Capulet's position echoes Protestant views on marriage. Here, for example, is Henry Smith in his sermon *A Preparative to Marriage*, written in 1591, just a few years before *Romeo and Juliet*: "To show the love which should be between man and wife, marriage is called *conjugium*, which signifieth a knitting or joining together; showing, that unless there be a joining of hearts and a knitting of affections together, it is not marriage indeed, but in show and name" (Matz 81).[2] Lord Capulet seems willing to rethink marriage along these Protestant lines for his daughter.

However, there is a qualification. Juliet is entitled to a "scope of choice." How large is that scope? When the choice of the young woman or man conflicts with the will of the parents, who should prevail? Smith has a clear response to children who are considering this question:

> Will you take your father's money, and will you not take his instruction? Marriage hath need of many counselors, and doest thou count thy father too many, which is like the foreman of thy instructors? If you mark what kind of youths they be which have such haste that they dare not stay for their parents' advice, they are such as hunt for nothing but beauty, and for punishment hereof they marry to beggary, and lose their father and mother for their wife.   (Matz 77–78)

Lord Capulet does not learn until the end of the play that Juliet has married Romeo. His anger toward her for refusing Paris does not derive from whatever residual animosity there is with the Montagues but rather from what Capulet views as Juliet's ungratefulness for his care and disobedience to his will. Marriage has gone from something the daughter should want to something the father arranges: "Doth she not count her blessed, / Unworthy as she is, that we have wrought / So worthy a gentleman to be her bride?" (3.5.143–45). When Juliet answers an evasive but respectful "no" to her father's question, Capulet thunders:

> Thank me no thankings, nor proud me no prouds,
> But fettle your fine joints 'gainst Thursday next
> To go with Paris to Saint Peter's Church,
> Or I will drag thee on a hurdle thither.
>   (3.5.152–55)

"Fettle" is a verb most often used in reference to horses or cattle and marks a transformation of Juliet into something like Capulet's animal property. Rather than arms and legs, she has an animal's "joints." The "hurdle" on which Capulet threatens to drag Juliet refers to a kind of platform on which traitors were carried through the streets to their execution, while also recalling lightweight fencing intended for penning up sheep. This fence, we might say, is the "scope" of Juliet's choice, and, having gone beyond that scope, she is reminded that she is less than human and that her father has the power to punish her if she does not accede to his will.

Notably, Capulet's wife is scandalized by this new position on marriage and by her husband's treatment of his daughter as if she were property: "Fie, fie! What, are you mad?" (3.5.157). There is much in the play that guides its audience to sympathize with Lady Capulet here. Nonetheless, even as the play celebrates Romeo and Juliet's love, we can see the outlines of Smith's suspicion that heady young people really will make poor marriage choices. The play may seem unsympathetic to the arranged marriage, but it can be read as equally skeptical of a more modern, romantic belief in the wisdom and power of youthful love. It takes instead a position like Smith's: marriage should be founded on love but within a limited scope of choice. Children who go beyond this scope or do not listen to their parents are likely to be overly hasty, superficial, and doomed to a bad end.

However, the conflicted attitudes toward marriage go deeper—both in *Romeo and Juliet* and in the culture that informs it—than this question of parental choice. Within sanctioned marriages, too, sexual desire and love were sources of conflicted attitudes. Protestants rejected the Catholic valorization of celibacy but remained uncomfortable with sex even in marriage. Marital sex was both central to marriage and a danger to it. William Whately writes in his 1623 marriage sermon *A Bride-Bush* that each spouse in the marriage must willingly pay the so-called marriage debt—that is, have sex with their spouse should the spouse desire it. But that is not to say that Whately affirmatively values sexual desire in marriage. Sex is a practical concession to human nature—our lack of the "gift of continency" (Matz 120). It is not a positive good, and it presents a danger to the married couple if it is treated as such:

> The married must not provoke desires for pleasure's sake, but allay desires, when they provoke themselves. They must not strive by words and gestures to enflame their passions, when were it not for such enforcements, they would be cool enough. . . . To incite themselves by mutual dalliances for pleasure's sake, and awake the sleeping passions, which nature had laid to rest, this is a fault, even betwixt yoke-fellows.   (124)

Excessive sexual desire transforms sex within marriage from something that God has ordained for specific purposes to the mere satisfaction of human appetite: "God hath ordained matrimony," Whately tells us, "not for pleasure's sake chiefly, but for the increase of mankind, and not to enkindle lustful desires, but to quench them" (Matz 123). Whately also warns that the excessively lustful couple are likely to put their desire before their duty: "Excessiveness disables them, without much unquietness, to endure separation upon just causes; moderation makes it easy to abstain when need requireth" (124).

Romeo's desire for his new "yoke-fellow" is excessive in the way Whately describes. He cannot moderate his desires, cannot without much unquietness endure a separation from Juliet when his banishment requires it:

>   Heaven is here,
> Where Juliet lives—and every cat and dog
> And little mouse, every unworthy thing,
> Live here in heaven and may look on her,
> But Romeo may not. More validity,
> More honorable state, more courtship, lives
> In carrion flies than Romeo. They may seize
> On the white wonder of dear Juliet's hand,
> And steal immortal blessing from her lips,

> Who even in pure and vestal modesty
> Still blush, as thinking their own kisses sin.
>
> (3.3.29–39)

It is hard to see Romeo as admirable in these lines, with his comparisons of his plight to the good fortune of cats, dogs, little mice, and carrion flies. To Renaissance ears, Romeo's intemperance sounds sinful as well. His excessive passion is for his own pleasure rather than circumscribed within God's ordinance for marriage. As a result, he substitutes the merely human for the divine. He thinks of Juliet as his own secular "heaven" and describes the "pure and vestal" Juliet as if she were his saint (as he has in the earlier courtship scene). Her lips, rather than God, become the source of "immortal blessing." But because Juliet experiences desire and inflames Romeo's, her lips end up providing not blessings but blushings.

We might think that this sexual sin within marriage stems from Romeo's youth and immaturity. Moving from character to cultural history, we might say that Romeo's sexual excessiveness marks the incomplete transformation of courtly love into marital chastity. I would suggest, however, that Romeo's improper desire reflects tensions within English Renaissance ideas of marriage, which rejected the Catholic preference for celibacy but still conceived of marital sex as liable to sin. Advice such as Whately's that the couple "must not provoke desires for pleasure's sake, but allay desires, when they provoke themselves" might, in actual married life, have been hard to follow. Would a couple be able to tell when the desires they felt "provoked themselves" rather than being also provoked by them? Moreover, Protestants' celebration of married love was in tension with the idea that human love was inferior to the love for God. Smith celebrates the love between husband and wife by reminding his audience that Paul in Ephesians compares the love between husbands and wives to that of Christ and his church (Matz 71). But something that can be compared to something else may also be too easily mistaken for it, as Romeo in comparing Juliet to a heavenly saint goes too far by treating her as if she were one. Likewise, Smith warns, "the man must take heed that his love toward his wife be not greater than his love toward God, as Adam's and Sampson's [sic] were" (81).

While the idea that a man's excessive love of his wife could be a form of spiritual adultery goes back to the early medieval period, we can imagine the fear of this possibility to have intensified as the celebration of married love did. Whately advises that

> for man and wife to have somewhat an over-good opinion of each other . . . is a thing so far from blame that it deserveth rather commendation; yea, for man and wife to be made so mutually blind with the liking each of other, as not to be able see some things that are amiss each in other, and to see things that are out of order, in as little a proportion and

shape as may be; this betwixt them two, is doubtless a praise-worthy
blindness.   (Matz 156–57)

Romeo and Juliet, however, cross the line from a benign overvaluation of each
other to a love so blinding to reason, judgment, and God's rule that their mutual
misapprehensions result in the tragedy, and sin, of suicide. One can say that
Romeo and Juliet take too far the injunction that the married couple share a
blinding love for one another. No matter how hard Friar Laurence seeks to contain their love, first within marriage and then within his good plans for their
safety, the very intensity of the love that grounds their marriage tragically undoes
it. Protestantism may have wanted holy marriage to capture human passion, but
the opposite was always at risk: human passion might capture holy marriage. I
am treating Friar Laurence here as if he were a figure of Protestant religion, but
it might be better to say that this danger within Protestant celebrations of marriage was more easily imagined by associating it with Catholicism and what the
English imagined to be Italian sexual decadence.

Finally, although Whately speaks of excessive desire as a sin husband and
wife potentially share, Smith does not: for Smith, this excess is a danger particular to men. For a woman to excessively desire her husband may be sinful,
but it does not upset gender hierarchies. A husband's excessive desire, however, threatens gender hierarchy, as Smith's references to Adam and Samson
make clear. The play is filled with suggestions that Romeo's love for Juliet
makes him less than a man and unable to fulfill his masculine duties. As Romeo
declares, "O sweet Juliet, / Thy beauty hath made me effeminate, / And in my
temper softened valor's steel" (3.1.112–14). Another version of this emasculation—
one not a product of sexual desire but of marital domestication—bedevils
the older generation of husbands, whom Shakespeare portrays as henpecked.
The nurse calls Lord Capulet a "cotquean" (4.4.6), a man who acts as a
housewife.[3] Lady Capulet mocks her husband for calling for a sword rather
than a "crutch" (1.1.71). Lady Montague physically restrains her husband from
fighting. "Hold me not: let me go!" Montague cries, but his wife remains firm:
"Thou shalt not stir one foot to seek a foe" (1.1.74–75). Renaissance married
couples were frequently reminded that husband and wife are one flesh, a conception grounded in Eve's creation from Adam's rib. Smith writes, "Therefore
she which should lie in his bosom was made in his bosom and should be as
close to him as his rib of which she was fashioned" (Matz 64). But when husband and wife live together intimately, it may be hard for the husband to
maintain his authority over his wife, even when—as is the case of the fathers
in Shakespeare's play—he is not enamored of her. Transforming the meaning
of Eve's creation from Adam, Smith recognizes this possibility: "Doth the rib
that is in man's side fret or gall him? no more him should she which is made of
the rib" (Matz 92). Romeo's love for Juliet effeminizes, while the fathers' married
loves domesticate.

Shakespeare finally celebrates marriage by leaving us only with its emblem. The statues of the lovers the fathers promise to erect provide an idealized version of Romeo and Juliet's love—with none of its messy contradictions. The lovers will no longer be imperfect flesh, sinfully or blindly loving of one another, but instead fixed monuments of "pure gold" (5.3.299). And even as Shakespeare's play idealizes and emblematizes the young lovers, it returns marriage to an institution controlled by fathers. Lords Capulet and Montague are the couple who join hands at the play's end and, in effect, arrange anew the marriage of Romeo and Juliet, who are no longer passionate, unruly children. Mothers are also gone. Lady Montague has died out of grief for her son's exile (5.3.210–11), and Lady Capulet disappears from the play, having declared in her final lines that the sight of the dead couple predicts her own death (5.3.206–07). Shakespeare ultimately gives us marriage without children, without flesh, without wives (J. Goldberg). This conclusion prefigures the more open violence of a later tragedy with marriage at its center, *Othello*.

NOTES

1. For a more detailed account of this question of continuity and change in ideas of marriage, see Matz 1–14.

2. When quoting marriage sermons in this essay, I have modernized their spelling and punctuation.

3. *Cotquean* was a derogatory word for a housewife that also came to refer to men acting as housewives, a usage first witnessed by the *Oxford English Dictionary* in this quotation; "Cotquean."

APPENDIX: PRIMARY SOURCES

Modern editions of these sermons are hard to come by. For Henry Smith's 1591 work *A Preparative to Marriage* and William Whately's 1623 work *A Bride-Bush*, I quote from versions that I edited (Matz), though a nineteenth-century edition of Smith's sermon is also available online in the *HathiTrust Digital Library* (H. Smith). Instructors with access to *Early English Books Online* can find original editions of several early modern English sermons, which means students can read the texts in modern typography, if not modern spelling and punctuation; perform keyword searches of the texts; and in some cases use a text-rendered table of contents. Sermons that may be of interest for further reading are Heinrich Bullinger's *The Golde[n] Boke of Christen Matrimonye*, Robert Cleaver's *A Godly Forme of Houshold Gouernment*, and William Gouge's *Of Domesticall Duties*.

Juliet's Age and Questioning Authority in *Romeo and Juliet*

Peter C. Herman

It happens like clockwork. Every time I teach *Romeo and Juliet,* I ask my class if they were told it was normal for people in Shakespeare's England to get married at a very young age. In fall 2020, I taught this play in two classes, Introduction to Literature, a general education course populated by non–English majors, and a Shakespeare survey for English majors. These were two very different groups with very different interests and preparation. But when it comes to the question of Juliet's age, they agreed. Using the poll function in *Zoom* (I taught these classes online because of the COVID-19 pandemic), I asked students whether they were taught that, for Shakespeare's time, marriage at the age of a little less than fourteen was normal. The results were similar between the classes: ninety-eight percent of the Intro to Lit students and ninety-two percent of the literature majors said yes. Asking my in-person classes yields the same results.

Obviously, this assumption guides how they wanted to talk about the play. I ask my students to write a blog post about the week's reading the day before we talk about it, and many ascribe the disaster at the play's end to fate ("star-crossed lovers") or Romeo's and Juliet's immaturity (one said that Romeo and Juliet acted like "dramatic teenagers"; another mentioned that a teenager's brain is not yet fully formed, "causing them to make rash decisions"). Underneath their views is a sense of superiority to Shakespeare's England: in our better, more-informed age, child brides are not allowed, and, while teen pregnancy obviously happens, underage sex is not something our society embraces as a positive. Such thinking likely explains why a summer 2019 production of *Romeo and Juliet* at the Old Globe Theater in San Diego silently changed "she's not fourteen" to "she's not sixteen." When the production's director, Barry Edelstein, visited my class, he had a simple explanation for the change: "I wanted to avoid the 'ick' factor." Baz Luhrmann's film leaves out these lines altogether.

But what if the "ick" factor is the whole point? To help students get a better sense of the play's themes, of how Shakespeare could be highly critical of his culture, and of how important it is to situate literature in its historical context, I ask the class to look at an excerpt from a letter dated 24 December 1575, by William Cecil, Lord Burghley, to George Talbot, the Earl of Shrewsbury. The earl had offered his son Edward's hand in marriage to Burghley's youngest daughter, Elizabeth. One might imagine that Burghley would have jumped at the chance to marry his daughter into the highest ranks of the nobility. But Burghley declines the offer for two reasons. The second has mostly to do with politics (Queen Elizabeth's jealousy and the suspicion such a marriage would cause), but the first is a different story:

> [M]y daughter is but young in years; and, upon some reasonable respects,
> I have determined (notwithstanding I have been very honorably offered
> matches) not to treat of marrying of her, if I may live so long, until she be
> above fifteen or sixteen; and if I were of more likelihood myself to live
> longer than I look to do, she should not, with my liking, be married before
> she were near eighteen or twenty.   (Lodge 2: 53)[1]

After I let this quote sink in (there's usually a minute or two of stunned silence),
I follow up with some facts from D. M. Palliser's social history of England, *The
Age of Elizabeth*: "Contrary to popular belief, youthful marriage was not the
norm, and child marriage was normally confined to aristocratic property trans-
actions, and was rare even in that circle" (40).[2] The average age for marriage
among aristocrats fits exactly with Burghley's expectations: late teens and early
twenties (Palliser 41). Commoners got married even later. On average, between
1550 and 1599, women were married at age twenty-five; the average rose to
twenty-six in the next half-century (41). For reasons that are unclear, London-
ers married early, between twenty-one and twenty-four. Shakespeare himself
married young, but he was eighteen at the time, still within Burghley's recom-
mendations. In sum, "a relatively late age of marriage was normal by Elizabeth's
reign" (41).

As the phrase goes, this changes everything. Armed with this background,
my students shift from looking at the play as a great romance to something
much more resonant and disturbing. As one student put it, the play is "tragic in
a much deeper way." It's not about fate or what happens when immature teenagers engage in sex, but a play about "a *really bad* society."

The first scene we look at is act 1, scene 2, when Count Paris comes to ask for
Juliet's hand in marriage. Students immediately recognize that Lord Capulet
responds exactly as Burghley did:

> My child is yet a stranger in the world;
> She hath not seen the change of fourteen years.
> Let two more summers wither in their pride
> Ere we may think her ripe to be a bride.
>   (1.2.8–11)

"Two more summers" would bring Juliet up to Burghley's minimum age of fifteen. By following Elizabethan marriage norms, Capulet shows that he is a
good father—for the moment. The next scene, however, goes in the opposite
direction. Lady Capulet and the Nurse repeat Juliet's age four times within
eleven lines (1.3.13–23). Thus, so far Shakespeare has told the audience no less
than five times that Juliet is "not fourteen." Given that no other specific ages are
stated in this play, it's fair to say that Shakespeare really wants the audience to
know Juliet's age. Knowing Juliet's age gives crucial specificity to Lady Capulet's remarks about marriage in the same scene:

Well, think of marriage now. Younger than you
Here in Verona, ladies of esteem,
Are made already mothers; by my count,
I was your mother much upon these years
That you are now a maid.

(1.3.71–75)

Comparing these lines with the Burghley quote shows students that Shakespeare's Verona is a world out of joint. When Lady Capulet says that women of Juliet's age "are made already mothers," I ask my students to do the math: these women must have gotten married at age 12 or so. It doesn't take a second before students realize that Lord Capulet's hesitancy about his daughter's marriage age is the exception rather than the rule in Verona. According to Lady Capulet, child marriage is in fact the norm in Verona, which should immediately alienate us from that society. Those in Shakespeare' audience who shared Burghley's view would have reacted the same way.

But there is more. Lady Capulet says that she was already a mother at Juliet's age, while Lord Capulet is repeatedly characterized as "old" in the play. When he tries to join the fray at the play's start, Lady Capulet says that he should be calling for "a crutch," not a sword (1.1.70–71), and Lord Capulet tells Paris "'tis not hard, I think, / For men so old as we to keep the peace" (1.2.2–3). If Capulet is as old as these passages imply, a number of questions jump out: How old is Juliet's mother? And how old was she when she married Juliet's father?[3] Apparently, not only are child brides acceptable in Verona, but so are marriages to men who are quite literally old enough to be their fathers, if not their grandfathers! Something has gone very wrong in Verona.

Strangely, Capulet knows that early marriage can be fatal. After he tells Paris that Juliet is too young, Paris responds with a horrific line that Juliet's mother later confirms: "Younger than she are happy mothers made" (1.2.12). But Capulet responds, "And too soon marred are those so early made" (1.2.13). We can assume from Capulet's response that he understands the dangers posed by pregnancy at age thirteen. "Marred" could mean permanent damage, or it could mean death. Given that he says "Earth hath swallowed all my hopes but she; / She's the hopeful lady of my earth" (1.2.14–15), chances are he means death. Either way, he understands full well the potential costs of children bearing children. At this point, I suspend the question of why Capulet, in 3.4, decides to abandon the Burghley rule (no marriage before age sixteen) and "make a desperate tender / Of [his] child's love" to Paris (3.4.12–13). Instead, I ask the class if there are any other causes for the catastrophe at the play's end. Who else, in other words, bears some responsibility for Romeo's and Juliet's death? Who else does not fulfill societal expectations and do their job? With these questions in mind, I lead the class in examining how each of the authority figures and institutions that should have protected the young ultimately fail them.

First up is the Prince. When he tries to stop the Capulets and Montagues from fighting in the street, it's clear that his authority does not extend very far: "Rebellious subjects, enemies to peace, / Profaners of this neighbor-stainèd steel—/ Will they not hear?" (1.1.76–78). True, eventually the warring parties stop their violence, but the Prince admits his inability to keep the peace when he says that both families "have thrice disturbed the quiet of our streets" (1.1.86). This riot, in other words, is the *fourth* such outbreak under his watch. As King James of Scotland puts it in his 1598 instruction manual on how to be a king, *Basilicon Doron*, the monarch's primary responsibility is to maintain "the well-fare and peace of his people" (James VI and I, 20). By that standard, the Prince clearly fails to do his job, just as Capulet fails in his duty as a father.

Next, we talk about the Nurse and Friar Laurence. For this section, I bring in another primary source: excerpts from the Bagot letters reprinted in Dympna Callaghan's invaluable edition of *Romeo and Juliet* (Shakespeare, Romeo and Juliet: Texts 315–42). These letters, detailing the domestic travails of the Bagot family, were written contemporaneously with Shakespeare's play, and, like the Burghley letter, they are an excellent guide to the social customs and mores of late-sixteenth-century England. In November 1589, one Richard Rugeley, god-son to Richard Bagot, got married without his family's permission. (It's worth pointing out that he was twenty-five or so at the time.) The parents were furious and threatened to disown their errant son, just as Lord Capulet does to Juliet. So, on 25 November, a local aristocrat and Rugeley's uncle, Lord Lumley, wrote to Richard Bagot to enlist his aid in calming things down. Here is the key passage: "[T]he young couple have with more speed than was meet coupled themselves in marriage without the consent and privity of their parents, to the utter subversion and undoing of the young couple, if it be not providently foreseen and wrought by some special friend of theirs." As in Shakespeare's play, a young couple (although not anywhere near as young as Romeo and Juliet) married without their family's permission. Clearly, the parents responded with the same fury as Capulet does when Juliet defies her father's demand that she marry Paris. Again like Romeo and Juliet, the Rugeleys face "utter subversion and undoing." So, Lord Lumley turns to a trusted third party, the young man's godfather, to intervene, "confer with their fathers," assure everyone that the property transfers "that have been delivered and made by the both may be performed accordingly," all "for the good of them all" (Shakespeare, Romeo and Juliet: Texts 319). Even though Lord Lumley and Richard Bagot are unacquainted, Lord Lumley asks Bagot to be that "special friend" and rescue the improvident couple from disaster.[4] Friar Laurence and the Nurse are in the same position Richard Bagot occupied in this matter: third parties who have an interest in Romeo and Juliet's welfare. They are exactly the "special friend" who could intervene with the warring families to calm things down. How well, I ask my students, do they do their job?

All the Nurse wants is for Juliet to get married: "An I might live to see thee married once, / I have my wish" (1.3.63–64). Even if the marriage will be to Romeo, she's perfectly fine with acting as a go-between. As for Friar Laurence, he, like Lord Capulet at the play's start, acts exactly as he should. After Romeo tells him that he now loves Juliet and wants the Friar to "marry us today" (2.2.64), Friar Laurence properly warns Romeo about undue haste, telling his charge that he did not mean for Romeo to switch out one obsession (Rosaline) for another (Juliet). Still, the Friar realizes that the match might have other benefits: "In one respect I'll thy assistant be, / For this alliance may so happy prove / To turn your households' rancor to pure love" (2.2.90–92). While not as precisely on point as the Burghley letter, the Bagot letter nonetheless shows that the Friar is acting according to expectations—he is willing to be the "special friend" who will intervene to not only incorporate the "improvident" young couple into the social network but reconcile the two warring families.

But once disaster falls and Romeo kills Tybalt after Tybalt kills Mercutio, again, like Lord Capulet, both go-betweens abandon societal expectation and respond with outrageous irresponsibility. The Nurse turns on a dime and, with alarming pragmatism, tells Juliet to forget about Romeo even though the Nurse knows full well that the two are married. He's banished, she tells her charge, so he can't come back "to challenge [claim] you" (3.5.215). Given Romeo's situation, or as the Nurse puts it, "since the case so stands as it now doth" (3.5.217), and given the Nurse's enthusiasm for Paris ("Oh, he's a lovely gentleman! / Romeo's a dishclout [dishcloth] to him" [3.5.218–19]), the Nurse's solution is simple: Romeo is gone; marry Paris, who is a better match anyway. At this point, I usually ask my class how they think Juliet feels. "Abandoned" and "unsupported" are milder responses. No wonder Juliet turns to thoughts of suicide as a last resort: "If all else fail, myself have power to die" (3.5.243). But before she has to resort to the most extreme solution, Juliet says she will "go to the Friar to know his remedy" (3.5.243).

Famously, or infamously, Friar Laurence's solution is an overly complex, Rube Goldberg–esque scheme. Rather than responding responsibly, as Burghley and Lord Lumley did—rather than acting as a "special friend" and marching Juliet back to her parents, telling them Juliet and Romeo are married, then doing what he could to resolve the situation—Friar Laurence comes up with the following idea (I always have some fun with this by speaking it as quickly as possible): "Juliet will take a drug that will make everyone think she is dead so she will be dressed in her best clothes and laid in the tomb. I'll send a letter to Romeo telling him that everyone will think Juliet's dead but she's not really dead, and he'll come back, and when Juliet wakes up he'll be right next to her. What could go wrong?" In short, everything. And as a result, Romeo kills Paris, then himself, then Juliet kills herself.

I end the classes on *Romeo and Juliet* by asking the students who is responsible. Is it "fate," as the Chorus says at the play's start? (Although I also point out that the Chorus is missing from the First Folio, which its editors, John Heminges and Henry Condell, claim reproduces the plays "as [Shakespeare] conceived them" [Shakespeare, *Mr. William Shakespeares Comedies*, sig. A3r], so perhaps Shakespeare did not want us to think in terms of fate.) Starting with the

Burghley letter clarifies for students that every authority in *Romeo and Juliet* that should protect the young couple fails them. Parental authority fails when Capulet does not act as Burghley did and refuse to allow his daughter's marriage before age fifteen. Secular authority, in the form of the Prince, fails by not keeping order. Religious authority and social responsibility fail when the Nurse and Friar Laurence do not act as "special friends" and prevent the "utter subversion and undoing of the young couple" (Shakespeare, *Romeo and Juliet: Texts* 319), which is of course exactly what happens in Shakespeare's play. At the end, my students do not feel resigned to fate, as perhaps a Greek tragedy might want them to be. Nor are they assured that vice is punished and virtue rewarded, as early modern theoreticians of tragedy would say. Instead, they are very, very angry.

Romeo and Juliet marks the beginning of Shakespeare's artistic maturity. While dating Shakespeare's play is an inexact science, at roughly the same time, he wrote *A Midsummer Night's Dream*, a play which seems fluffy but is in fact a sharp-edged treatment of misogyny, and *Richard II*, Shakespeare's deep dive into the roots of the Tudor dynasty. Shakespeare's coming into his own, in other words, meant writing plays that ask the audience to question authority and look hard at his culture's failings. If my students learn nothing else, I hope that's what they take away from the class.

NOTES

1. Sadly, Elizabeth would die before her father did. I have silently modernized the spelling in the early modern letters quoted in this essay.

2. It's worth noting the persistence of the "popular belief" in youthful marriage; Palliser 40. Even though Palliser's book is over thirty years old, high school students are still taught that early marriage was conventional in Shakespeare's England.

3. Zeffirelli's and Lurhmann's film versions as well as the 1978 BBC television version of *Romeo and Juliet* all cast Lady Capulet as distinctly middle-aged (*Romeo and Juliet* [Zeffirelli]; *William Shakespeare's Romeo + Juliet*; *Romeo and Juliet* [Rakoff]). While the actors playing Lord Capulet are all definitely older, the gap is not so great as to strike the viewer as obviously inappropriate.

4. Lord Lumley, as Callaghan notes, was partly successful. The negotiations over property continued for at least a year after the marriage was performed (320). Nonetheless, it seems that the couple's marital bliss was allowed to continue. Nobody threw them out or disowned them.

Individualism and the Character Turn in *Romeo and Juliet*

Meghan C. Andrews

Much like the sonnets that structure its first half, *Romeo and Juliet* possesses an important, tenor-changing turn shortly before its end. I do not mean the oft-noted generic shift from comedy to tragedy between acts 2 and 3; rather, the turn I refer to is the character evolution that Romeo and Juliet both undergo between acts 3 and 4, a change that can be harder to perceive but that is just as pivotal for the play's tragedy. Unlike the generic turn, this character turn is often difficult for students to identify and analyze. This essay discusses strategies for helping students understand it, ranging from writing assignments to the selective screening of two major adaptations, Franco Zeffirelli's *Romeo and Juliet* and Baz Luhrmann's *William Shakespeare's Romeo + Juliet*. Writing assignments that track character development hone students' ability to interpret narrative because they help students see how character is critical to understanding a text's major themes. Such assignments also help students make the jump from close reading a single speech or scene to weaving together readings of multiple scenes to arrive at a larger reading of a text as a whole, sharpening students' critical reading and analysis skills. Moreover, analyzing film versions of a play provides students with an introduction to adaptation and acquaints them with the idea that every performance presents a certain reading of a play—the idea that a performance's creative choices convey, or even change, the meaning of a text.

I teach *Romeo and Juliet* in both upper-division Shakespeare and non-Shakespeare Renaissance literature seminars as well as in lower-division topic-centered courses for non–English majors. The time we spend on the text varies from five (for the upper division) to eight or nine (for the lower division) sixty-five-minute periods. But, no matter the class, my fundamental approach to the play remains constant. I teach *Romeo and Juliet* as a powerful tragedy of individualism, a combination of coming-of-age story and quintessential Renaissance narrative about creating an individual identity distinct from one's inherited or socially ascribed identity. I choose to focus on character in *Romeo and Juliet* for three reasons. First, and most important, it provides an accessible way into the text for students. Even in upper-division courses, students have varying levels of preparation for reading Shakespeare (and *Romeo and Juliet* is usually the first text I teach in Shakespeare seminars). Not every student is ready for discussions of the play's generic mixture of comedy and tragedy, but every student has a reaction to the characters themselves, especially since the majority of my students are not much older than Juliet and Romeo. Second, I see character as key to discussions of gender, a major strand of my teaching of the play. From Romeo's ultimately disastrous determination to establish his masculinity to Juliet's increasing defiance of early modern social scripts for women, I suggest to students that what we see in *Romeo* is an almost total subversion of early modern gender norms. Understanding how Juliet and Romeo grow as characters is key to understanding the play's querying of gender norms. Third, *Romeo and Juliet* is tragic for many reasons (and we always have a productive last day of discussion on these reasons), and I suggest to students that one of the biggest reasons is that Juliet and Romeo both establish unique individual identities and fully mature into adults just in time to die, thus ending when they should be beginning. However, it is their successful individuation and maturation, and their final agency over their own bodies and fates, that lends them tragic gravitas and contributes to their depiction as transcendent by the play's end. *Romeo and Juliet* thus derives much of its tragic power from Romeo's and Juliet's character development. For all these reasons, it is character that we spend the vast majority of our time discussing.

Our discussions always go very well for at least the play's first half, as we note that both Romeo and Juliet begin by acting in accordance with cultural scripts that prescribe identities for them. My students find Juliet, in particular, highly engaging—they are much more interested in her than in Romeo—and readily grasp that her introductory scene in act 1, scene 3, frames her as a version of the perfect Renaissance daughter; she speaks just seven of the scene's 107 lines and subordinates her own desires to her parents' wishes: "I'll look to like, if looking liking move; / But no more deep will I endart mine eye / Than your consent gives strength to make it fly" (1.3.99–101). Students therefore recognize how immediately her character begins to grow when she meets Romeo, from flirting with him to manipulating the Nurse into discovering his identity to expressing her own desire for him immediately and intensely. Students also have no difficulty recognizing that the balcony scene continues this evolution. As we work through the balcony scene in sections, with volunteers reading Romeo's and Juliet's lines throughout (always a course highlight), students unanimously agree that Juliet—with her sophisticated musings on identity and love, forthright statements of desire, rejection of social conventions, pragmatism, and intensity of feeling—is almost unrecognizable from the Juliet of 1.3.

Similarly, students easily recognize Romeo's character growth over the first two acts. In the class meeting prior to beginning *Romeo and Juliet*, I give students a brief primer on Petrarchism along with a handful of sonnets from Petrarch's *Rime Sparse*; alert students have no trouble identifying the Romeo of 1.1 as a caricature of the Petrarchan lover.[1] While this initially makes students skeptical of his feelings for Juliet, those with a finely tuned poetic ear realize that as soon as the lovers meet his language moves away from stale Petrarchan clichés and toward powerfully individual and more genuine sentiments of love. This linguistic evolution is matched by character evolution, as students acknowledge that Romeo's actions in the rest of acts 1 and 2—from approaching and conversing with Juliet, to risking death to see her, to listening to and honoring her desires, to arranging for the marriage, to, most importantly, his commitment to a reciprocal relationship of equals—make a sharp contrast to his actions with Rosalind. In effect, the Romeo of act 1 becomes a foil to the more mature lover of act 2.

Our conversations on acts 1 and 2 thus center on how both Romeo and Juliet reject cultural scripts in favor of their own nascent individual identities. With some prompting, students are able to carry this discussion into act 3 and see that Romeo's and Juliet's major dilemma remains the same: whether to side with their newfound private identities or their public identities determined by their biological families and Verona's gendered social norms. At the beginning of act 3, this dilemma is particularly acute for Romeo, who must choose between being a "man" who prioritizes his obligations to Juliet and a "man" who proves himself through violence and participation in the feud (Kahn, *Man's Estate* 82–118); by the act's end, the dilemma is more acute for Juliet, who learns she will be disowned by her family unless she agrees to marry Paris. Notably, Romeo and Juliet have different initial reactions to this dilemma. While Romeo initially chooses loyalty to Juliet, Mercutio's death leads him to privilege his public identity as a violent Montague; it is this choice that steers the play into tragic territory, illustrating the dangers of unthinkingly acting in accordance with social norms. In contrast, Juliet initially sides with her family while mourning Tybalt—I point out to students that her speech at 3.2.73–85 is full of the Petrarchan paradoxes the play earlier associates with inauthenticity—before quickly aligning herself with Romeo. Their wedding night, like their earlier marriage, then serves as a rite of passage that renews their commitment to each other and continues to move them into adult life, a process that is marked by their burgeoning individuation and movement away from their families. Further, after Romeo leaves, how much Juliet's character has grown is marked in 3.5, when her double-speak with her mother successfully hides her intentions and when she confidently tells her parents she will not marry Paris.

So far, so good. However, the first several times I taught *Romeo and Juliet*, difficulties arose in acts 4 and 5. Perhaps because they were fresh off of discussing Romeo's and Juliet's seemingly melodramatic, juvenile responses to the news of Romeo's banishment, students tended to take this view of the lovers as immature into the final two acts and thus to see Romeo and Juliet ending the play as dumb teenagers whose rashness is responsible for their demise. While the lovers' impatience is certainly an important element of the tragedy and should not be ignored, another equally powerful reading is one that sees Romeo's and Juliet's decisions to kill themselves as the final step of their maturation into adults choosing individualistic self-determination over socially dictated roles. When we read the play this way, I suggest to students, it is both more satisfying on a character level—for we see both Juliet and Romeo complete their character arcs—and more tragic, because Juliet and Romeo achieve full individualism just in time to die. Further, reading the lovers as attaining full individuation helps activate the reading of them as triumphant and transcendent at the play's end. If students simply think of Romeo and Juliet in the play's two last acts as dumb teenagers, all this is lost. Thus, the more I taught *Romeo and Juliet*, the more I realized that my task was to help students see the character turn that Juliet and Romeo undergo in the final two acts. I now do this in two ways, one involving a traditional writing prompt, and one involving film.

First, in advance of our discussion of acts 4 and 5, I assign students a simple writing prompt as homework, which in its broadest form reads, "Compare Juliet in 4.1 and 4.3 with Juliet in 3.2 and 3.5, and compare Romeo in 5.1 and 5.3 with Romeo in 3.1 and 3.3." These scenes share surface-level similarities, and yet, when prompted to read them comparatively, almost all students will write that Juliet's character changes very much between acts. Romeo tends to fare less well in student assessments, but stronger students will glean that his character, too, follows the same general outline as Juliet's: a movement from overwrought Petrarchan statements about banishment and death in act 3 to a more mature experience of true grief in acts 4 and 5, which replaces poetic posturing with actual suicide. This change is accompanied by Juliet's final rejection of her Capulet self—when she takes the poison, she seemingly makes a decisive break with her Capulet identity—and determination to take possession over herself and her body, rejecting first her parents' and then Friar Laurence's plans for her in favor of deciding her own fate once and for all.

I estimate that about eighty-five percent of students at least begin to get at these ideas thanks to the prompt, which I have found facilitates much better discussion. For example, one particularly perceptive student noted that in contrast to 3.2, in 4.3

> Juliet is by comparison somber. Her actions are well thought out and she is not riding the emotional turmoil of a recent revelation. . . . Here Juliet acts almost like an adult. She is, certainly, still immature, but has taken great strides in maturity between the two scenes. . . . In 3.2, Juliet is a juvenile that has been told some bad news, and has reacted as juveniles will. In 4.3, Juliet is a young adult with a plan of action and a rational thought process.

Another wrote:

> The Romeo of 3.1/3.3 is more dramatic, while the Romeo of 5.1/5.3 is less talk and more action. . . . [In 3.3], much like the earlier Juliet, this Romeo relies on Friar Laurence to form a plan for him while he is in distress. However, the Romeo of 5.1 does not rely on Friar Laurence at all. Within his first three lines after learning of Juliet's "death," Romeo has already put his plan into action. . . . Similarly, in 5.3 Romeo sounds like a cold and calculating man who just wants to get his job done. . . . This new Romeo . . . speaks through his actions rather than running his mouth.

Not every student will be capable of this depth of analysis or eloquence, but even if students just scratch the surface of Romeo's or Juliet's evolution in the last two acts they are more prepared to discuss the completion of their character arcs and to consider how these arcs contribute to the play's tragic denouement.

On the day of the discussion itself, film becomes an immensely useful teaching tool, paradoxically, thanks to what it excludes instead of what it includes. The two most popular film versions of the play—Zeffirelli's and Luhrmann's—*do* cast the lovers' actions in acts 4 and 5 as the rash actions of immature children. However, they heavily cut the text to justify this interpretation, which students perceive when we compare film to text. Further, by cutting Juliet's part more, both films truncate her character arc as it is charted in the text. I therefore always begin my discussion of act 4 by telling students that I would love to show them either the Zeffirelli or the Luhrmann version of Juliet's great soliloquy in 4.3, but that I cannot because both films cut it. As she drinks the potion, Zeffirelli gives Juliet just a single line—"Love give me strength"—transposed from 4.1.126, while Luhrmann mingles just four lines of the soliloquy with Juliet's farewell to her mother. This naturally leads me to ask my students, "What is lost if we lose Juliet's final soliloquy?" The students' answers—an illustration of her courage and commitment in the face of terror, her rejection of her family's wishes, a continuation of her intelligent pragmatism, and ultimately her determination to decide her own destiny— all lead students to see how her "deathbed" soliloquy completes Juliet's evolution into a fully individualized, self-determining character.

I then backtrack to Zeffirelli's adaptation of 4.1 through 4.3 (though one could easily replace this with Luhrmann, since both films extensively cut act 4) and ask the same question: "What do you notice has been omitted, and how does that change our sense of Juliet's character?" Students almost always notice that the adaptation (no matter which) cuts almost all of Juliet's testy stichomythia with Paris, a verbal duel that the Juliet of 1.3 would have been wholly unable to engage in and that, like her double-speak in 3.5, measures how far she has come. Not coincidentally, both films also cut that double-speak and make cuts to 3.5 that eliminate Juliet's more thoughtful, less emotional objections to marrying Paris. Both films then either entirely or functionally cut both Juliet's first long speech to Friar Laurence, stating that *if* he cannot help her, she is determined to die (4.1.50–67), and then her "Oh, bid me leap" speech (4.1.77– 88); Zeffirelli entirely cuts the former and significantly shortens the latter, while Luhrmann shortens the former and cuts the latter. The overall effect, students agree, is to cast Juliet as far more helpless and emotional and far less self-possessed and intelligent than she is in Shakespeare's text, where she repeatedly states she will kill herself only *if* the Friar cannot help her.[2] And in classes where I have screened either or both films fully, we note that the cuts to 3.5 do the same work: they foreground lines that make Juliet seem hysterically emotional and cut lines that cast her as more measured. (And while Zeffirelli at least retains Juliet's refusal to fly with the Friar in 5.3 and her final lines that underscore her final self-possession, Luhrmann cuts all of her dialogue, which casts her suicide as "defeat rather than triumph, helplessness rather than control" [Scott 144].)

On the whole, I have found the Zeffirelli and Luhrmann films highly useful tools for teaching the character evolution of Juliet in particular. Romeo's parts tend not to be cut to the same degree, and so in both films it is easier to see that Romeo has left posturing behind when faced with what he believes to be Juliet's real death, which spurs him into aggressive action for the first time in the play, motivated by a more emotionally real recognition that he truly does not want to live without Juliet. However, I do discuss with students how the omission in both films of Romeo's duel with Paris and lying to Balthasar, and Zeffirelli's additional omission of his buying poison, also detract from his arc (even if they make him more appealing and innocent) by omitting the symbolic murder of his former, inauthentic Petrarchan self (Paris); by diminishing the part of Romeo that finally stops talking and starts doing; and by casting his decision to kill himself as less measured. Overall, I suggest to students that these cinematic adaptations work hard to cast the lovers as dumb teenagers and that the extent of these cuts reveals just how far these young lovers actually change in Shakespeare's text. With stronger classes, this can then spur productive discussions of *why* Hollywood has wanted to portray the lovers as foolish adolescents and *Romeo and Juliet*'s cultural place as the ur-narrative of passionate first love.

Along these same lines but more broadly, Luhrmann's film is also useful because its emphasis on Romeo at the expense of Juliet can retroactively help students understand that the play itself is in many ways about Juliet more than Romeo (R. Jackson 220–21; Lehmann; Donaldson 165–71). After we read the play, I usually screen the Luhrmann film in its entirety, and before we watch I ask students to prepare by identifying Juliet's and Romeo's three most important speeches each. We review the class's answers together, and I ask students to pay particular attention to these speeches and how they are adapted. Students are often surprised and dismayed that most of what they have identified as Romeo's major moments—his opening lovesickness for Rosaline, his protestations of love in the balcony scene, his anguish at being banished in act 3, and his jolt into action at the start of act 5 and then lengthy death speech—generally survive, if not unscathed, with their spirit intact, but that many of the moments they identify as important for Juliet's character are either entirely cut or so deeply changed that her character arc is fundamentally altered. Students generally identify Juliet's standout moments as 1.3, the balcony scene; Juliet's epithalamium and then anguished response to Romeo's murder of Tybalt in 3.2 and breaking away from her family in 3.5, 4.1, and 4.3; and her last lines in 5.3. As noted above, the film fundamentally cuts or alters 3.5, 4.1, 4.3, and 5.3, and it is also worth noting that both Luhrmann and Zeffirelli functionally cut Juliet's epithalamium as well as the vast majority of her dialogue in 3.2. The only major moments for Juliet that survive unscathed are 1.3 and the balcony scene.

In other words, through discussion the students come to realize that the Luhrmann film in particular, whether consciously or not, minimizes Juliet's character arc and role even as it leaves Romeo's fundamentally untouched, and in fact makes Romeo more attractive—less whiny, more active, and more accepting of the consequences of his actions—than in Shakespeare's text. Students keenly sense that Luhrmann's Romeo is "the subject through whom the story is told" (Lehmann 211) and "a more complexly drawn character than . . . Juliet" (Anderegg 61, 71n4), despite the fact that in the text "Shakespeare's Juliet has so far outgrown Romeo by the end of the play" that she has become the center of dramatic interest (Weis 61). And here we should note that the functional omission of Juliet's epithalamium is also particularly striking given that Luhrmann's film can hardly be said to be prudish—and the same might be said of Zeffirelli's, which cuts the epithalamium entirely. Juliet's epithalamium can be overlooked by students given everything else that happens in act 3, but it, too, serves as an important moment for Juliet and richly rewards close reading as a class, as her spiritual expression of adult eroticism is another important step in her maturation. The functional omission of this speech not only detracts even more from Juliet's character; it also, I suggest, hints at a larger discomfort with such a forthright, assertive statement of female desire—one perhaps mirrored in students, who sometimes giggle nervously when we close read the speech. That both directors seem more comfortable with a topless Juliet in bed with Romeo than with one who speaks alone and assertively of her desire is telling. And, again, in stronger classes this can lead to a discussion of popular culture's discomfort with female sexuality more broadly.

Overall, the students and I thus frame Luhrmann's film as a fantastic adaptation of Shakespeare to the modern day but as a highly flawed reading of *Romeo and Juliet*, one whose privileging of Romeo over Juliet in defiance of Shakespeare's text is no doubt rooted in Hollywood's deep-seated sexism and skepticism of female-led films. Recently, a student remarked that Luhrmann's film reminded her of a superhero movie in the way it made Juliet more passive, more reactive to Romeo, and overall weaker than in Shakespeare's text: the "girlfriend" or damsel in distress to his hero. This is a perceptive comment, but I also suggest to my students that there may be hope on the horizon, given the relatively recent box office success of women-led superhero blockbusters such as *Wonder Woman* and *Captain Marvel*. At the writing of this essay, it has been twenty-five years since Luhrmann's film, almost equal to the twenty-eight years between Zeffirelli and Luhrmann. Hopefully another magisterial adaptation of *Romeo and Juliet* will appear soon and will give Juliet her due, telling the tale of Juliet and her Romeo.

NOTES

1. For suggestions about how to incorporate Petrarch into a class on *Romeo and Juliet*, see the essay by Joshua Reid in this volume.

2. Both adaptations retain Friar Laurence's lauding of Juliet's "strength of will" (4.1.72) but omit his implication that she has masculine bravery and "valor" (4.1.120–21).

An Intersectional Approach
to Girls and Girlhoods in Shakespeare's Verona

Ariane M. Balizet

Shakespeare's Juliet brings out some of my students' most entrenched beliefs about gender in the Renaissance: people married younger, women were considered property, women had no say in marriage. Students usually talk about Juliet's girlhood by suggesting that marriage marks the threshold where girls become women. They conclude that Juliet dies because she could not fulfill the only social purpose available to girls: marriage and motherhood. This reading of *Romeo and Juliet* troubles me because it asserts a false narrative of social progress between the sixteenth and twenty-first centuries: the mechanisms of Renaissance patriarchy (emblematized by Juliet's arranged marriage to Paris) uniformly oppressed all girls and women in the past, until modern advancements in gender equality (emblematized by the presence of white women in lucrative professions) uniformly liberated all girls and women today. In the wake of the 2022 United States Supreme Court decision in *Dobbs v. Jackson Women's Health Organization*, this narrative seems more misleading than ever. Moreover, this postfeminist interpretation of history also ignores other girl figures in the play—such as Rosaline, the servant girls secretly admitted to the Capulet feast, and the Nurse's lost infant, Susan—and thus elevates Juliet as the only girl who matters in the play. The diverse social positions occupied by characters in *Romeo and Juliet* whom we might now call "girls" are shaped not only by gender and age but also by race, class, sexuality, and other social dynamics that subordinate all of these figures to Juliet. I invite students to place Juliet within a constellation of girls and girlhoods in Shakespeare's Verona and to examine girlhood not as a stable category of identity marked by thresholds of age and gender but as a process of social valuation along multiple axes. In this way, my pedagogical aim in focusing on girls in *Romeo and Juliet* is to practice intersectional analysis with my students.

Juliet is a white, wealthy, noble-born girl who clearly expresses heterosexual desire and consents to marriage within the Roman Catholic Church to the white, wealthy, noble-born Romeo. An analysis that reduces Juliet's tragic ending to gender-based oppression in a Shakespearean past rehearses what Kimberlé Crenshaw calls "single-axis analysis" (139). From this position, characters with fewer markers of racial, class, and sexual privilege are even further marginalized, as though the modern study of Renaissance girlhood cannot consider individuals who were Black, poor, queer, or servants. Crenshaw argues that "dominant conceptions of discrimination condition us to think about subordination as disadvantage occurring along a single categorical axis" (140). In the study of Shakespeare, gender is very often the single axis upon which students understand historical oppression. By contrast, Crenshaw, with Sumi Cho and Leslie McCall, argues that intersectionality is an analytic "sensibility" or "disposition" that adopts

> an intersectional way of thinking about the problem of sameness and difference and its relation to power. This framing—conceiving of categories not as distinct but as always permeated by other categories, fluid and changing, always in the process of creating and being created by dynamics of power—emphasizes what intersectionality does rather than what intersectionality is. (Cho et al. 795)

Exploring the dynamic nature of girlhood in *Romeo and Juliet* helps students develop intersectional readings of early modern literature and culture. The point is not to define the early modern "girl" but rather to use girlhood as a starting point to examine and understand marginalized subjectivities in Shakespeare's Verona.

The study of girlhood as "always creating and being created by dynamics of power" begins with the understanding that gender cannot be separated from other forms of identity and representation in the play. That is, we cannot make any assumptions about "all girls" because the language of girlhood is itself interpellated with the rhetoric of age, race, class, and sexuality. *Romeo and Juliet* includes more than a dozen terms that might apply to young female characters, including "maid," "madam," "woman," "lady," "child," "daughter," "wretch," "wench," "mistress," "bride," "fair creature," and, of course, "girl." Juliet is addressed or described by all of these terms, as well as by misogynistic epithets that do not denote age ("harlot," "hilding," "baggage") and titles directly related to her secret marriage ("wife," "widow"). As Deanne Williams notes, with these many terms to choose from, "Shakespeare typically uses the term 'girl' when a character's relationship to authority is complicated or troubled" (*Shakespeare* 4). For example, after Juliet feigns compliance with the plan to marry Paris, Lord Capulet exclaims, "My heart is wondrous light / Since this same wayward girl is so reclaimed" (act 4, scene 2, lines 46–47). Even with respect to children more generally, there was no stable girl/boy binary in the English Renaissance. As

Jennifer Higginbotham demonstrates, any child could be described by the term "girl" in Middle English, and it was not until the early sixteenth century that the term "had come to refer exclusively to female individuals" (21). Alternately, in Shakespeare's *The Winter's Tale*, a shepherd comes across an abandoned infant and exclaims, "A boy or a child, I wonder?" (3.3.68). Instead of starting from a stable category of "the girl," students might ask, How and why are young people valued or devalued as girls, maids, ladies, or daughters?

Romeo's first love, Rosaline, is described as a "woman" who "hath sworn that she will still live chaste" (1.1.199, 212). Students often assume this means Rosaline intends to become a nun, but "chaste" could denote her rejection of extramarital sexual activity as well as religious celibacy. Her invitation to her uncle Capulet's feast—and Benvolio's confidence she will attend—point to the possibility that the unmarried Rosaline has rejected Romeo in particular and not romance in general. But Rosaline's chastity does not prevent Mercutio from composing a crude anti-blazon of her body to "conjure" Romeo:

> —I conjure thee by Rosaline's bright eyes,
> By her high forehead and her scarlet lip,
> By her fine foot, straight leg, and quivering thigh,
> And the demesnes that there adjacent lie
>
> (2.1.17–20)

Rhetorically, Mercutio considers Rosaline only in terms of sexual possession, concluding his attempt to arouse Romeo's spirit with the image of the "demesnes"—a synonym and near-homonym for "domains"—adjacent to Rosaline's "quivering thigh[s]." Like the Montague maids whose assault is the subject of fantasy for two Capulet men in the first scene, Rosaline's social value is determined through sexual possession by men of the enemy house.

Before Romeo dismisses Rosaline entirely—"He jests at scars that never felt a wound" (2.1.43)—the play's chorus announces that her value has decreased after comparison with her cousin: "That fair for which love groaned for and would die, / With tender Juliet matched, is now not fair" (2.0.3–4). This moment captures the constant sense of competition for superior (and supreme) whiteness between girls in Shakespeare's Verona. My students typically read the word "fair" in the play's opening lines as a reference to justice and, to a lesser extent, beauty. But the white-light connotations of "fair"—used not just as a synonym for but as a comparative measure of beauty—dominate its usage in the play. In the first scene, Benvolio counsels Romeo to forget Rosaline "by giving liberty unto [his] eyes, / Examine other beauties" (1.1.222–23). Romeo responds:

> 'Tis the way
> To call hers, exquisite, in question more.
> These happy masks that kiss fair ladies' brows,

> Being black, puts us in mind they hide the fair.
> He that is strucken blind cannot forget
> The precious treasure of his eyesight lost.
> Show me a mistress that is passing fair:
> What doth her beauty serve but as a note
> Where I may read who passed that passing fair?
> (1.1.223–32)

Romeo argues that viewing other beautiful faces will only draw heightened attention to Rosaline's "exquisite" features. The illustrative metaphor that follows—black masks hiding fair brows—characterizes the young friends' discourse as one in which whiteness is used to identify a singular beauty. Benvolio argues that Rosaline is "fair" only when perceived alone: "compare her face with some that I shall show," he dares Romeo, "and I will make thee think thy swan a crow" (1.2.89–90). In Shakespeare's Verona, beauty *is* whiteness and registers most clearly in contrast to Blackness. Crucially, this contrast is not a stable binary with respect to girls' attractiveness; Rosaline is fair only until she is compared to "some other maid" (1.2.100), and without ever appearing onstage she swiftly becomes the "crow" or "black mask" that sets off Juliet's fair, white beauty.

In the past, some of my students have been reticent to read Romeo's praise of "the white wonder of dear Juliet's hand" (3.3.36) in racial terms. One student argued that whiteness is a marker only of class distinction in Renaissance England because tanned or darker skin tones indicated labor outdoors, whereas ladies of the higher classes could stay inside and preserve the "white wonder" of their hands. However, as Kim F. Hall reminds us, "[t]he language of fairness and darkness is always *potentially* racialized, and it does an injustice to the richness of the language to insist out of fear or ignorance that texts exist as 'pure,' above ideologies of race" (261). I remind my students that insisting on a class-based analysis that excludes racialized fairness both presupposes white skin as normal (darkened by the sun) and still centers and reasserts whiteness as an aspirational quality inherent to both beauty and class.

Romeo's lines when he first glimpses Juliet offer an excellent opportunity for students to abandon the notion of Shakespeare's plays as "pure" and "above" race and to practice multiple-axis analysis:

> Oh, she doth teach the torches to burn bright!
> It seems she hangs upon the cheek of night
> As a rich jewel in an Ethiop's ear,
> Beauty too rich for use, for earth too dear.
> So shows a snowy dove trooping with crows
> As yonder lady o'er her fellows shows.
> (1.4.155–60)

In this passage, Romeo raises the racialized subtext to the surface, explicitly linking the light/night and dove/crow motifs to the image of a "rich jewel in an Ethiop's ear." For Joyce Green MacDonald, the play pointedly racializes darkness, "as a fragment of an otherwise sanctioned black body becomes the expressive vehicle for the impact of Romeo's sudden flash of emotional and erotic insight" (47). By describing Juliet as "a rich jewel in an Ethiop's ear," Romeo articulates her value specifically in terms of whiteness and in contrast to both an African and her Veronese peers.

Considering the Ethiopian's "sanctioned black body" in this passage can further hone students' ability to read girls in Shakespeare's Verona intersectionally. Hall's work on the popularity of Black cameos[1] in the sixteenth and seventeenth centuries offers us a visual example of the Ethiopian profile Romeo imagines upon first meeting Juliet. Hall explores in detail the early modern English practice of acquiring, wearing, and exchanging jeweled images of Africans as an expression of wealth and status. For Hall, these depictions suggest "that long before England gained a foothold in the Atlantic slave trade, blacks played an important role in the symbolic economy of elite culture" (211). Students may find it useful to consider who in the play might have access to such adornment, or why it is Romeo (and not Benvolio, Mercutio, nor even Capulet, who also use dark/light binaries to distinguish between girls) who so directly contrasts Juliet with a Black woman. Inviting students to explore how Juliet's "fellows" are subordinated to her in terms of skin color helps them see how whiteness is a racialized process of valuation in Shakespeare's Verona.

While girls' fairness and beauty are always determined by comparison, the play stresses Juliet's singularity by repeatedly reminding the audience of Juliet's age. Before Juliet appears or is named, Lord Capulet describes her with language emphasizing her youth:

> My child is yet a stranger in the world;
> She hath not seen the change of fourteen years.
> Let two more summers wither in their pride
> Ere we may think her ripe to be a bride.
>
> (1.2.8–11)

Paris rebuts Capulet's call for patience by projecting "happy mother[hood]" onto others of Juliet's age and younger, to which Capulet insists that motherhood at such a young age "mars" young brides. My students are eager to read Shakespeare's specificity about Juliet's age as indicative of her innocence and naivete—an interpretation that accords with their condemnation of the protagonists as impulsive and immature. At the same time, the fact that Paris and Capulet disagree about Juliet's readiness for marriage jars their general sense that "everyone got married earlier in those days." These considerations reveal that ideas of youth, maturity, and innocence were not understood in terms of clear thresholds but were interpellated in other forms of identity and social valuation.

We can examine Juliet—just two weeks shy of her fourteenth birthday—as neither "too young" nor "too old" but rather in the middle of a process through which her social value is changing dramatically.

Turning fourteen, in fact, marked a significant milestone in the lives of early modern girls. Citing the seventeenth-century midwife Jane Sharp, Ursula Potter notes that "the stages of life are measured in seven-year stretches and . . . the year fourteen holds particular significance for girls" (421). In early modern England, medical writers were "atypically unanimous . . . when it came to marking and describing the moment of female puberty: when a girl reached the age of fourteen or fifteen, her body began to heat up, her breasts began to swell, and she began to menstruate" (Bicks, "Incited Minds," 185). Because menarche was expected at fourteen, Capulet's reminder that Juliet "hath not seen the change of fourteen years" may reflect concern about her ability to conceive. But Capulet's wife and Juliet's Nurse—like Paris—see Juliet's age in a different light. In her first line, the Nurse claims that she herself became sexually active at an even younger age, vowing by her "maidenhead at twelve year old" (1.3.2). Likewise, Capulet's wife echoes Paris when she reminds Juliet:

> Younger than you
> Here in Verona, ladies of esteem,
> Are made already mothers; by my count,
> I was your mother much upon these years
> That you are now a maid.
>
> (1.3.71–75)

If Juliet is still a "maid," and the play's constant reminders that she is "not fourteen" (1.3.13) imply that she has not begun menstruating, Juliet is in fact an unusual case in the Capulet home and, by her mother's account, among Veronese "ladies of esteem." In sixteenth-century England, the average age of marriage for women was twenty-six (King 87), so the notion that Juliet's mother may be nearing that age as her daughter approaches fourteen suggests that there is no bright line between girlhood and motherhood. Though Capulet may view Juliet as not yet "ripe to be a bride," her mother, wet nurse, and suitor suggest that she is overdue to leave behind her maidenhead and become a "happy mother" and "lady of esteem." I ask my students to consider why Juliet's parents might hold such varied opinions about her age and why the Nurse and Paris are in agreement about Juliet's readiness for marriage despite their vast differences in class and status.

The Nurse's lengthy monologue recalling the day of Juliet's weaning offers students another excellent opportunity to consider girlhood as a process of social valuation. As her title suggests, the Nurse was first employed by the Capulet family as a wet nurse for the newborn Juliet, a position that included not only breastfeeding but rearing the child through toddlerhood. Although most children of Juliet's class and status would have been sent away to live with the wet nurse's family until they were weaned, the Nurse's memories of Juliet's early years suggest that Juliet was raised by the Nurse within the Capulet household. In recalling Juliet's infancy, the Nurse also laments the loss of her own infant daughter, Susan, whose brief life physically enabled her mother to be a wet nurse:

> Come Lammas Eve at night shall she be fourteen.
> Susan and she—God rest all Christian souls—
> Were of an age. Well, Susan is with God;
> She was too good for me.
>
> (1.3.19–22)

The practice of wet-nursing is profoundly alien to most of my students, so drawing attention to the Nurse's lasting grief over the loss of her own baby girl helps students better understand the complex emotional ties between wet nurses and the families who employed them. Gail Kern Paster describes the "material history implied by this narrative," including

> two "blood" parents, the two surrogate "milk" parents of nurse and husband, and the infant girl in their care. Juliet, of course, is herself a surrogate for the baby Susan whose (presumably very early) death brought her mother, grieving and lactating, into the Capulets' employ, along with her now-dead husband. It is likely that the Capulets sought a nurse the "gender" of whose pregnancy matched their own and whose "new" milk would be highly desirable.
>
> (221)

As I have argued elsewhere, although many early modern wet nurses took in new charges as their own children were weaned, Susan's early death would have made the Nurse highly attractive to her future employers (Balizet, "Breastfeeding" 232). With Susan gone, Juliet would not have to share her Nurse's milk—milk that would be particularly appropriate in terms of moral and physical health for Juliet, another girl "of an age" with Susan. In other words, the death of one infant girl may be read directly in terms of her perceived value to the wealthy family who seeks to employ her mother.

The account by the Nurse of Juliet's traumatic weaning also raises the specter of her deceased husband, whom the Nurse recalls exchanging a ribald joke with the toddler Juliet, who was in tears after falling on her face:

> And yet I warrant it had upon it brow
> A bump as big as a young cock'rel's stone—
> A perilous knock—and it cried bitterly.
> "Yea?" quoth my husband. "Fall'st upon thy face?
> Thou wilt fall backward when thou comest to age,
> Wilt thou not, Jule?" It stinted and said "Ay!"
>
> (1.3.54–59)

Most editions of *Romeo and Juliet* gloss the husband's "Thou wilt fall backward" as a reference to sexual submission; when Juliet "come[s] to age" and "ha[s] more wit" (1.3.34), she will take her proper place on her back. Juliet's knowing response to the joke suggests that, even at the age of three, Juliet had already learned from her "milk" parents that her value would ultimately be determined through her sexuality.

The name "Susan" itself becomes another of the play's many terms that register variable notions of girlhood. Like the Nurse's daughter Susan, Rosaline, and the ladies invited to the Capulet feast (1.2.65–73), the two servant girls secretly admitted to the Capulet house do not appear onstage. As he instructs his fellows to transform the hall into a dancing space, the Head Servingman also names two unseen characters: "Away with the joint-stools! Remove the court-cupboard! Look to the plate!—Good thou, save me a piece of marzipan, and, as thou loves me, let the porter let in Susan Grindstone and Nell" (1.4.118–22). Prudently keeping an eye on the Capulet's possessions ("look to the plate"), the Head Servingman allows himself a small indulgence ("save me a piece of marzipan") and sanctions the admittance of "Susan Grindstone and Nell." I ask my students what girlhood and an intersectional "analytic disposition" might help us understand about these two figures. The name "Grindstone" (like "Potpan") seems to align this Susan with a particular form of domestic service, although it may also serve as a nickname that alludes to her sexual availability. Are these girls, like the marzipan, emblematic of an illicit indulgence for the male servants? Are they called for to assist with service—commodities within the Capulet house like the plate, joint-stools, and court-cupboard? Could they be both, and, if so, how does the play distinguish between domestic employment and sexual labor? Usually, my students eagerly note the recurrence of the name "Susan" as meaningful in the depiction of class in Shakespeare's Verona, although they are troubled by the notion that the name signals subservience and invisibility within a wealthy household.

Teaching *Romeo and Juliet* with a focus on girls and girlhoods helps students appreciate that although Juliet is the only girl we see onstage, hers is not the only girlhood that matters in Shakespeare's Verona. Indeed, the play draws upon complex and often contradictory forms of social valuation connected to racial and class identities as well as gender and age to elevate Juliet at the expense of other figures we would now call girls, emphatically rejecting the notion that girlhood is a category that can be generalized along a single axis. Studying girlhood as a dynamic process of valuation and subordination gives students confidence in approaching early modern literature and culture from an intersectional perspective.

NOTE

1. See, for example, the mid-sixteenth-century cameo *Diana as an African Woman* (Osenbruck).

Juliet and Girl Power

Natalie K. Eschenbaum

Taylor Swift's hit song "Love Story," taught me that I had been teaching Shakespeare all wrong. This was about a decade ago, when I was still pretty fresh to my first faculty job at the University of Wisconsin, La Crosse, and scheduled to teach the course Shakespeare's Early Works each semester. At that time, I was eagerly engaging with resources provided by the university's Center for Advancing Teaching and Learning and discovering that I had never been purposefully taught how to teach. I knew nothing about the science of learning, and I assumed I would be a successful teacher if I just taught as I had been taught, through mini lectures and faculty-led discussion. In an effort to practice some of what I was learning about teaching, I scaffolded three assignments. First, I put students in small groups—each assigned to a different play—and asked them to work together to write an annotated bibliography of six recently published critical articles on their play. Second, they gave a presentation on their play and led the class in discussion based on what they learned through their research. Third, they used this same research to write their own critical essays. This assignment sequence worked for what it was designed to do—to get students in conversation with current scholarship—but the assignment results, especially the presentations, made me realize how out of touch I was with the ways in which my students engaged with Shakespeare.

The *Romeo and Juliet* group opened their presentation with Taylor Swift's video for "Love Story." Swift stands on the balcony of a small castle in a cream-and-gold, corseted, Renaissance-style gown, singing about a Juliet and Romeo who live happily ever after. The video moves back and forth between this balcony scene and a costume ball where Swift's Juliet and Romeo meet and fall in love. I had not seen the video or heard the song despite the fact that it was a best-selling single at the time. I blamed my ignorance on the hermit-like lifestyle I had adopted to survive the last years of graduate school and the first years on the tenure line—and on my distaste for country music. Unlike me, though, every student in the class knew the video well, and they were excited to talk about it. I felt like an outsider in my own class.

If I am honest, I felt like an outsider in part because I believed "Love Story" was an awful representation of Shakespeare's play. I thought to myself, "The song is fine in its own right, but it is not Shakespeare." I did exactly what Douglas Lanier says many Shakespeare instructors do, to the detriment of our students' learning: too often, we begin "with the proposition that adaptations should be read against the 'original,' that they are supplemental to or dependent upon 'real' Shakespeare" (23). My original reading of "Love Story" was that it represented a version of Shakespeare I wanted students to unlearn. Nearly all of them had encountered the play in high school—thanks to the Common

Core—and they described the story as being about two immature, impulsive children who rashly, albeit tragically, commit double suicide. Most wondered why such a story has endured and why they are asked to read it, again and again. The old me wanted to show students how their reading of the play was too simplistic, but my method was to prove this through Shakespeare's text and its contexts alone. I read their dismissal of the play as an example of "inappropriate prior knowledge" that was locking them into just one reading of the play (Ambrose 20). But then I started to wonder, What if the "Love Story" version of *Romeo and Juliet* is exactly where we should start? And what if we looked at the adaptations not just as means to understand Shakespeare better but rather as part of a constellation of texts that artistically represent youth—specifically, girlhood?

Swift's "Love Story" is more than a decade old, but thanks to her continued success as a pop icon, the song persists in our students' imaginations. It has charted more than six million downloads; it was rerecorded and rereleased in February 2021 to "swift sales," according to *Billboard* (Caulfield). The song has also been featured in a number of media, including a film (*Letters to Juliet*) and a commercial for the website *Match* ("Match Made in Hell"). I now incorporate "Love Story" and other adaptations regularly in my teaching of *Romeo and Juliet*. My current two-hour lesson plan includes the recent commercial for *Match*, Swift's "Love Story," and clips from Baz Luhrmann's *William Shakespeare's Romeo + Juliet*. This lesson is informed by recent scholarship on Shakespeare and girls' studies, and it follows a structure recommended by Ariane Balizet: "The pedagogical frame I propose comprises three overlapping priorities: modern adaptation as starting point, analysis of girlhood across multiple historical contexts, and considerations of girlhood intersectionality through the centering of marginalized figures or attention to systems of marginalization" (*Shakespeare* 157). It also purposefully engages at least two of the seven research-based principles for smart teaching in Susan A. Ambrose and her coauthors' *How Learning Works*: "Students' prior learning can help or hinder learning" and "[s]tudents' motivation determines, directs, and sustains what they do to learn" (4, 5). At the end of this lesson, students should be able to articulate why encounters with various "Juliets" matter. Ultimately, students should be able to analyze different "Shakespeares" for the power they hold, including the power to reshape or undo past versions and interpretations.

An in-class screening of the actor Ryan Reynolds's commercial "Match Made in Hell" begins the lesson. Released in December 2020, and inspired by the COVID-19 lockdown, the commercial opens with the words "11 Months Ago." Satan—red, horned, muscular—is sitting in his burning, fiery pit, clearly bored, when his cell phone buzzes. Match.com, an online dating service, has found him a perfect match. Swift's newly rereleased "Love Story" begins as the commercial cuts to Satan standing under a bridge in the rain. A woman approaches and says, "Satan?" He responds, "Hi. Two-zero-two-zero?" With a smile, she says, "Please, call me twenty-twenty"; thunder claps, and the two begin a whirlwind romance (picnicking in an empty stadium, stealing rolls of toilet paper from a bathroom, taking selfies in front of a dumpster fire), all accompanied by Swift's lyrics. Students, of course, get the joke immediately and enjoy a good laugh. Then I ask, "Why do you think Reynolds chose to use Taylor Swift's song?" We talk about Reynolds's particular brand of sarcastic humor and about love sometimes having dire effects, but we then focus on the idea that Romeo and Juliet are code for love. The specifics of Shakespeare's version of the tale matter little in this context; simply the names "Juliet" and "Romeo" in the commercial signal something like the greatest love of all time.

We do not linger with Reynolds's commercial; it functions as a prompt to get students thinking about their previous encounters with Romeo and Juliet—the characters, the play, and their or its adaptations. Students put their minds together for a brief small-group chat and then scribble everything they can think of on a whiteboard. They inevitably include a few references I have never heard of but also Luhrmann's *Romeo + Juliet*, the animated film *Gnomeo and Juliet*, and Swift's "Love Story," along with concepts of romance, love, foolishness, and childishness. The purpose of this exercise is to "deliberately activate students' prior knowledge," which will "help them forge robust links to new knowledge" (Ambrose 18), and to reveal how Shakespeare's plays function as a Deleuzoguattarian rhizome (Lanier 28).

Students' own experiences with *Romeo and Juliet*, together with the theoretical concept of Shakespeare as a rhizome, are what bring us to girls' studies. Prior to class, the students have read Ariane Balizet's introduction to *Shakespeare and Girls' Studies*, where she powerfully argues that the water sustaining this rhizomatic Shakespearean root structure is girlhood, or girlishness: "To understand Shakespeare's place in 21st-century popular culture, I propose, we must acknowledge the deep entanglement between the history of appropriating Shakespeare into other forms and media and the cultural impulse to shape, through narrative example, the expression and experience of girlhood" (1). In the case of Juliet, Balizet suggests that we "distinguish between figures like the Juliet of Shakespeare's play and 'Juliet,' a modern media property that evokes not only Shakespeare's cultural authority but also fantasies of girlhood (past and present), attitudes towards heteronormative desire, anxieties of 'risky' adolescent behavior, fears of teen suicide, and traditions of performance, including the celebrities who have portrayed Juliet on large and small screens" (7). The students discuss how Balizet's theory applies to their brainstormed whiteboard list of encounters with Juliet, specifically.

Our conversation then focuses on Swift's "Love Story," considering both the music video visuals and the lyrical text. We begin by talking about youthful love, because the song begins with the singer saying that she and her "Romeo" were young when they met. The video features Swift in front of a high school, holding a stack of books and locking eyes with Justin Gaston, her mop-haired Romeo, whose appearance echoes the most recognized filmic Romeos: Douglas Booth, Leonardo DiCaprio, Leonard Whiting. The video then flashes to scenes from a Renaissance past—or the filmic version of a Renaissance past—with Swift as Juliet, her hand joining with Romeo's ruffle-cuffed hand, her eyes peeking over a fan, and then the two of them moving together to dance. The video cuts to a small, fairy-tale castle with Swift's Juliet alone on a balcony, singing about the scene at the costume ball when Romeo (whose name she did not yet know) sought her out in the crowd. She relays that her father warned Romeo off after noticing his attentions to her. The video takes us back and forth among the settings of Swift's Juliet singing from her castle balcony, the ballroom, and Romeo and Juliet sneaking away in the garden; we then see him finding her castle, presumably the next day, and them both frolicking in a grassy field. The video ends back at the high school, in the present day, with the two lovers walking toward one another.

As the students talk about the details of the video, I share a few quotations about the song in my *PowerPoint* presentation. In an interview with *Time*, Swift said that it was inspired by a boy she liked whom her family and friends disapproved of: "For the first time, I could relate to that Romeo-and-Juliet situation where the only people who wanted them to be together were them. That's the most romantic song I've written, and it's not even about a person I really dated" ("Ten Questions"). We talk about how, for Swift, Romeo and Juliet represent forbidden, youthful love. The song opens and closes with references to their youth and specifies her father's disapproval. Even though Romeo asks Juliet to marry him, we discuss how the youthful context makes us read the marriage plot as a fairy-tale fantasy rather than a serious proposal. The video confirms this reading: the "real" setting is high school, and the fantasy setting—where the love story and proposal occur—is a dreamlike flashback to another era.

Swift was eighteen when *Fearless*, the album featuring "Love Story," was released. All of the songs in the album focus on youth, specifically girlhood. One is called "Fifteen" and is about being a fifteen-year-old girl. In class, I show a quotation from Lizzie Widdicome's *New Yorker* article on the projection screen: "The setting, on her first two albums, is high school, but the lyrics are layered with dreamy images that could have come from the romantic imagination of a much younger child—princes, fairy tales, kissing in the rain." Swift's success came through her appeal to girlishness. The fact that she turned to Shakespeare's *Romeo and Juliet* is thus not surprising, since, as Balizet has pointed out, "girls, girlhood, and girlishness" have been "instrumental to Shakespeare's sustained and enduring cultural capital" (*Shakespeare* 21). A girl today "might read a YA novel like Suzanne Selfors' *Saving Juliet* and watch Baz Luhrmann's *Romeo + Juliet* several times before reading Shakespeare's play in her ninth-grade English class and then, at age 18, produce her own web series inspired by this network of Shakespearean intertexts" (9). For Swift, it was a song rather than a web series, but the crucial point is the same: girlhood has played a key role in keeping Shakespeare current for our students.

Balizet suggests that when teaching Shakespeare alongside girls' studies we should center the question, "How does the scene/film/video/novel/text define who counts as a girl?" (*Shakespeare* 158). This is where my lesson goes next, and it is part of the project of girls' studies at large. The students look again at Swift's video to define who counts as a girl and to directly address the construction of girlhood. According to Swift's "Love Story," girls are pretty and they love beautiful boys, but they respect their fathers. The song clearly privileges heteronormativity but also whiteness and wealth. Although the students in the blurry background of the high school scenes that frame the video may show a more diverse group, Swift and her Romeo are white, and the flashbacks to the dance show only white dancers in elaborate ball gowns. Students always comment that the whiteness, especially, reflects the whiteness of Shakespeare's own play and time. Here, we turn to Shakespeare's text. The purpose is not to prove the students wrong, because they are right that the scene where Romeo and Juliet meet also privileges whiteness, heteronormativity, and wealth. Rather, I want students to see how their reading of who counts as a girl in Swift's video is equally applicable to Shakespeare's play.

Girlhood, whiteness, heterosexuality, and wealth are linked and mutually reinforce one another in the cultural imaginary—today and in Shakespeare's time. The association of girlhood with purity and innocence in turn reinforces the association of girlhood with whiteness. True girlhood is white girlhood, according to these cultural texts. I ask the students to discuss a few moments in act 1, scene 4, including Capulet's call to all to dance, but especially the girls: "A hall, a hall! Give room!—And foot it, girls!" (1.4.138). Capulet is shown to be the powerful father and lord who attempts to create a space of youthful joy and energy because, he admits, he is "past" his "dancing days" (1.4.142). We then consider Romeo's first view of Juliet, in all her wealth and whiteness:

> It seems she hangs upon the cheek of night
> As a rich jewel in an Ethiop's ear:
> Beauty too rich for use, for earth too dear.
> So shows a snowy dove trooping with crows
> As yonder lady o'er her fellows shows
> (1.4.156–60)

We then look at the sonnet Romeo and Juliet write when they meet and add *Christian* to our list of things that define Juliet's girlhood. Juliet's insistence on prayer and the description of her as a saintly statue who is passively kissed by Romeo mark her as both Christian and pure and thus, again, white (1.4.204–17).

After lingering with the text, I turn to another adaptation: Luhrmann's *Romeo + Juliet*. Luhrmann's film includes more diversity in its cast, but whiteness, heteronormativity, wealth, and Christianity are again used to define Juliet's girlhood. Balizet suggests that we also ask, "When and where does girlhood begin and end? Who controls these boundaries?" (*Shakespeare* 158). In Swift's video, the boundary is high school and the person in control is her father. In Luhrmann's film, multiple figures dictate Juliet's actions: mostly Lady

Capulet and Juliet's nurse, but also Tybalt, Lord Capulet, and Paris. Some students argue that Juliet's girlhood ends when Juliet sees Romeo: desire (some are willing to call it love) is the beginning of the end of her girlhood. In Luhrmann's film, Juliet sees Romeo first, through a fish tank that separates the boys' and girls' restrooms. Perhaps she is just looking at the fish, but perhaps she is actively searching for a boy—one who is *not* chosen by her father. This independence—and willful disobedience—is crucial to understanding Juliet's character. I point the students to Deanne Williams's analysis: "The word 'girl' often appears in Shakespeare as a label for a young woman's independence, willfulness, and resistance" (*Shakespeare and the Performance of Girlhood* 6). In other words, we may see independence as moving a girl toward womanhood, but this same independence is also a key marker of "girlishness." The students and I muse together on whether this remains true today. On the one hand, "girl" is still frequently used as an insult; on the other, it is the signifier of the "girl power" countermovement.

The lesson concludes with a discussion of the balcony scene alongside Carolyn Brown's article "Juliet's Taming of Romeo," which students have also read in advance. We keep Balizet's same questions central to our conversation and focus on the boundaries of girlhood. Brown's piece considers Juliet's maturity by looking closely at the falconry imagery to demonstrate how Juliet "tames" her Romeo. Arguing against the common characterization of Juliet as "naive" or "immature," Brown finds instead that Juliet is a "self-willed, courageous, intelligent young woman who initiates and controls action in her struggle to preserve her integrity and autonomy in a world that is hostile to women" (333). In a sense, Brown argues that Juliet's ability to tame Romeo is what makes her a "young woman" rather than a "child" or girl. Brown suggests that the falconry imagery reverses Romeo's and Juliet's genders: "Shakespeare establishes a reading that draws parallels between Romeo and trainable falcons (usually females) and between the way Juliet treats Romeo and the methods falconers (usually males) use to train their birds" (334). Students find the article accessible and the historical context fascinating, and it helps them see the way in which Juliet controls the dialogue with Romeo. They notice that Juliet is the one who proposes marriage. Some students are then reminded of Swift's Juliet, who similarly gets Romeo to propose by questioning his commitment to her. I ask the students to consider whether Juliet's statements and actions (in the play and in Swift's song) mark her as a powerful girl or as a young woman—or, as Brown suggests, as taking a position usually occupied by a man. The discussion helps students to see how identity markers shift over time and are sometimes used as weapons. In the end, I want them to expand their definition of "girl" to include independence, maturity, creativity, and power rather than to presume that a powerful girl has to be something other than a girl (a young woman, a girl acting like a man).

Over the past decade, I have regularly called up the "outsider" feeling Swift and my students inspired. It reminds me that my students have much to teach me and that Shakespeare lives in our students' imaginations in ways he does not live in mine. I have also come to believe that the Shakespeare I was taught—a Shakespeare that focused on the text and was informed by history—cannot be the only Shakespeare of the future. I agree with Lanier, who states powerfully, "Foregrounding the trope of adaptation . . . offers a useful way forward, a means for reconceptualizing Shakespeare as a disciplinary field, but only if we place the Shakespearean text and the authority it seems to provide firmly within the orbit of adaptation" (23). We can no longer justify teaching Shakespeare if we don't also teach the racist, sexist, and colonial structures that have enabled his continued success. Beginning lessons with adaptations can help to shift the balance of power away from Shakespeare in productive, necessary ways.

As I think about teaching this lesson again in the future, I am eager to see Carey Williams's film *R#J*, which was released at the 2021 Sundance Film Festival. It's a modernized adaptation, told mostly through social media and virtual platforms, and features an incredibly diverse cast. In an interview with *Variety*, Francesca Noel, who plays Juliet, says, "I personally really wanted to bring reality to Juliet; I wanted to make her tumultuous and hormonal and fueled by all of these emotions you get when you are seventeen and things are so heightened and you want to kill yourself over someone that you just met" ("'R#J' Cast"). In a future iteration of the lesson, *R#J* is where we will end. Noel marks Juliet as a youth once again but this time uses hormones and emotions to mark the contours of girlhood. She also speaks about the importance of being biracial and cast alongside a Romeo who is Black, something she says would not have been possible twenty-five years ago, or a generation ago, when Luhrmann's film was released. Noel's Juliet will offer students more answers to the question of who counts as a girl (Balizet, *Shakespeare* 158), and I hope that she will start to live in our students' imaginations alongside Claire Danes, Hailee Steinfeld, and Taylor Swift. Every Juliet helps us to see how power structures, gender hierarchies, and intersectional identities define girlhood in new ways. And every Juliet helps to prescribe how and to justify why we continue to study and teach this incredible play.

Queering *Romeo and Juliet* with Film Adaptations

Anthony Guy Patricia

There is little doubt that Romeo and Juliet love each other genuinely and passionately despite the extreme brevity of their courtship. Such is the power of the kind of "love at first sight" by which they are enchanted. But at the ages of sixteen and fourteen, respectively, the lovers are very young and arguably incapable of making the careful, rational decisions that might be expected of older, more experienced people who know a thing or two about life. Hence the problematic tragedy of their end: death by suicide because they cannot bear to be apart. That Romeo and Juliet are, to their peril, dangerously immature and impulsive should be of concern to audiences, but such apprehensions are too often elided by the idea that *Romeo and Juliet* is one of the greatest love stories ever told.

Addressing this reputation of the play, Shakespeare scholars working from a queer theoretical perspective would hasten to point out that *Romeo and Juliet* is considered one of the greatest *heterosexual* love stories ever told—a crucial distinction. A distinction of this sort is, in fact, a necessary first move in the larger project of queering a dramatic text such as *Romeo and Juliet*. Like many theoretical approaches to literature, queer theory can, at least initially, seem so abstract and so esoteric as to be impossible to work with, especially in the classroom. However, a productive viewpoint can be achieved by keeping in mind that, at its simplest, the premise of queer theory means thoroughly challenging, questioning, critiquing, and problematizing heterosexuality as the be-all and end-all of human interpersonal relationships it is purported to be. This critique does not mean that heterosexuality is a material concept or lived reality that must be destroyed; it means, rather, that other sexualities—homosexuality, bisexuality, and asexuality, to name three—are equally valid and valued sexual identities and ways of being in the world, and they demand to be treated as such.

The task at hand then becomes one of praxis. To that end, this essay will show how *Romeo and Juliet* can be queered in the classroom, what is accomplished by doing so, and why such work is still necessary in the twenty-first century. In my experience, this type of demonstrable queering can be achieved most effectively by incorporating film into the pedagogical mix. I have found film to be a particularly supple medium for introducing college or university students to queer theory in relation to Shakespeare in ways that are memorable, relatable, and impactful. So situated, the films that I recommend considering include George Cukor's 1936 *Romeo and Juliet*, Franco Zeffirelli's 1968 *Romeo and Juliet*, Baz Luhrmann's 1996 *William Shakespeare's Romeo + Juliet*, and Alan Brown's 2011 *Private Romeo*. Each of these individually, and the group collectively, sheds light on Shakespeare's *Romeo and Juliet* from a queer point of view and thus adds immeasurably to the study of the play overall.[1] This approach has the further benefit of allowing students to see how queerness has been dealt with in film adaptations of Shakespeare over a historical progression of some eighty-five years. They will also be able to grapple critically with the idea that sexuality is fluid rather than fixed and immutable, if not for themselves, then certainly for others; that there is really nothing threatening about queerness and, in fact, that queerness is liberating for everyone; and that love and fulfillment in relationship with another human being, regardless of their sexuality or gender, is not the sole province of straight people. If nothing else, the approach teaches students about empathy, something we need much more of in this world.

I recommend working through the movies selected in chronological order, thus beginning with Cukor's production. This is a film that immediately presents us with two extratextual aspects that warrant thinking about in a queer context: first, the film is in black and white, and second, the actors in the lead roles, Leslie Howard and Norma Shearer, are noticeably older than the young teenage characters in Shakespeare's play. I have noticed in recent years an increasing resistance on the part of students to engage with black-and-white films, especially those made nine decades ago. My guess is that this is because, in most cases, they have only been exposed to color movies laden with computer-generated images and other kinds of special effects. Therefore, watching a black-and-white film like Cukor's *Romeo and Juliet* is a decidedly queer, destabilizing experience because it is so far outside their frame of reference. A black-and-white film is simply not the norm for them, and they think they cannot relate to such old movies. Even so, I tell them, that does not give them a pass to forgo watching the Cukor film. To this I add that the film, like just about everything else in life, has a history; it existed long before they did, and knowing something about that history can only contribute to their developing cultural literacy and sophistication.

For the second aspect, I ask students to keep a journal during the *Romeo and Juliet* unit. The first entry requires them to write their own definition of love—they are specifically instructed not to consult a dictionary. Once they do this, they consider how love has affected them in their own lives and what they think *Romeo and Juliet* has to say about love. It is often worthwhile to share students' insights about love anonymously and have them compare notes. Then we watch Cukor's film, usually over two or three class periods. As with the reluctance toward black-and-white movies, at least some of my students are reluctant to watch "older" people (at the time, Shearer was thirty-seven and Howard was forty-two, seemingly ancient to some young people) act out the rituals of falling in love on screen, especially if there is much physicality. The "ick" factor of feeling like they are watching their parents performing courtship rites can be difficult to surmount. I respond by arguing that if they are stuck on the ages of Romeo and Juliet, they are in effect saying that love is not for "older" people, that it is only for young people like themselves—and that does not seem fair or equitable. This is another thing I ask students to reflect on in their journals as we consider Cukor's *Romeo and Juliet*.

Zeffirelli's *Romeo and Juliet*, which is in glorious color and stars the age-appropriate seventeen-year-old Leonard Whiting and fifteen-year-old Olivia Hussey, generally fares better in my classroom than Cukor's, despite the fact that it premiered a little over fifty years ago. My experience with Luhrmann's *Romeo + Juliet* has been similar. Students tend to respond positively to this film because it was made at the height of the MTV era in the mid-1990s and, like the music videos of that time, it unfolds at a breakneck pace, features a pulsing score, presents a feast of psychedelic color, and, perhaps above all, stars Leonardo DiCaprio and Claire Danes (like Whiting and Hussey, also age appropriate). For Zeffirelli's and Luhrmann's films, we spend two or three class periods viewing each. While we are doing so, I ask students to pay particular attention to Romeo and Juliet as they meet for the first time at the Capulet ball; their quick courtship, complete with a simultaneously innocent but passionate first kiss; their equally quick decision to marry; Romeo's vengeful slaying of Tybalt and subsequent banishment from Verona; and, ultimately, the tragedy of their deaths in the Capulet tomb.

After screening these three mainstream productions, my students and I review the premise of queer theory that we started this unit with. With that in mind, they are directed to complete the following journal writing assignment: Did they notice anything that could be considered queer in any of the three films? Responses tend to vary wildly once discussion begins. I think this depends very much on whether or not students have any familiarity with the concept of queerness prior to taking my Shakespeare class. In any case, I point out aspects of the films that could be considered queer, which fall into three broad categories. The first is that Romeo and Juliet, in their love for each other, are a lot like LGBTQIA+ couples by virtue of the fact that their relationship goes against everything their families and their society stand for. But still they choose to stay together, even going so far as getting married in order to circumvent Juliet's betrothal to Paris, her father's favorite choice of husband, no matter what. The second queer aspect is the films' respective treatments of Mercutio as being enamored with Romeo in a way that calls to mind the stereotypical (but no less poignant) story of the gay guy being head over heels in love with his straight male friend whom he can never "have." And the third involves paracinematic elements like the fact that Shakespeare himself is largely thought to have been what we would call a bisexual man; the fact of Cukor's homosexuality, Zeffirelli's bisexuality, and Luhrmann's metrosexuality; Luhrmann's staging of Mercutio as a fierce, cross-dressing drag queen; and Whiting's backside nudity in the aubade scene in Cukor's film, which makes a male character the object of the "male gaze" (Mulvey). Often, the writing and discussion here lead to requests to rewatch certain parts of the films as students make connections between the theory and what they see on screen.

At this point in the course, we are well positioned to move on to independent film director Alan Brown, who, in 2011, released a radical, queer, cinematic appropriation of *Romeo and Juliet* called *Private Romeo*. This is a film about an all-male group of military high school students who, while their fellow cadets are away, are required to maintain their regular routines, including class attendance. In one of these classes (presumably English or drama), the young men must read Shakespeare's *Romeo and Juliet*. As would be expected in a same-sex environment, some of the young men take on female roles—like that of Juliet—in the play. This extended reading of Shakespeare's play is one of the major conceits of *Private Romeo*; in fact, it provides the basis from which the bulk of the movie's plot develops.

Private Romeo is, I tell my students in a brief lecture before we watch the film, *Romeo and Juliet* thoroughly queered. Brown accomplishes this in four ways.[2] First, he uses an all-male cast. This is not necessarily revolutionary, but it does harken back to the original conditions of staging Shakespeare's plays. In early modern London, for a number of reasons, women were not allowed to act on stage, so all roles in publicly performed dramas were played by men and (especially for female roles) prepubescent boys. What makes Brown's casting queer in this case is the fact that women are no longer prohibited from the profession of acting; Brown could have chosen to cast women in the female roles but did not. The second way in which Brown queers Shakespeare's play is by using what can only be described as a hypermasculine setting: the McKinley Military Academy for high-school-aged young men. A great deal of ink has been spilled about such all-male military purviews; suffice to say here that Brown represents this environment as a natural catalyst for homoerotic and homosexual bonds.

The third and the fourth ways Brown queers *Romeo and Juliet* in *Private Romeo* are interrelated. Given the setting of an all-male military academy, the characters are almost always dressed in some form of military clothing, most often featuring camouflage patterns or, at the very least, olive-green solid colors. Furthermore, these military costumes remain consistent throughout *Private Romeo*; there is no cross-dressing like there would have been in Shakespeare's day. In addition, Brown did not change the pronouns of any of the characters. So, for example, when the character Glenn Mangan (Matt Doyle) plays Juliet in the cadets' class study and reading of *Romeo and Juliet*, the character is always addressed as "she" or "her" rather than "he" or "him" even though Glenn appears as a handsome young man. In regard to gender and voice, then, Brown makes no attempt in *Private Romeo* to normalize—to straighten—things through cross-dressing or pronoun switches or by making his actors use artificial falsettos to indicate femininity.

Arguably, this quadruple queering of *Romeo and Juliet* is most visible in the scene in which Romeo (played by Seth Numrich, in the role of the cadet Sam Singleton) first lays eyes on Juliet/Glenn. My students and I watch as this meeting happens at a typical military cadet party—complete with poker and beer—which substitutes for the Capulet ball in Shakespeare's play. It is a party that, as you might expect, the cadets' superior officers have no idea is occurring. In the scene, Juliet/Glenn has left the main crowd for an outdoor patio; Romeo/Sam sees *him* and says, "What lady's that which doth enrich the hand / Of yonder knight?" (1.4.153–54). As he walks toward Juliet/Glenn, Romeo/Sam says, "Did my heart love till now? Forswear it, sight, / For I ne'er saw true beauty till this night" (1.4.163–64). This is the first time in *Private Romeo* that Romeo/Sam has admitted out loud that he is in love with someone who is of the same gender (male) as himself. This is where Brown's queer blurring of all-male casting, hypermasculine setting, male clothing with no cross-dressing, and no change in pronouns has a powerful impact—especially for LGBTQIA+ folk who do not often see themselves represented on screen (although that is starting to change for the better, but there is a long way to go). What the audience is able to witness in this scene—and what they are also able to enjoy vicariously, if they so wish—is two young men falling in love. To me, this is the very definition of what it means to queer something: by showing a nonheteronormative configuration of first love in a wholly positive way, as I argue to my students.

As *Private Romeo* continues, Romeo/Sam tries to lean in and kiss Juliet/Glenn. It is a sweetly flirtatious moment between the two young men that leaves Juliet/Glenn a bit taken aback and Romeo/Sam blushing in a bit of embarrassment. But Juliet/Glenn, astonished though he may be, proceeds to reveal his own interest in Romeo/Sam, whom he tells, again using Shakespeare's words from *Romeo and Juliet*:

> Good pilgrim, you do wrong your hand too much,
> Which mannerly devotion shows in this;
> For saints have hands that pilgrims' hands do touch,
> And palm to palm is holy palmers' kiss.
>
> (1.4.208–11)

So saying, Juliet/Glenn reaches out and takes Romeo/Sam's hand in his own so that their palms are in fact touching. This encourages and emboldens Romeo/Sam, who responds, cheekily:

> ROMEO/SAM. Have not saints lips, and holy palmers too?
> JULIET/GLENN. Ay, pilgrim, lips that they must use in prayer.
> ROMEO/SAM. O then, dear saint, let lips do what hands do:
> They pray; grant thou, lest faith turn to despair.
> JULIET/GLENN. Saints do not move, though grant for prayers' sake.
> ROMEO/SAM. Then move not while my prayer's effect I take.
>
> (1.4.212–17)

Then Romeo/Sam kisses Juliet/Glenn full on the lips. When they separate, both young men seem rather surprised by what they have just done. "Thus from my lips, by thine, my sin is purged" (1.4.218), Romeo/Sam offers by way of another apology for being so forward. But Juliet/Glenn smiles broadly at Romeo/Sam, steps closer to him, and says, "Then have my lips the sin that they have took"

(1.4.219). To which Romeo/Sam replies, "Sin from my lips? O trespass sweetly urged! / Give me my sin again" (1.4.220–21), then he reaches out and takes Juliet/Glenn's face between his hands and kisses him again, this time more passionately. And Juliet/Glenn responds by kissing Romeo/Sam back with just as much ardor.

This is one example of queerness at its most visceral and, at least potentially, its most transformative. It shows the world that two young men can and do kiss one another (if they are so inclined) and that there is nothing sick or disgusting about them doing so. In fact, it shows the world that it is just as natural and beautiful for two young men to kiss one another as it is for a man and a woman. There is no capitulation to heteronormative imperatives in *Private Romeo*; there is only resistance to those imperatives. Even so, this is when I often find myself bracing for trouble in the queering *Romeo and Juliet* unit of my course. Despite the many warnings given orally and in writing about what is to come in *Private Romeo*, there is a big difference between the idea of two young men kissing each other and the reality of them doing so on screen directly in front of students, some of whom may take offense and complain that they are being compelled to accept this nonheteronormative content. In this day and age, I have very little patience for such posturing, and I refuse to let anyone turn my classroom into anything other than a safe space. Any students who react this way to *Private Romeo* are firmly reminded that they are in the course by choice and, therefore, they do not have to remain in it if they are so offended. That usually takes care of the problem, which, thankfully, does not happen as often as I fear it will. By taking such a position, it is my hope, too, that LGBTQIA+ students in the class will feel that they are supported and that someone will stand up for them when necessary—and when they may not yet be able to stand up for themselves. I also hope that they will find some kind of validation in the representations available in *Private Romeo* and the other films we study from a queer perspective, since all too often our society attempts to delegitimize their very existence by chipping away at their self-esteem, their emotional and mental well-being, and even their physical being.

As we continue screening the film, my students and I discover that Brown's queering of *Romeo and Juliet* does not stop with the romance and (same-sex) marriage between Romeo/Sam and Juliet/Glenn. Having created an entirely believable representational realm in which male same-sex love is paramount, Brown also manages to generate a significant amount of suspense for those audience members who have become invested in the two characters—and especially for those who are familiar with the tragic ending of Shakespeare's play. The expectation for *Private Romeo* is, of course, that Romeo/Sam and Juliet/Glenn will die, just like their counterparts do in *Romeo and Juliet*. However, Brown, in a virtuoso—and, I argue, totally queer—move, thwarts these expectations.

Act 5, scene 3, unfolds in a large, deserted lecture hall at the McKinley Military Academy. There, Romeo/Sam rushes in to find his beloved Juliet/Glenn sprawled on the instructor's desk, seemingly dead. His anguish is immediate and heartbreaking to witness. Thus, it is completely understandable when

Romeo/Sam drinks the last of the (supposedly) drugged water that Juliet/Glenn left in his canteen; he is quickly overcome and dies while spooning Juliet/Glenn in his arms in an all-encompassing embrace that epitomizes Romeo/Sam's love for Juliet/Glenn. But, moments later, Juliet/Glenn awakes and finds Friar Laurence/Cadet Adam Hersh (played by Adam Barrie) hovering nearby and urging him to leave at once. Juliet/Glenn sends the Friar away, insisting that he will not be parted from Romeo/Sam. After the Friar is gone, Juliet/Glenn says, "I will kiss thy lips: / Haply some poison yet doth hang on them / To make me die with a restorative" (5.3.164–66). Then he kisses Romeo/Sam. As he is doing so, Romeo/Sam starts to kiss Juliet/Glenn back. Then his eyes flutter open. Thus, astonishingly, neither Romeo/Sam nor Juliet/Glenn die as Romeo and Juliet do in Shakespeare's original. The gay, male, same-sex couple lives. And we are left to presume that they will live happily ever after. This ending is perhaps the queerest thing of all about Brown's *Private Romeo* because it completely jettisons the heteronormative master narrative and literally gives life to the gay male love story.

I like to end this unit by rewatching the scene in which Romeo and Juliet meet for the first time and fall so deeply in love with each other in all four films that we have considered in this context over the last few weeks, from Cukor's to Brown's. After we do this, I ask students to revisit their definitions of love that they wrote in their journals. In particular, I instruct them to reflect on whether or not there is any difference—other than gender—in the love as it's portrayed by a male-female versus a male-male Romeo and Juliet, given that the language—Shakespeare's—is exactly the same. It is my hope that, rather than turning them gay or queer, as some ridiculously fear about this kind of pedagogy, the way we have studied the play on film has allowed my students to understand that when it comes to love, straight or LGBTQIA+, we are all pretty much the same. Providing the means for students to develop their empathy for others in this way is, I believe, a crucial part of higher education today. This is especially true since, as I write this piece, a half dozen American states (and, no doubt, more to follow), driven by conservative religious extremism and cynical Republican politics, are seeking to enact bills that, under the guise of parents' rights, would literally make it illegal for educators, even at the university level, to teach the lessons detailed here. That cannot be allowed to happen, but if it does, as seems all too likely, continuing to queer *Romeo and Juliet* through film is one way to fight back.

NOTES

1. For more on queer theory and Shakespeare, see Patricia, "Queer Studies"; Sanchez.

2. I discuss Brown's queering of the play at greater length in Patricia, "(Un)Queering" and *Queering*.

Rediscovering the Familiar: Comedy in *Romeo and Juliet*

Stephanie Pietros

As most instructors will attest, sometimes it is difficult to teach a text that students have read before. They feel they have it all figured out and are closed to new readings, sometimes even to reading it again at all. I find this is especially the case with *Romeo and Juliet*, particularly given the status of Shakespeare as a cultural icon. At the College of Mount Saint Vincent, every spring I teach a 300-level Shakespeare survey course required by the English major. While the class is primarily composed of English majors and the occasional English or theater minor, it usually contains one or two non–English majors taking it as an elective. I always begin by surveying students about their previous study of Shakespeare. I find it helpful to know what they might have read (or in some cases performed) and hence what preconceived notions regarding Shakespeare they may have. Although I am occasionally surprised (the student who read *Titus Andronicus* in high school comes to mind), typically students have read a handful of the major tragedies, rarely a comedy, and always *Romeo and Juliet*. Even for students from disadvantaged schools (which are well represented in my classroom), *Romeo and Juliet* is a near-universal secondary school experience.

My goal then is to open up the play in new and exciting ways and to encourage students to dig deeper and see things they didn't in the ninth grade. In this respect, where I place the play in the Shakespeare survey course is especially important. (Indeed, different groupings of the plays help me see plays I have read many times over with new eyes.) Pairing *Romeo and Juliet* with a later play centered on a more mature and far less idealized couple, such as *Antony and Cleopatra* or *Troilus and Cressida*, is one such approach that I have used. By far the most successful pairing, however, is with *A Midsummer Night's Dream*, as very few, if any, students have encountered this play or any other Shakespeare comedy in high school. In this essay, I discuss how I teach *Romeo and Juliet* in relation to the conventions of comedy, showing students that, at least at the beginning of the play, it almost appears to *be* a comedy. This approach enables students to see the play they think they know so well in an entirely new light while also reinforcing their newly gained knowledge about the less familiar genre of comedy. While *Romeo and Juliet*'s indebtedness to comedy and the pedagogical benefits of pairing it with *Midsummer* are well documented, my approach highlights the class implications of genre. In doing so, I introduce students to important concepts regarding genre and literary conventions while showing them that these concepts are not mere academic abstractions.

Approaching the play through the lens of comedy is hardly novel from a critical perspective. Indeed, it is in some ways an older, classic approach to the play that is particularly effective in the classroom. As Susan Snyder argues in her 1970 article "*Romeo and Juliet*: Comedy into Tragedy," the reversal of fortune in the play, which she pinpoints to Mercutio's death, is so drastic as to actually constitute a change in genre from comedy to tragedy (391). As in a conventional comedy, the main conflict in *Romeo and Juliet*—the feud—is extrinsic to the main characters; it does not stem from an intrinsic flaw of theirs as in a conventional tragedy. The movement of the titular characters toward social regeneration and marriage is, according to Snyder, likewise comic (391–92). Snyder details numerous other ways in which the play is more comic than tragic: Romeo's turn to a possible, realistic love; the attempts by Friar Laurence and the Nurse to move the play toward a typical comic resolution. Even though this resolution fails to materialize, the double suicide at the end of the play, like that of the later *Antony and Cleopatra*, is more indebted to the conventions of comedy than tragedy (Rozett). *Romeo and Juliet*'s comic resonances are well established, as is the play's influence on later comedies (Bly).

In my Shakespeare course, I deliberately teach the plays in chronological order so that my students have read two comedies (including *A Midsummer Night's Dream*) before we get to *Romeo and Juliet*. Moreover, I place *Midsummer* and *Romeo and Juliet* in direct succession so that they can more easily be read as a pair. By pairing the plays and teaching them as a unit, I follow the tradition of scholars like Thomas P. Harrison, who argues that the plays are companion pieces that contain not only many linguistic similarities but ones of plot as well. The similarities between *Romeo and Juliet* and the Pyramus and Thisbe play in *Midsummer* are clear: the family feud, the concluding setting of the tomb, the false assumption of death and subsequent suicides. As in the scholarship, there is a pedagogical tradition of teaching the plays alongside one another. In making his case for the value of teaching *Romeo and Juliet* in light of its indebtedness to other genres, Douglas Bruster argues that it is ideal to teach it together with *Midsummer* (61).

When my students read *Midsummer*, they are delighted to discover that the inset play performed by the mechanicals, "Pyramus and Thisbe," bears a striking likeness to the *Romeo and Juliet* they remember from high school. The story of Pyramus and Thisbe, told in Ovid's *Metamorphoses*, is commonly acknowledged as similar to that of *Romeo and Juliet*, if not one of its direct sources. Original audiences likely would have recognized this similarity given that both *Midsummer* and *Romeo and Juliet* were written and performed around the same time in the mid-1590s. (Although critics have long debated which came first, the two plays are undeniably linked regardless of sequence.)[1] Once we engage with these fairly obvious similarities, I then ask students to identify how "Pyramus and Thisbe" in *Midsummer* differs from their recollection of *Romeo and Juliet*. Clearly, the mechanicals are a source of much humor, as terrible actors who feel the need to overexplain every aspect of the play lest the audience take it too literally—their interpretation of "Pyramus" is part of the humor. In addition, the play is incongruously called "The most lamentable comedy and most cruel death of Pyramus and Thisbe" (act 1, scene 2, lines 11–13). While the contradiction inherent in "lamentable comedy" escapes the mechanicals' notice, Theseus picks up on it immediately when he and Philostrate are considering their choice of entertainment for the evening. Theseus considers the mechanicals' description of their play:

> "A tedious brief scene of young Pyramus
> And his love Thisbe; very tragical mirth."
> Merry and tragical? Tedious and brief?
> That is hot ice and wondrous strange snow!
> How shall we find the concord of this discord?
> (5.1.56–60)

Much like the phrase "lamentable comedy," the description of the play contains a number of seeming contradictions, which Theseus questions. As he elaborates on these contradictions, he adds some of his own—"That is hot ice and wondrous strange snow!" Theseus's addition of the oxymoron "hot ice" could be lifted right out of a Petrarchan sonnet, which often deploy such seeming contradictions in their description of the beloved. Since I begin the semester in Shakespeare with some sonnets, astute students will often pick up on this connection. At this point in our reading of *Midsummer*, I tell them to file away this aspect of Petrarchan convention for future reference, as we will continue our discussion of it when we move on to *Romeo and Juliet*.

Beyond its linguistic malapropisms, students are quick to recognize other factors that make "Pyramus and Thisbe" funny despite its resemblance to tragedy: its bad poetry, the terrible acting of the mechanicals, their insistence on the insertion of prologues, their metatheatrical language that makes it difficult for the audience to believe that the action they see on the stage is real (Elizabethan antitheatrical writers had repeatedly criticized the theater for its supposed ability to confuse drama with reality). Performance only heightens the comic effect, as any number of productions of *Midsummer* on stage and in film reveal.[2] Students generally enjoy these productions, and viewing them fosters rich discussion on how the final act of the play turns away from its lovers and toward a consideration of the conventions of the theater itself through the inset play.

Following our study of *Midsummer*, I begin our discussion of *Romeo and Juliet* by asking students how the start of the play is different from the start of other tragedies we have read or they are familiar with, and how it is more like comedies. Having read two Shakespearean comedies, my students are at this point pretty comfortable with their generic conventions. Rather than immediately introduce us to our tragic protagonists at their height, *Romeo and Juliet* begins, like a comedy, with a physical conflict, staging a public brawl between servants from the Montague and Capulet families. Moreover, this "comic" conflict is played out first by the *servants* rather than the aristocratic figures. That the comic characters are servants in the play betrays the fact that there is a class element to genre—an aspect of genre with which students are generally unfamiliar but are keen to discuss once it is pointed out to them. As act 1 progresses, we are also introduced to another conflict: Romeo's unrequited love for Rosaline. At this point, the play almost seems to produce the expectation that, as in a comedy, whatever is separating these characters will ultimately be resolved and the play will end with a marriage. The opening scenes of the play also explicitly refer to another possible future marriage: that of Juliet and Paris. Structurally, then, with a conflict-filled opening and a gesture toward future marriage(s), the play begins more like a comedy.

Furthermore, Romeo and Juliet do not possess the stature that we typically expect of a tragic hero whose fall happens over the course of the play; as my students note, the play's focus on a pair of young lovers is more similar to the comedies we have read than the tragedies. Romeo and Juliet are young teenagers from aristocratic families and do not possess any particularly heroic qualities (unless one counts the ability to speak in really ornate poetry). In fact, because my students have just finished reading *Midsummer*, which concludes with the mechanicals' production of "Pyramus and Thisbe," even the famous ornate poetry in *Romeo and Juliet* falls a little flat. The Petrarchan language that Romeo spouts in the play's opening acts, first in regard to Rosaline and then Juliet, seems so textbook as to be almost parodic, much like Shakespeare parodies Petrarchan convention in his description of "Pyramus" in *Midsummer* as a "lamentable comedy." Given what students have just learned about class and comedy, they might start to wonder if the parody of Petrarchan convention, first in *Midsummer* and now in *Romeo and Juliet*, is also a critique of poetry written by aristocratic *gentlemen* poets. Students who have read Shakespeare's sonnet 130—which makes much of the hackneyed potential of Petrarchan poetry—are especially likely to pick up on this critique.

Romeo is in the throes of puppy love, and his lines, while poetically beautiful, can feel as though he is simply parroting things he has read without any sense of what they really mean. He speaks, much like he kisses, "by the book." For example, when Romeo first enters the play toward the end of 1.1, following the brawl, he laments his lovesick state to Benvolio, explaining that sad hours are long because he lacks "that, which, having, makes them short," namely Rosaline's love (1.1.159). As he continues his discussion of love and hate with Benvolio, his language evokes Petrarchan poetry:

> Why, then, O brawling love, O loving hate,
> O anything of nothing first created,
> O heavy lightness, serious vanity,
> Misshapen chaos of well-seeming forms,
> Feather of lead, bright smoke, cold fire, sick health,
> Still-waking sleep that is not what it is—
>
> (1.1.171–76)

In the various oxymorons Romeo employs to describe his lovesick state—heavy lightness, serious vanity, feather of lead, bright smoke, cold fire, sick health, still-waking sleep—he mimics the language of Petrarchan love poetry that so famously employs such oxymorons. While Benvolio does not take Romeo to task for this, Mercutio later in the play certainly does: "Now is he for the numbers that Petrarch flowed in; Laura to his lady was a kitchen wench—marry, she had better love to berhyme her—Dido a dowdy, Cleopatra a gypsy, Helen and Hero hildings and harlots, Thisbe a gray-eye or so" (2.3.36–40). Mercutio explicitly references Petrarch here, noting that Romeo favors his particular brand of poetry and believes his beloved Juliet to be far superior to other famous romantic heroines, including Petrarch's beloved Laura and numerous fictional ladies, most notably Thisbe. Moreover—and this speaks crucially to my earlier point about genre and class—Mercutio's caricature of Petrarchan oxymorons operates by distinguishing royal, aristocratic women from lower-class ones: kitchen wenches, gypsies, and so on.

That Romeo as a lover may be a bit of a parody and an almost comic figure in the early acts of the play is a revelation for my students. While such a reading does not necessarily make the play's ending less tragic (in fact, it could be argued that it heightens the tragedy of the ending through contrast), it enables students to see him in a new way and to recognize the class implications of the play's rehearsal of different genres. In addition to helping students look at the play with fresh eyes, approaching *Romeo and Juliet* through the lens of comedy helps them to think about Petrarchan conventions and about generic conventions more broadly. My approach to *Romeo and Juliet* infuses the traditional study of genre in the play with a heightened focus on social class. This approach is especially effective pedagogically for a number of reasons. This classic focus on genre, while hardly revelatory to scholars, is still novel for my undergraduate students who typically know little of generic conventions or the wider Shakespeare canon. It provides them with a grounding in the play that can then serve as a solid foundation for their research papers, as inevitably many choose to write about the play with which they are most comfortable. Now they can approach recent research on the play with more solid critical footing than they might otherwise have the time to acquire in the span of a semester. Moreover, discussions of the class implications of genre provide an entry point into Shakespeare that is especially relevant for my students, many of them first-generation students of color who, even if they are English majors, view Shakespeare with a great deal of trepidation. Shakespeare's iconic reputation means that many students regard his work as having some kind of elite status. Therefore, they are delighted to discover not only that Shakespeare plays were popular culture in his day but also that he parodied more "elite" genres. Having seen the play in a new light, they hopefully take forward with them the lesson that there is always more to see even in that which we think we know so well.

NOTES

1. Whether *Romeo and Juliet* or *A Midsummer Night's Dream* was written first has long been a debate among scholars, and the issue of genre has been considered a deciding factor in which play influenced which. See, for example, Riess and Williams, who argue that *Romeo and Juliet* is the earlier play and that Shakespeare used tragedy to enhance the comedy of *Midsummer*.

2. In particular, I have had success using Michael Hoffman's 1999 film *A Midsummer Night's Dream* and a recording of the 2013 Shakespeare's Globe production of the play directed by Dominic Dromgoole.

"Love at First Sonnet": Romeo and Juliet's Collaborative Sonnet in Context

Joshua Reid

As with most Shakespeare courses, my class on *Romeo and Juliet* zeroes in early on Romeo and Juliet's courtship scene in act 1, scene 4—a structural, formal, and thematic crux of the play. I project the following text and ask my students whether the form looks familiar, maybe with an added prod to count the lines and chart the rhyme scheme:

ROMEO.	If I profane with my unworthiest hand
	This holy shrine, the gentle sin is this:
	My lips, two blushing pilgrims, did ready stand
	To smooth that rough touch with a tender kiss.
JULIET.	Good pilgrim, you do wrong your hand too much,
	Which mannerly devotion shows in this;
	For saints have hands that pilgrims' hands do touch,
	And palm to palm is holy palmers' kiss.
ROMEO.	Have not saints lips, and holy palmers too?
JULIET.	Ay, pilgrim, lips that they must use in prayer.
ROMEO.	Oh, then, dear saint, let lips do what hands do:
	They pray; grant thou, lest faith turn to despair.
JULIET.	Saints do not move, though grant for prayer's sake.
ROMEO.	Then move not while my prayer's effect I take.

(1.4.204–217)

While the answer is common knowledge for Shakespeare teachers, it is not for many students. For them, this is a retrieval practice question that draws on previous material we have covered and applies it to a new context. Invariably, a few students raise their hand and recognize this moment as "love at first sonnet" (Garber, *Shakespeare after All* 194).

This essay covers teaching strategies I have used in Shakespeare undergraduate survey courses and high school classrooms to excavate the full import of this embedded sonnet. First, I explore with students the literary context via the sonnet craze of the 1590s. This backdrop prepares students for a close-analysis group project where they dissect the structure, word choice, and sonic traits of Romeo and Juliet's collaborative sonnet. After this activity, which reinforces the relationship between form and meaning, the discussion moves outward to the play as a whole, to explore how the embedded sonnet prepares the audience for the play's obsession with metalanguage, wordplay, artifice, and world-building.

What's in a Sonnet?

The richness of the discussion of Romeo and Juliet's collaborative sonnet correlates closely with the contextual background the class has covered up to that point. I have found that the most effective preparation is a previous unit on Shakespeare's sonnets, although the material can be compressed into a previous class session or even into a much-abbreviated lesson on the same day. As Shakespeare's sonnets and *Romeo and Juliet* are commonly covered in university and high school curricula, the integrated pairing of the two will be natural.

Students should understand that during the same time *Romeo and Juliet* was likely first performed (circa 1595), the English literary scene was in the midst of a sonnet craze that started with the publication of Sir Philip Sidney's 1591 *Astrophil and Stella* and peaked during the years 1593–97, during which approximately eighteen sonnet sequences appeared. I typically show my students a slide of the number of sequences published during this period to illustrate the genre's popularity.[1] Shakespeare's own collection of sonnets was not published until 1609, but he clearly was writing them all through these years, along with other works like *Venus and Adonis*, in 1593, and *The Rape of Lucrece*, in 1594, that were partly prompted by the closing of the theaters because of the plague. The new Cambridge edition of the sonnets, *All the Sonnets of Shakespeare*, edited by Paul Edmondson and Stanley Wells, organizes the sonnets by conjectural composition date, allowing readers to see that most of Shakespeare's sonnets were drafted during this peak time.

After establishing this historical and generic context, we discuss a healthy sampling of Shakespeare's sonnets along with representative sonnets from Sidney, Barnabe Barnes's *Parthenophil and Parthenophe*, Giles Fletcher's *Licia*, Thomas Lodge's *Phillis*, Samuel Daniel's *Delia*, Michael Drayton's *Ideas Mirrour*, Richard Barnfield's *Cynthia*, and Edmund Spenser's *Amoretti*.[2] It helps to have the heights of a Spenser alongside the exquisite bathos of a Barnes to provide students with the breadth of the sonnet in practice. The learning objectives for this unit that best prepare students for *Romeo and Juliet* include identifying Petrarchan commonplaces, analyzing the rhetorical structure of a sonnet, and thinking through the commonalities and differences between the lyrical and the dramatic.

The Petrarchan commonplaces discussed include the lover-poet's often unrequited and hyperbolic adoration of the beloved, conventional metaphors and conceits (e.g., sun, moon, fire, ice, sea, seasons, hunt, warfare, religious ritual), and literary devices such as antithesis, oxymoron, and blazon.[3] A Petrarchan-commonplace scavenger hunt activity has worked well in the past: students take a list of Petrarchan conceits and devices and document their use in the assigned sonnets for the week. A bonus question in the scavenger hunt asks students to identify a Petrarchan remnant in a contemporary song. The assignment works well out of class and perhaps even better in class if there is time, as you can have teams compete for timed completion. Students emerge with a better grasp of how ubiquitous a particular conceit, such as love compared to a storm-tossed ship at sea, is across different sonneteers, but also how a device like the blazon, while prevalent, can be used in self-consciously playful ways (e.g., in sonnet 130).

My students also learn to closely analyze the structure and rhyme scheme of this simultaneously fixed yet supple form, exploring what Stephen Regan calls the "dynamic internal structure" (5) of divisible yet linked units of octave and sestet, which further divides into three quatrains and a couplet, expressed through alternating (in the Shakespearean sonnet) or envelope (in the Petrarchan sonnet) rhymes. The alternating rhyme scheme of the Shakespearean sonnet encourages patterns of parallelism and antithesis, and the quatrains enable vibrant movements of sequencing, contrast, and accumulation. The form seems particularly suited for the unfolding of logical argumentation and imagistic contrasting. We discuss the volta and how it acquired special potency as a rhetorical shift into the final quatrain, and we discuss the concluding couplet with its epigrammatic powers of encapsulation, reversal, and distillation. By reading Shakespeare's sonnets next to those of his contemporaries, we can see where Shakespeare either follows convention or breaks free from it. Class discussion and written analysis assignments of individual sonnets complement one another and enrich our understanding of the sonnets' properties.

For the written assignments, I typically ask students to choose and analyze one of Shakespeare's sonnets along with one from his contemporaries so I can rely on those students to be class "experts" on a particular sonnet for that day's discussion. In the prompt, I ask variations on these questions:

> What is the theme or argument of the sonnet, and how does the sonneteer explore that theme through word choices, literary devices, and structure?
>
> If the two poems you have chosen use the same theme, how do they approach it differently?
>
> What word choices seem significant, and why? (Explore connotation as well as denotation, consider the sonic traits of the word, and look up at least one in the *Oxford English Dictionary*.)
>
> How does the poem use literary devices (alliteration, allusion, antithesis, blazon, enjambment, metaphor, oxymoron, onomatopoeia, parallelism, personification, pun, etc.) and to what effect?
>
> What are the focal points of the quatrains, how do they build on each other and develop the theme, where and how does the sonnet "turn," and what does the couplet accomplish for the sonnet as a whole?
>
> What Petrarchan devices and conceits do you see, and how are they used?
>
> Does the sonnet play with reader expectations?
>
> What is the most powerful moment in the sonnet, and why?

This writing assignment typically produces some of the most detailed close reading of the semester, as thinking with and through a sonnet elicits heightened awareness of the text's *how* (devices, lexicon, form, structure, style) as incarnation of its *what* (content). Like a linguistic cubic press, the sonnet compacts the conventional lump-of-coal theme into a multifaceted diamond demanding granular attention.

This exploration of the formal properties of the sonnet prepares students for a broader discussion of the relationship between the lyric properties of the sonnet and the dramatic action of a play. While lyric poems and plays may seem to operate quite differently in terms of time, space, and narrative, the generic borders were porous for Elizabethan writers. For example, the sonnets "offered the fledgling drama characters, attitudes, and poses for the 'love game,'" and the length of the sonnet helped calibrate and condition the "average mid-length speech" of a play (Barry 15). The sonnet sequence could take on the form of a dramatic character experiencing the trials and travails of love, and many of the sonnets, particularly Shakespeare's, deploy theatrical conceits. Edmondson and Wells describe how Shakespeare may have used the sonnet as "a collection of fourteen-line monologues . . . sketchbooks for characterization, or character studies in miniature" (*Shakespeare's Sonnets* 101, 103). One possible activity (using the Edmondson and Wells edition of the sonnets) would be to select sonnets that were written closest to a particular play's performance date; a related activity would be to find dramatic analogues for a particular sonnet. At this point in the class, I will often introduce a few sonnets that Shakespeare embeds in his plays, particularly in *Love's Labor's Lost*, as its historical proximity to *Romeo and Juliet* makes for useful contrast later. What happens when a sonnet enters the dramatic-play space? Are we reading a "poem or speech?" (Barry 13). *Love's Labor's Lost* provides three sonnets as dramatic props read to the audience as well as a playfully ironic moment where Biron, forswearing "maggot ostentation" (5.2.410) and straitjacketed formalism (like sonnets), makes his declaration of unadorned love to Rosaline in a festooned sonnet. Many in Shakespeare's original audience, living in an environment saturated with sonnets in print and manuscript, surely would have recognized Biron's speech as a sonnet when spoken.

But Soft, What Sonnet through Yonder Play Breaks?

After the unit on sonnets, students are primed for an application of this material to *Romeo and Juliet*, particularly to the play's collaborative sonnet. To prepare for the meeting of Romeo and Juliet in 1.4, I ask students to identify in the preceding scenes examples of Petrarchan commonplaces and any gestures toward the sonnet form. Of course, there is the play's prologue, a plot spoiler in the form of a sonnet spoken by the Chorus, which allows for a fascinating discussion of a sonnet form wrenched from its conventional love frame and co-opted for narrative—the "star-crossed" inevitability of the play represented in miniature by the preordained structure and rhymes. The chaos put orderly in those four-teen lines proceeds to erupt on the stage with Samson and Gregory's aggres-sively stichomythic punning.

Students will then point out the Petrarchan language infusing the play, par-ticularly the oxymoronic cascade from Romeo, which one student called "down-right [Barnabe] Barnesian":

> Why, then, O brawling love, O loving hate,
> O anything of nothing first created,
> O heavy lightness, serious vanity,
> Misshapen chaos of well-seeming forms,
> Feather of lead, bright smoke, cold fire, sick health,
> Still-waking sleep that is not what it is—
> This love feel I, that feel no love in this.
>
> (1.1.171–77)

"Dost thou not laugh?" (1.1.178), Romeo asks Benvolio at the completion of this poetastery, and it is difficult for my students not to do so themselves. They also point to other lines from Romeo that seem directly drawn from the sonnet sketchbook:

> She will not stay the siege of loving terms,
> Nor bide th'encounter of assailing eyes,
> Nor ope her lap to saint-seducing gold.
> Oh, she is rich in beauty; only poor
> That, when she dies, with beauty dies her store.
>
> (1.1.207–11)

Romeo's ending couplet here sounds just like the procreation argument of the first seventeen of Shakespeare's sonnets. Students easily identify Romeo's mop-ing as a stylized aping of Petrarchan language: as Mercutio puts it, "Now is he for the numbers that Petrarch flowed in" (2.3.36–37). After having read so many sonnets themselves, students can detect the exhausted "Neo-Petrarchan kitsch" (R. Wells 915) of Romeo's rhetoric and how the play seems to be "pulling the same [Petrarchan] rabbit out of the same hat" (Levenson, "Definition" 22). Like the sonneteer's object of desire, Romeo's beloved is conspicuously absent and exists as a verbal construct, and she has the most commonplace of names for literary beloveds: Rosaline, which appears (also as the variant Rosalind) in Lodge, Spenser, and two other Shakespeare plays. With a little extra prodding, students can see how the opening scenes contain phantom references to the sonnet form itself: Romeo and Benvolio duel about the merits of Rosaline in sestets (1.2.85–96). And, one might ask, what age is Juliet about to turn, mentioned five times in twelve lines when she is introduced? Fourteen.

Wherefore Art Thou Sonnet?

Students by now are ripe for the identification of Romeo and Juliet's courtship scene as a sonnet. They are also informed enough to discuss just how sui generis this moment is, both as a sonnet and as a dramatic encounter. Unlike the stilted artificiality of the prologue sonnet (which is separated from the dramatic action, and even excised entirely in the First Folio) and the prop-like sonnets in *Love's Labor's Lost*, this sonnet is fully integrated in the dramatic action so as to be almost undetectable. And yet, as a sonnet that activates a well-known rhythmic formula for audiences, it reveals itself as a distillation moment—a dramatic as well as a lyrical centering.

As a class, we analyze the sonnet wisely and slowly, as they stumble that run fast. A productive early question for students concerns the mixing of genres: What has the dramatic reprocessing done to the all-too-familiar sonnet? In what ways does the play ensure that the "sonnet will never be the same again once it has passed through its essentially theatrical body" (Schalkwyk 64)? Students comment right away that this is no longer some private monologue to an audience of oneself: "the Petrarchan habit of speaking of one's beloved, or to one's beloved, or behind the back of one's beloved, is replaced by the reciprocity of speaking *with* one's beloved" (67). Which one is the poet and which the beloved? Both take turns in each role. The dialogic and mutual nature of this particular sonnet makes it virtually unprecedented in the genre. (Students who have read Spenser's *Amoretti* 75 may be able to compare that poem's remarkable reciprocity between poet and beloved.)

The centerpiece of the class hour is a group analysis task, where I ask the students to work through the following prompts:

> How does the sonnet structure and rhyme scheme help us chart the development of Romeo and Juliet's relationship?
>
> Underline or make a list of the words that Romeo and Juliet share with each other.
>
> Underline or make a list of the words that start with *p*.

Then, together as a class, we discuss and develop the results. Having had practice analyzing the structure of Shakespeare's sonnets, most students are able to make cogent points about the quatrain-quatrain-quatrain-couplet and the octave-sestet dialectic. Romeo has eight lines and Juliet six, just like an octave and sestet. Romeo leads with one quatrain and Juliet follows with her own, both echoing the "this"-"kiss" rhyme. In the third and final quatrain, Romeo and Juliet alternate lines, signaling a closer syntactic proximity as they move from a discussion of hands to lips. The volta is a question, which signals a more intimate shift in their rhetorical interactions as well. By the end of the quatrain, they are now rhyming with each other instead of miming rhymes (Juliet's "prayer" and Romeo's "despair").

And the resolution couplet gives each character a line, rhyming together in a coupling that links works and action, culminating the sonnet's movement from "palms" to "lips" to "kiss." This is the "body sonnetized," where "voice and flesh reciprocate, both through the bodies of the lovers and the body of the poem they speak" (Whittier 35).

The list of shared words—*hand, pilgrim, touch, kiss, lips, saints, move, prayer*—deepens students' understanding of the playful game of the two lovers, who hand words off to one another across the linear boundaries and redeploy them in new signifying contexts. Students gain an appreciation for ploce (the deliberate repetition of a word for rhetorical emphasis) and connotative nuance as we explore the subtle shifts in meaning as one character repurposes the words of the other for coy defense or offense. This is also an opportunity to discuss the preponderance of religious words and the sacralizing effect of the conceit they construct together.

Many of those religious words account for the *p* alliteration throughout: *profane* (one), *pilgrim* (four), *palm/palmers* (four), *pray/prayer* (four). We can add in for good measure the four instances of consonance with *lips*. As I often explain to my students, in addition to its sonic effect, alliteration creates a conceptual covalent bond through consonants. When these words are arranged in sequence, they create a mininarrative thread in the sonnet—*profane* to *pilgrim* to *palm* to *palmers* to *pilgrim* to *prayer*—a chiasmus-like structure that emphasizes the movement (pilgrimage?) from the profane to prayer with a pun on *palm/palmer* in the center. We also chart the intensification of the sounds: there are four *p* alliterations in the first seven lines and nine in the last seven lines; there are three in line 8, where the central *palm/palmer* pun occurs. It is the climax of the second quatrain, just before the sestet where Romeo and Juliet begin to share sections (a similar alliterative climax occurs in line 8 of sonnet 12, "Borne on the bier with white and bristly beard"). We can then discuss the sonic effect of the plosive *p* sound, including the important fact that the shaping of the word involves the pursing of lips, like a kiss, before the pushing of air.

For Never Was a Sonnet of More Woe

Moving from analyzing the collaborative sonnet's structure to individual word choices to phonemes, students reinforce previous knowledge from the course to apply it in this new context. They are also uniquely situated to understand the significance of this moment for the play. Out of the sterile Petrarchan language from the previous scenes springs a new language of love, both natural and artful. Romeo and Juliet build a sonnet together but also a room, a little world, a moment's monument, both encapsulating and sublimating the sonnet form and its discourse of love: "the sonnet tradition of unattainable or unrequited love is turned inside out, and the artifice of conventional language goes with it" (Garber, *Shakespeare after All* 194). It is both a dramatic moment that moves the relationship forward and yet one that arrests it in lyric.

But it cannot last. We then move to the next four lines, which seem to start another sonnet quatrain, with ever more bonding through language:

ROMEO.	Thus from my lips, by thine, my sin is purged.
JULIET.	Then have my lips the sin that they have took.
ROMEO.	Sin from my lips? Oh, trespass sweetly urged!
	Give me my sin again.
	[*He kisses her.*]
JULIET.	You kiss by th'book.
	(1.4.218–21)

Students note the continuation of the religious rhetoric from the previous sonnet as well as the handing off again of words, such as "my lips" and "sin." And the back and forth of the lines in the shared quatrain builds to a shared final line, where each contributes a half. One gets the sense that they would go on sonneteering, and kissing, in perpetuity, but the Nurse intrudes on the sonnet and separates them. This is the moment Romeo learns Juliet is a Capulet. Romeo and Juliet's stanzaic bubble has been punctured by external forces, which presages the intrusion of factionalism that will turn their comedy into a tragedy. They will of course speak to each other again, but never with the same mutual composition, and their final death scene acts as a horrific inverse of their initial meeting: two bodies next to one another but no longer in antiphonal rhythm—each monologuing to an absent (whether drugged or dead) beloved, ending both speech and life with unreciprocated kisses. Each set of once-feuding parents promise to build a commemorative statue for the other's child, a poor, gilded substitute for the moment's monument of Romeo and Juliet's sonnet courtship, and a marmorealizing gesture that is—as my students by now know—a well-worn Petrarchan conceit. Is this a play that manages to transform and transcend the Petrarchan stranglehold on the Elizabethan rhetoric of love, or is it ultimately confined and defined by it? That is a question for my students to decide.

NOTES

1. Spiller provides a list of sonnet sequences in his appendix (198–99).

2. Shakespeare sonnets typically assigned include 1, 12, 18, 19, 20, 23, 29, 30, 33, 35, 53, 55, 60, 62, 65, 71, 73, 74, 80, 87, 94, 97–99, 105, 106, 110, 113, 116, 127–30, 132, 135, 136, 138, 144, 146, 147, and 152–54. Generous samplings of sonnets by the other sonneteers can be found in M. Evans and in Sylvester and online in Arber and Seccombe. Popular English literature anthologies, such as Black and Prescott or Greenblatt, have a smaller but still useful selection of sonneteers from this period.

3. See Earl for a list of Petrarchan traits, including examples from English sonneteers and connections to *Romeo and Juliet*.

Editing *Romeo and Juliet* in the General Education Shakespeare Course

Rebecca Olson

In 2018 I oversaw the creation of a student-edited, online textbook of *Romeo and Juliet*. Our conflated edition, published by Oregon State University's Open Educational Resources Unit and revised by a second group of students in 2020, was designed to engage teenagers and support Oregon classrooms in particular; we deemed *Romeo and Juliet* the play most likely to be taught to new readers of Shakespeare and thus most in need of a fresh, free online text. From the start, I knew that I would adopt our open educational resource (OER) in the general education Shakespeare course I offer every year, both on campus and online, and thus reduce the textbook costs of a class perennially popular with non–English majors looking to satisfy humanities requirements. What I did not anticipate is that my experience preparing advanced students to become editors—by way of experiential instruction in topics including book history, educational access, and antiracist pedagogy—would transform my approach to teaching *Romeo and Juliet* in the introductory course as well.

My general education Shakespeare course now includes a unit on editing the play that puts to good use the fact that, for many new readers of Elizabethan drama, the strangeness of the language makes for a slow-going and often alienating experience. When we empower students to edit *Romeo and Juliet* at this early stage, we change expectations: students are not asked to adapt to Shakespeare but rather to develop language *with* Shakespeare. As Paula Blank observes, "We cannot entirely help hearing Shakespeare's language through or against or alongside our modern vernacular, creating a friction between two 'Englishes'—one that was ours, has influenced ours, yet is not quite ours" (4). In line with Blank's recommendation, I invite my students to take "an anachronistic disposition toward Shakespeare" and actively compare his language with their own (Blank 5). This essay provides an overview of the learning outcomes and activities of the editing unit in my general education Shakespeare course, all of which are designed to help students experience firsthand—and take seriously—Juliet's seemingly facetious "What's in a name?"

As I explain, editing requires that students read very closely but simultaneously think of the big picture: they must consider individual words—and even individual punctuation marks—not only in the context of the play as a whole but also in light of the audience they aim to serve. While my advanced students spent weeks engaged with primary and secondary sources prior to producing the online *Romeo and Juliet*, my approach in the general education course is very different. I basically throw my students—most of whom are not English majors and many of whom are in their first year—into the deep end of a pool they did not know existed, largely because I want to avoid putting pressure on them to do it "right." My goal is to engage students in puzzles presented by the complicated textual history of Shakespeare's plays, raise their awareness of the extent to which the expertise or biases of individual editors shape our experiences of those plays, and create an opportunity for them to take ownership of the Shakespearean material and its ongoing legacy.

My editing unit takes advantage of the increasing number of excellent online resources and technologies; we make use of digital humanities projects like the University of Victoria's Internet Shakespeare Editions, websites including the online *Open Source Shakespeare*, and document-sharing applications like *Box*, among others. However, editing Shakespeare with the specific goal of validating student perspectives has a long history that predates the digital age. Take, for example, the work of Katherine Lee Bates, who was one of at least seventy women who edited Shakespeare before 1950 (Yarn 199). In contrast to Shakespeare editors who foregrounded their own opinions, Bates—who in the late nineteenth century edited student editions of *The Merchant of Venice*, *A Midsummer Night's Dream*, and *As You Like It*—took a decidedly learner-centered approach. As Molly Yarn explains, Bates's editions invited students to participate in making meaning of the text: "She invited engagement with the text's material history by deflecting the assumption of a single, authoritative reading . . . and by capitalizing on students' pre-existing propensity to mark up their schoolbooks, encouraging them to take on an editorial role by writing in their preferred readings and emendations" (194). My editing unit takes a similarly student-centered approach and destabilizes not only the assumption of a single, authoritative reading but also the assumption of a single, authoritative text. For the most part, undergraduates are used to treating "the text" as a starting point for analysis and discussion, and this unit productively unsettles that premise. The fact that there are different early modern versions of *Romeo and Juliet* and that nobody can definitively say what Shakespeare actually wrote can come as a real shock.

Like Whitney Taylor, I find that editing assignments advance the goals of critical pedagogy. When designing her own successful editing assignment, for instance, Taylor was committed to "placing students in a position of authority to make Shakespeare's work more approachable, learning more interactive, and students more comfortable making their own critical interventions." She hoped, moreover, that the assignment would give students "common ground and confidence" (131). Indeed, when editing takes the form of an experiential, collaborative, community-facing project, it represents the kind of high-impact educational practice that can be especially engaging for underrepresented students in higher education (Whitley et al. 35). For instance, Ayanna Thompson finds that first-generation students in particular can benefit from editing exercises: "They seem to get that the power resides in the editor, who may be making things up (!), and they wonder how they too can grab that power" ("Response" 185). Especially for students who struggled with *Romeo and Juliet* in high school, editing provides an opportunity for a do-over—a chance to "grab that power" and literally rewrite passages and footnotes that previously left them unmoved, angry, or even feeling bad about themselves.

By the time we get to the editing unit in the fourth week of my general education course, students have already spent a week reading and discussing *Romeo and Juliet*. They know about the play's textual variants, having participated in an online discussion that asked them to explain the significance of a specific variation in Juliet's speech in act 4, scene 3, as printed in the first quarto edition of 1597 (Q1) and the First Folio of 1623. They have also, in an earlier unit focused on *A Midsummer Night's Dream*, explored the potential impact of compositional or transcription error for early modern printed texts; each student has engaged with online resources devoted to either original pronunciation or early modern paleography, has completed a multimedia practice quiz on that topic, and has offered an example, in an online discussion post, of a word that would be easy to mistake for another in the early modern period.

The first learning activity in the editing unit introduces the class to the online *Oxford English Dictionary* (*OED*) by way of a practice quiz that asks them to find specific information about twenty-first-century entries as well as early modern terms. I find that even after five or ten minutes navigating the *OED*, most students are far more likely to seek period-appropriate definitions of unfamiliar Shakespearean words than to rely on modern online dictionaries or other scholarly editions of the play. This hands-on activity is complemented by a brief lecture (filmed for the asynchronous online version of the course) in which I narrate the history of the Oregon State OER edition, provide a summary of the student editors' main objectives, and share examples of various formats they considered. I also walk us through a passage that proved especially challenging— the dialogue between Lord Capulet and his servant in 4.2—and explain how the student editors resolved those challenges by conflating Q1 and the second printed quarto of 1599 (Q2).[1] By the end of this presentation, my general education students can explain why editing the entire text took a great deal of training, attention to detail, and collaboration. They understand that their own projects will be much smaller in scale but that they, too, will become actual editors.

And then, without further ado, they edit! In the first of the unit's three assignments, each student chooses twelve to thirty lines in *Romeo and Juliet* to work on. The first step is to review the digital images of the passage in both Q1 and Q2. Students are encouraged to make sure they understand the passage (looking up phrases as needed in the *OED*, for example). All editing decisions are theirs to make: they must consider which base text to use, how to format the page, whether or not to modernize punctuation or spelling, and which words or phrases require a marginal gloss or footnote. Some students opt to "translate" the language into twenty-first-century speech altogether; most prefer to tweak an early modern edition, replacing only the most obsolete or misleading words.

The finished editions are then attached, as pdf files, to students' submissions of the second assignment, which is a graded discussion post. In two hundred words or less, they address the following prompt: "Give us an example of one decision you had to make while editing your passage. Be sure to be specific: this should be a particular word or phrase, choice of punctuation, or formatting element. ('I modernized the language' is too broad to be effective.)" Most students describe how they dealt with variations between the early printed editions; those differences are often subtle, such as a word they found capitalized in one printing and not the other, but sometimes students describe a surprising discrepancy, such as a line reassigned to a different character. Once everyone has posted, each student responds, in one or two sentences, to at least one other person in their small group. I provide a clear expectation for this response, as follows: "In your reply, let the author know what one of their decisions suggests to you about their intended audience. Who, in other words, would benefit from the particular editing decision they describe or from the general format of their edition? Here again, be specific: 'anyone' is too broad." The discussion post is graded with a rubric that includes the following criteria: presentation of the edition, signs of difference from the base text, discussion of editorial decisions, and reply to their peer.

Such editing exercises advance my course's ongoing conversation about Shakespeare's cultural status even as they introduce students to literary close reading and why it matters. In fact, this online discussion is the first assignment in which many students successfully demonstrate close reading, presumably because it forces them to focus on a very specific textual detail. Moreover, and in line with Taylor's observation that editing can meet many of the same objectives as a formal essay (136–39), their editions almost always evidence deep engagement with the play. I find that combining an editing assignment with an essay can be especially beneficial when it comes to helping students understand the wider applicability of the skills required for literary analysis. To this end, the final assignment in the *Romeo and Juliet* editing unit is an essay that asks students to situate their own experiences as editors in a wider social context. Here is how I introduce the assignment:

> Now that you are an experienced editor of Shakespearean drama, it's time to think more critically about the role editing plays in our reading

experience. How do the choices that you made encourage readers to interpret the play differently than they would if they were reading someone else's edition? Describe, in two to three pages, one way that your edited passage differs from the Oregon State OER edition. Your essay must also address one of the following questions:

> What does that difference tell us about your interpretation of the passage?
>
> What does that difference suggest about the two editions' target audiences?

The essay assignment reinforces a mindset I seek to cultivate throughout the course: all students bring expertise developed both inside and outside of our class to the study of Shakespeare. Here, students are asked to articulate the value their knowledge of a particular passage of *Romeo and Juliet* might have for others, such as those in their home or online communities.

The essays written in response to this prompt have deepened my understanding of what it is about *Romeo and Juliet* my students find most engaging and why my previous approaches to teaching the play often fell flat. For instance, most of the students who choose to answer the first question—"What does that difference tell us about your interpretation of the passage?"—write about characterization, something I habitually neglect: many have made persuasive and passionate arguments about how slight changes in wording, punctuation, or capitalization impact our understanding of a particular character's emotion or motivation. Such essays build on our earlier discussion about the differences between early modern printings of the speech Juliet delivers before drinking the sleeping draft; in that assignment, students often articulate why their preferred version seems more in line with Juliet's representation elsewhere in the play. But it is not until they actually edit the play for themselves that many students come to appreciate the differences between one character's speech and another's. To my surprise, students have typically avoided the play's most familiar passages and have instead chosen to edit relatively obscure dialogue that includes minor characters (the banter between musicians after Juliet's wedding to Paris, for example). In an online section of the course, my student Lucinda Boyle explained the decision to keep a line delivered by Romeo to the Apothecary as it appears in Q1—"I pay thy poverty, but not thy will"—to support what Boyle saw as the scene's quick pace and intensity; unlike our textbook's "I pay thy poverty and not thy will" (5.2.76; Shakespeare, *Romeo and Juliet: A Textbook Edition*), which is based on the 1623 First Folio edition, Q1 reintroduces the word "but," which appears in the Apothecary's preceding line. Ultimately, the student explained in a detailed analysis, the word "but" reinforces the scene's depiction of Romeo's agitation and social privilege. Even a brief encounter with editing hastens students' comfort with *Romeo and Juliet*'s rich language, in part because even as they acclimate themselves to reading Shakespeare, they develop sensitivity to the way the play codes characters, especially in terms of gender, class, and age. In our follow-up conversation, asking "Who had a character in their passage who was hard to edit, and why were they hard?" produces a reliably vibrant dialogue that paves the way for further investigations of the play's representations of various categories of identity.

While the essays that address the prompt about interpretation often present sophisticated considerations of a character's social position in Verona, many students who choose to answer the second question—"What does that difference suggest about the two editions' target audiences?"—attend instead to editorial positionality, including their own. Some, for example, have argued that specific vocabulary in the online edition's footnotes indicates an expected level of education or assumes whiteness. Students with backgrounds in theater are often quick to point out places where the edition fails to support actors or take performance into account. Interestingly, several students have argued that the OER created by my advanced students, despite its stated objective to engage young people, takes for granted an interest in the play that many readers encountering Shakespeare for the first time, and especially those required to read the play in ninth-grade language arts, do not share. Others have pointed out that the edition's retention of now-obsolete early modern words such as "thou" betrays its orientation toward older readers, who may value historical authenticity more than clarity. Such critique of the student editors' assumed "American student" illuminates the drawbacks of generalizing readers in a way that is helpful for future conversations in the course: we can hold one another accountable for complicating categories like "early modern playgoer" or "postcolonial adaptor," for example.

Before we conclude our editing unit, I lead the class in a discussion about how they approached any elements in their passage that were racist, misogynist, classist, or ableist. I bring a variety of editions to this session so that we can compare scholarly treatments of those same passages. Students who entirely rewrote Shakespeare's language are invited to share how their own perspectives impacted their word choices and consequently their representation of the character's social standing. That conversation supports two important points: first, editors are people with their own perspectives, expertise, and implicit biases; and second, even seemingly insignificant language choices can ultimately support oppressive social systems.

Students tasked with editing even a few lines of text, and who are looking closely at differences between the quartos, begin to see *Romeo and Juliet* as a narrative continually and collectively rewritten, not only in performance but also on the page. Most helpful for their success in the course, however, is the fact that being thrust into editing hastens my students' cultivation of the seemingly paradoxical ability to both emotionally connect to Shakespeare's characters and, at the same time, recognize the fundamental differences between their modern lives and those represented in the world of the play. Their analyses are stronger once they have developed a more editorial orientation to the past and to Shakespeare—one that maintains sensitivity to historical context and its norms without ever ignoring the realities of our present moment and the lived experiences of people with whom we share it.

NOTE

1. Two of our original editors discussed this example in a presentation at the 2019 Oregon State Undergraduate Humanities Conference.

Benvolio Must Die:
Q1's "Conceited" *Romeo and Juliet*

Sarah Neville

for Steven Urkowitz, of course

William Shakespeare's *Romeo and Juliet* first made it into print in 1597. That book, known to scholars as Q1, was published by London stationer John Danter, who chose to advertise the play as an "excellent conceited tragedy" and to highlight on its title page that it had often been performed "with great applause." Two years later, in 1599, another edition of the play (Q2) was published by a different London stationer, Cuthbert Burby, who advertised his edition as "newly corrected, augmented, and amended." The Q2 text is not only twenty percent longer than Q1, but it also contains over eight hundred lines that vary significantly from their earlier equivalents; this substantive difference between the two editions verifies Burby's claim. The longer Q2 version of the play was reprinted in 1609 (Q3) and again in 1622 (Q4). A third version of the play appeared in the First Folio of 1623 that mostly copied Q3 but also offered a few interesting variants of its own.[1]

The longer 1599 text forms the basis for most modern editions of the play, making it the version most frequently taught in schools, most frequently written about by scholars, and most frequently performed onstage. The present essay suggests that there are significant benefits in bringing the unfamiliar 1597 edition, sometimes known as the play's "bad quarto," into the classroom. I contend that by enabling students to engage with the debates around so-called bad quartos, seemingly familiar texts can be made new and uncanny in surprising and often productive ways. To show how bad quartos can create opportunities for investigative, discovery-based learning, I approach them by demonstrating productive intersections between performance as research, textual scholarship, and book history. The goal in all three methods is to destabilize right-answerism—the notion that Shakespeare's text is a complicated interpretive puzzle that has already been solved by centuries of learned scholars. While both instructors and students can fall prey to right-answerism, it can be easily defeated by examining the ways that broad narratives about provenance exist only because of the elision or exclusion of certain types of textual and performance-based evidence. In the case of Shakespeare, such broad narratives around bad quartos give instructors an opportunity to demonstrate firsthand that scholarly activities themselves have a history—one that is often exploratory, argumentative, defensive, trendy, and recursive. Testing some of the claims made about bad quartos enables students to be active participants and peer reviewers in the scholarly process. By investigating the truth claims that underpin literary metanarratives, students both better understand the historicity of texts and become more adept at close reading. In other words, bad quartos can lead to good pedagogy.

What Is a "Bad Quarto"?

Romeo and Juliet is not the only Shakespeare play that exists in multiple versions: *Hamlet, Henry V, Richard III, 2 Henry VI, 3 Henry VI, King Lear,* and *The Merry Wives of Windsor* all have early quartos that differ substantively from later editions. In fact, half of the plays in the First Folio had been previously printed, and all of Shakespeare's plays contain substantive variants among their early editions. In the first half of the twentieth century, bibliographers collated the differences between early and later editions and grouped several quartos together based on the similar ways that these texts differed from later versions of the same play (Kirschbaum). Though these early quarto editions had mostly the same plots and characters as their longer versions, they shared similar types of variance with one another: substantively shorter texts, unique stage directions, flexible approaches to entrances and exits, and a greater divergence from metrical norms. Scholars often cited the First Folio paratexts to explain these similarities. Here, in "To the great Variety of Readers," John Heminges and Henry Condell, who had collected Shakespeare's dramatic works for publication, claimed that the Folio plays were superior to earlier editions: "where, before, you were abused with diverse stolen and surreptitious copies, maimed, and deformed by the frauds and stealths of injurious impostors that exposed them—even those are now offered to your view cured, and perfect of their limbs" (Shakespeare, *Mr. William Shakespeares Comedies* sig. πA3r). Some scholars suggested that the curious early quartos were the "surreptitious copies" that Heminges and Condell warned about, and they recast these editions as "maimed and deformed" versions caused by nefarious publishers rushing unauthorized texts to print. Bibliographers named these editions "bad quartos," a moniker that has persisted in scholarship despite later attempts to recuperate these books. Bad quartos thus came to be seen as imperfect transmissions of Shakespeare's fuller and more perfected dramas.

Once the deficiencies of the bad quartos had been established, scholars proposed a variety of explanations to account for the provenance of the texts that appeared in them. One theory held that the texts were shorter because they were "memorial reconstructions," or transcripts commissioned by agents trying to remember verbatim the text as it was heard onstage (Kirschbaum). Another theory held that the bad quartos were the result of audience members taking shorthand as they watched a play (Stern, "Sermons"). Though sometimes quite complicated, these theories all suggest that, regardless of how garbled the texts might have become, their origins began in the theater. Bad quartos thus came to be seen as evidence for the way that Shakespeare's plays appeared onstage, particularly in their early incarnations, which is why they often include more detailed stage directions than those of later editions. For example, in act 2, scene 5, Juliet's entrance in Q2 is marked in a stage direction simply as *"Enter Juliet"* (2.5.15), but Q1 offers a direction that is much more dynamic and even prescriptive, hinting perhaps at the way the scene played out in performance: *"Enter Juliet, somewhat fast, and she embraces Romeo"* (2.5.8).[2] Such evidence suggests that bad quartos might be the closest thing we have to a record of what early modern audiences really experienced in the theater.

While some critics still dismiss the bad quartos as literary accidents or as corruptions in the typical processes of textual transmission, others now see the bad quartos as evidence of how Shakespeare's plays simply changed as part of the theatrical process, with bad quartos as the surviving products of Shakespeare's usual writing habits rather than a sign of something gone awry (Urkowitz). Scholars have also suggested another possibility: bad quartos are not garbled forms of longer texts but simply earlier *versions* of plays that were later expanded and changed. Some argue that Shakespeare was an unusually frequent reviser, which is why his printed plays, more so than the plays of any other Renaissance playwright, were often advertised on their title pages as "corrected" or "augmented" (Farmer). Others have suggested that when his company had the chance to perform his plays at court, Shakespeare revised them to suit the tastes of his royal audience (Dutton). Shakespeare's variable editions show us explicitly that early modern play texts were not fixed but mutable—plays could shift as a result of company need, direct or indirect collaboration between playwrights, theatrical trends, or audience reactions to the first performance (Stern, *Documents*). The diversity of the evidence used to support claims about bad quartos means that even the most experienced Shakespeare instructors have cause to reconsider many of their basic premises about Shakespeare; examining these unfamiliar quartos through a variety of performative, textual, and book-historical methods allows instructors an opportunity for learning alongside their students by engaging in a shared process of discovery.

Teaching Textual Variance through Performance

As many theater scholars recognize, performances of Shakespeare's plays can explain curiosities that confuse or bedevil literary critics. For example, commentators upon *Romeo and Juliet* have long puzzled over an early exchange between Romeo and Benvolio after the latter urges Romeo to forgo his love for the disinterested Rosaline:

ROMEO.	Your plantain leaf is excellent for that.
BENVOLIO.	For what?
ROMEO.	For your broken shin.
BENVOLIO.	Why, Romeo, art thou mad?

(Q1 1.2.42–45)

A similar exchange appears in Q2. Commentary on the passage often discusses the plantain as an herbal remedy and considers Romeo's medicalized response a sardonic refutation of Benvolio's string of aphoristic love advice. While these notes are not wrong, major editions of the play have too often missed the implicit stage direction in Romeo's remarks: he is *literally kicking his friend in the shin*, a comedic bit of stage business. The embodied practice of theater often allows practitioners to locate similar insights into stage action, character motivation, and dialogue, ultimately broadening our sense of Shakespeare as an artist.

Bad quartos are especially valuable fodder for these kinds of theatrical investigations, and scholars often celebrate the insights these texts provide about performance. Q1 *Romeo and Juliet* is particularly suggestive in exactly this way; as Lukas Erne says, "[I]f we are interested in getting close to a Shakespeare play as it was performed as well as in the process which turned Shakespeare's original drama into a workable performance script, then there is no better text to turn to than the first quarto of *Romeo and Juliet*" (25). Yet despite scholars' acknowledgment of the theatrical provenance of these early quartos, few theater companies have taken the next investigative step of staging them. Lord Denney's Players (LDP), the academic theater group at Ohio State University that I founded and manage, uses theater as a lab space to enable undergraduate and graduate students, staff and faculty members, and recent alumni to engage in intensive experiential learning and research around the annual production of an early English play. We often choose to perform early quarto texts of Shakespeare to evaluate how well they work onstage, and in the past we have performed plays such as the 1597 text of *Richard II* (dir. Sarah Neville, 2015) and the 1602 quarto of *The Merry Wives of Windsor* (dir. Sarah Neville, 2018). As theatrical experiences for engaged student audiences, LDP productions allow for buy-in from multiple courses across the English department, including introductory and upper-level Shakespeare as well as our British literature surveys. In spring 2019, LDP mounted a full production of the Q1 text of *Romeo and Juliet* (dir. Cat McAlpine) in a rented theater in downtown Columbus.[3]

Our six-night run of Q1 *Romeo and Juliet* invited audiences to notice how this version of Shakespeare's famous play offered new ways of considering the relationship between the lovers and the violent world in which they find themselves. Because Q1 covers the same narrative ground as Q2 but has only eighty percent of its lines, it is demonstrably faster; here, the breathless pace of the lovers is matched by the audience's experience of seeing a well-known story on fast-forward. One local theater reviewer remarked that though the Q1 version "still feels like a rough draft," because of its "rough edges and contradictions" our production "crackled with a breathless intensity" (Sanford). LDP's semester-length investment in producing and performing the text also allows company actors to see firsthand how a play's popular reputation can sometimes be at odds with its actual form or structure. In a filmed interview, Lior Livshits, who played Romeo, recounted his initial impressions of the play as being a kind of "chocolate box love story" (Merritt et al.) but discovered when we started rehearsal that he and Juliet (played by Jordan Booker) are actually rarely onstage together, too often separated by violent politics and family dynamics.

As Andrew Hartley points out, performances alone don't enable students to see the inherent variance in possibilities that a text puts forward, as the overarching ethos of a director and their team can condition audiences to see the play in only a single, preinterpreted way. Performances, then, can produce an explicitly *textual* effect. But performances of bad quartos, presented by producers and directors through the lens of performance as research, allow audiences to see how particular interpretations of Shakespeare's plays can be undermined by other texts of the very same play. As they are designed from an explicitly pedagogical angle, LDP's productions of early quartos allow student and public audiences alike to read these performances alongside the standard texts they have previously encountered in their English classes. Like Hartley, I am interested in enabling students to "find a way . . . to explore Shakespeare as something which they can own . . . to discover a methodological approach that might go some way to escaping the hierarchically inflected coercion of the script" (123). Taught alongside classroom readings of their "good" brethren, performances of bad quartos demonstrate that Shakespeare's plays were malleable forms even for their author.

Audiences of Q1 *Romeo and Juliet* often note that the frequency of substantive variants between it and Q2 increases in the second half of the play. One of the more noteworthy distinctions is that Q1 has a special provision for what happens to Benvolio. At the conclusion of all three texts, Lord Montague announces his wife's death immediately upon his arrival at the Capulet tomb. The Q2 speech continues with his explanation: Lady Montague died of grief, for "my son's exile hath stopped her breath" (5.3.211). In Q1, however, the cause of Lady Montague's death is more ambiguous, and she does not seem to have died alone: "Dread sovereign, my wife is dead tonight, / And young Benvolio is deceasèd too. / What further mischief can there yet be found?" (5.3.140–42). Benvolio is present in both texts from the first scene of the play, and he often functions as a figure who verifies instances of conflict for characters who arrive after the fighting has begun. His name means "well-wishing," and the Q2 text positions Benvolio as a reluctant fighter who initially draws his sword only to defuse the skirmish between rival servingmen. Yet his first line in Q2 has no Q1 equivalent: "Part fools, put up your swords; you know not what you do" (1.1.60–61). Coupled with the absence of Benvolio's peacemaking, his death in Q1 suggests that the civic broils at the end of the play are perpetual, making this play more violent than the longer version. This impression is reinforced in the final scene by a two-word variant in Montague's response to Capulet after the latter offers a handshake in lieu of Juliet's dowry. In Q2, Montague says, "But I *can* give *thee* more" (5.3.298; my emphases), and he proposes a statue in Juliet's honor. Q1's Montague promises the same statue, but the recipient of the gift is different. He says, gesturing at the dead lovers, "But I *will* give *them* more" (5.3.209; my emphases), and this change suggests that Q1 ends less on a note of newfound concord than on one of continued competition.

Inspired by Benvolio's death and by the perpetuation of the play's closing conflict, the LDP director Cat McAlpine characterized the Verona of Q1 as reckless in the show program, an observation that was reflected in her production's evocation of recent youth protests against gun violence in the wake of the 2018 Parkland shooting. In the LDP production, Benvolio's death results from an observed change to his previously "well-wishing" character: after Mercutio and Tybalt died, Benvolio drew his sword and charged offstage. To prepare audiences for the later announcement of Benvolio's death, the director also added an invented interstitial scene between 5.2 and 5.3, where a loud, riotous clamor accompanied an obviously wounded Benvolio as he limped across the stage. Classroom comparison of the two roles of Benvolio allows students to consider whether his status as a well-wisher was inherent to Q1 or was instead a later Q2 invention.

In special-topics Shakespeare courses, which include English majors, we are able to examine textual variants in greater depth to consider the ways that such variants play out in performance. For example, in the first two quartos of *Romeo and Juliet* the plot and the names of the characters are the same, though scenes and individual speeches generally run shorter in Q1. For example, while the final scene of the play is 310 lines long in Q2, the same scene in Q1 takes only 220 lines of dialogue. These disparities often lead to major differences in characterization or pacing that can shift the way the play's themes are understood. The significant variance in Juliet's entrance in 2.5, discussed above, allows audiences to see Juliet as a more active figure in the play's development, which the dialogue of Q1 serves to amplify. As Q1 Romeo notes, the lovers' appointed meeting was Juliet's idea: "This morning here she pointed we should meet / And consummate those never-parting bands" (Q1 2.5.4–5). This Q1 speech has no equivalent in Q2. Even more noteworthy, Juliet's entrance in Q1 is preceded by Friar Laurence's observation that "[y]outh's love is quick, swifter than swiftest speed" (Q1 2.5.9); when immediately followed by Juliet's *"somewhat fast"* entrance, the Friar's metacommentary takes on a jocular tone that justifies the Q1 title page's identification of the play as "conceited," or witty (Levenson, introduction 49–52). In comparison, the Friar Laurence of Q2 is considerably more ominous: "These violent delights have violent ends, / And in their triumph die like fire and powder, / Which as they kiss consume" (2.5.9–11).

Not all textual variants are as clearly significant as the ones outlined above, but they still provoke pedagogical openings. Even as their individual speeches tend to be shorter, bad quartos often provide alternatives in dialogue that offer opportunities for instructors to generate low-stakes debate. For example, the prologue to Q2 has "A pair of star-crossed lovers take their life" (line 6), while the corresponding line in Q1 puts the pair in the past tense: "A pair of star-crossed lovers *took* their life" (line 6; my emphasis). Instructors might ask students about the effect of beginning the tragedy with an outline that makes explicit the finality of the plot. Likewise, in the more familiar Q2 text, Romeo famously asks, "But soft, what light *through* yonder window breaks?" (2.1.45;

my emphasis). In contrast, in Q1 he asks, "But soft, what light *forth* yonder window breaks?" (2.1.44; my emphasis). While this minor difference might seem insignificant, it allows instructors in a general education class an opportunity to introduce students to language resources like the *Oxford English Dictionary*; a more advanced English class for majors might encourage students to use an online Shakespeare concordance, such as the one in *Open Source Shakespeare*, to investigate Shakespeare's usage of the same word elsewhere.

Performance and Book-Historical Approaches

In my English classroom, I also like to create opportunities for discovery by allowing students to explore curiosities in the printing of Shakespeare plays and to collate the differences that exist among the advertising of quarto versions. For example, students in my introductory Shakespeare course might come to class already aware that *Romeo and Juliet* is one of Shakespeare's best-known plays, but they are often surprised to learn that when the tragedy was first printed, Shakespeare's name did not appear on the title page of its first two editions. Examination of the Q1 and Q2 title pages allows students to see that *Romeo and Juliet*'s first two publishers didn't think that "William Shakespeare" had enough star currency of its own to sway customers to purchase their playbook. Instead, the title pages of Q1 and Q2 appealed to potential customers' familiarity with Shakespeare's theater company, right down to the identity of its patron. But the Q1 and Q2 title pages also differ in the words they use to describe Shakespeare's tragedy. This distinction made it into the pages of our Q1 production's review, where the reviewer noted that "hints of what's in store start with restoring the publisher's full title . . . before 'conceited' became the 'lamentable' we're all accustomed to and when Juliet's name loomed as large as Romeo's" (Sanford). Bringing into the classroom (and the theater) Q1's anonymous title page allows students to better contextualize its publisher's boast that the play contained within its pages "hath been often (with great applause) played publicly by the Right Honorable the Lord Hunsdon his Servants." This exercise helps students see that critical and historical work derives directly from the information contained within surviving documents, and it also helps students realize that Shakespeare's fame and reputation were not inevitable.

As well as demonstrating the way that early modern playbooks often trumpeted their textual origins in the theater, this small detail about Lord Hunsdon on Q1's title page helps scholars date the text of the play. The second Baron Hunsdon, George Carey, was the patron of Shakespeare's company for only a brief window between July 1596 and April 1597 before he became the lord chamberlain and the company's name returned accordingly to the Lord Chamberlain's Men. The wording of the title page thus suggests that the play was set into type (or that the manuscript behind the printed copy was written) during this period. Moreover, the playbook promises that the drama is "An Excellent *Conceited* Tragedy" (my emphasis), a word that suggests that Danter, its publisher, hoped to advertise the play's witty wordplay. This was a curious choice, because though *conceited* was often used in early English title pages to describe comedies, Q1 *Romeo and Juliet* remains the only early modern English tragedy to be advertised in this way. When the play was reprinted in a second edition in 1599, its new publisher, Cuthbert Burby, swapped the word "conceited" for "lamentable," perhaps because Burby feared that book purchasers might find this explicit appeal to comic wit confusing for a tragedy.

I was able to make these claims about Q1's and Q2's title pages easily because of a freely available online tool: *Deep: Database of Early English Playbooks*, created by Alan B. Farmer and Zachary Lesser. *DEEP* transcribes the language of playbook title pages and couples it with other theatrical and bibliographic information about editions to allow users to create customized investigations of "the publishing, printing, and marketing of English Renaissance drama" through 1660. Via *DEEP*, students can compare the Q1 and Q2 editions of *Romeo and Juliet* not only to each other but also to the other plays circulating in the London book trade around the same time, providing a crucial context for understanding Shakespeare in print during his own lifetime. Students can use *DEEP* to explore freewheeling questions about genre (What sort of language characterizes tragedy?), character (Whose plots are described in detail?), authorship (When did Shakespeare's name start appearing on title pages?), or publisher behavior (How did Cuthbert Burby usually market plays?). By allowing students to think of playbooks not just as transcriptions of stage events but also as literary commodities (as publishers themselves thought of them), *DEEP* can help students bridge the gap between stage and page (Neville and Dalea).

A pedagogical approach to *Romeo and Juliet* that puts its material variability forward in performative, material, and textual terms celebrates the play's potentiality, allowing students to see how a directorial, commercial, or editorial decision could just as easily have gone in a different direction. Textual variance particularly destabilizes the notion of the perfect linguistic work produced by a timeless and flawless author like Shakespeare, pushing back against Heminges and Condell's claim to have "scarce received from him a blot in his papers" (Shakespeare, *Mr. William Shakespeares Comedies*, sig. πA3r). Highlighting Shakespeare's variance signals him as a working playwright instead of a timeless genius, subject to changing his mind as he changed his scripts. The advantage of using bad quartos in the classroom is not merely that they disrupt students' right-answerism but that they destabilize the right-answerism and the familiarity that career teachers can unwittingly bring to their teaching of well-known texts. Instructors, too, can benefit from teaching variant playtexts: by disrupting familiar works, bad quartos allow teachers to learn alongside their students.

NOTES

1. For a comprehensive overview of the textual history of the play, see Levenson's introduction to her edition (96–125).

2. All quotations from the Q1 text of the play are taken from Shakespeare, *Romeo* (Levenson), which features both Q1 and Q2 texts. Quotations from Q2 are taken from Greenblatt et al.

3. For a full recording of the LDP production of Q1 as well as the program and associated promotional materials, see "Excellent and Conceited Tragedy."

Teaching *Romeo and Juliet* with Cue Scripts

Marguerite A. Tassi

Long before students read *Romeo and Juliet*, they know it is a tragic story of "star-crossed lovers" set in the midst of a feud, with a romantic balcony scene, a secret marriage, and a double suicide at the end. This sensationalized version of the play, generally speaking, is how popular culture represents *Romeo and Juliet* and how students remember it when they come to the university. To defamiliarize this well-known tragedy, I teach the play using a fascinating historical method of acting, the cue-script technique, which allows students to encounter the play in the same manner that Shakespeare's actors did—through intimate study of their own characters' roles and spontaneous performance of scenes. We know that Shakespeare's actors received only their own parts, handwritten on pasted-together strips of paper, with a few cue words preceding each speech. Approaching *Romeo and Juliet* with cue scripts gives students a personal stake in the play, since it gives each student exclusive knowledge of their character's part while also giving them a collaborative sense of discovery through performance. In the spontaneity of unrehearsed dialogue, students are able to draw out the play's themes, discover key words and lines that define its characters, and find answers to questions such as, To whom am I speaking? What patterns and rhythms are occurring to help move the dialogue along? What should my character be doing to dramatize this moment? I have used cue scripts rather than a modern edition of the play in undergraduate Shakespeare courses for English majors and nonmajors and in upper-division Western drama courses focused on historical conditions of performance. My students love discovering *Romeo and Juliet* through this highly adaptable approach, which invites them to practice close reading skills while giving them a hands-on introduction to the performance conditions of Shakespeare's playhouse.

Evidence for the historical use of cue scripts in professional and amateur productions in Europe and Great Britain dates as far back as the fourteenth century (Palfrey and Stern 15–39). Surprisingly, though, only one professional player's part from England is extant from Shakespeare's time: the title role from Robert Greene's play *Orlando Furioso* (1591), which was owned by the actor Edward Alleyn. This part is lengthy, contained in a scroll of eighteen feet or so, with cues of one to three words before Orlando's speeches and stage directions occasionally indicated in the left margin (Foakes). While the cue script fell out of favor by the nineteenth century, it has been used occasionally by theater companies since then. London's Original Shakespeare Company, for example, performed Shakespeare plays with cue scripts from 1990 to 2000. The company's research and practical discoveries have been documented by its cofounder, Patrick Tucker, in his book *Secrets of Acting Shakespeare*, which I recommend as a valuable guide for teaching with cue scripts.

A fruitful way to introduce cue scripts to students is to start by discussing Shakespeare's formative years as an actor in the London playhouses, which served as training ground for his playwriting. His familiarity with using cue scripts to play roles would have taught him how character parts were written like blueprints for performance, rich with verbal nuances, implicit stage direction, and distilled elements of the larger drama. In this way, Shakespeare gained both rhetorical and practical knowledge to draw upon as he began to compose individualized parts for his own dramas. By 1594–95, the period in which Shakespeare wrote *Romeo and Juliet*, he was a member of a tight-knit ensemble of players known as the Lord Chamberlain's Men, which included the rising star Richard Burbage (likely his Romeo). Shakespeare wrote parts for this group of men, whose personalities and performance skills he knew well.

Shakespeare filled his dramas with references to actors' parts and cues, and pointing out a few examples can be enlightening for students. For example, in *A Midsummer Night's Dream*, the amateur theatrical manager Quince assigns parts to a motley crew of players: "masters, here are your parts, and I am to entreat you, request you, and desire you to con [memorize] them by tomorrow night" (1.2.81–83). When they are rehearsing, "everyone according to his cue" (3.1.64), Flute mistakenly "speak[s] all [his] part at once, cues and all" (3.1.86–87). This comic moment reveals that cues were memorized and therefore in danger of being spoken accidentally. Similarly, in *Twelfth Night* the disguised Viola states, "I can say little more than I have studied, and that question's out of my part" (1.5.158–59). This line reflects how the player knew only what was "in" his part and would be put on the spot when receiving cues that were not in the part. Finally, when Othello says "Were it my cue to fight, I should have known it / Without a prompter" (1.2.84–85), we learn about the key position of the prompter in the theater.

Unlike the modern theater, Elizabethan playhouses worked successfully without a director. Actors were primarily on their own and came together for rehearsals that were practical and kept to a bare minimum (Stern, *Rehearsal* 46–123). In rehearsal, they learned for the first time how they were to interact with other characters and how their own miniature dramas fit within the larger drama. Performances were managed by the theater's prompter, or bookkeeper (the "book" was the entire playscript). As Arthur Kinney indicates, the bookkeeper would have handled all matters involving the dramatic text and stage management, from hiring copyists and scribes to making fair copies of the plays and parts, to adding in stage directions and assigning minor parts, to overseeing properties and directing the players with the stage "plot" (or "platt"), a large sheet of paper hung backstage that listed the play's scenes along with actors' names, their entrances, and props (Kinney 43; Ioppolo). He would have managed performances like a "conductor, unifying actors who had learnt their roles away from their fellows" (Stern, *Rehearsal* 94).

After giving this theater history in class, I set the scene for a cue-script performance of the first 105 lines of *Romeo and Juliet*. The scene has energetic exchanges of wit, provocative cues, swift movements, multiple entrances, high emotion, and confusion—all tailor-made for demonstrating the challenges and spontaneous discoveries brought about by the cue-script method. Before class, I prepare cue scripts for the ten parts in this scene, as well as multiple copies of a two-line part for Citizens. Cue scripts can be made by typing lines and cues from a modern edition such as the Folger Shakespeare Library one (which I used to create Gregory's part below) or copying and pasting text from an online source. Gregory's part works well for a first demonstration, as his script fits easily on two letter-sized pages, which can be taped or stapled together and then rolled into a scroll. When I hand out copies of the part, I draw attention to the rolled script as the likely inspiration for the word *role*, which by the early seventeenth century could refer to a character played by an actor or to the written part itself. I ask students to imagine themselves as members of the Lord Chamberlain's Men who have gathered in the theater to be cast in a new Shakespeare play. When they unroll Gregory's part, students are looking at an approximation of what a Lord Chamberlain player would have been given in the 1590s to prepare for performance.

> *Enter Sampson and Gregory, with swords and bucklers, of the house*
> *of Capulet.*

______________________________ not carry coals.

    No, for then we should be colliers.

______________________________ we'll draw.

    Ay, while you live, draw your neck out of collar.

______________________________ being moved.

    But thou art not quickly moved to strike.

______________________________ Montague moves me.

    To move is to stir, and to be valiant is to stand. Therefore,

    if thou art moved, thou runn'st away.

______________________________ maid of Montague's.

    That shows thee a weak slave, for the weakest goes to the wall.

______________________________ maids to the wall.

    The quarrel is between our masters and us their men.

______________________________ cut off their heads.

    The heads of the maids?

______________________________ sense thou wilt.

    They must take it in sense that feel it.

___________________________ piece of flesh.

  'Tis well thou art not fish; if thou hadst, thou hadst been

  poor-john. Draw thy tool. Here comes of the house of Montagues.

Enter Abram with another Servingman.

___________________________ will back thee.

  How? Turn thy back and run?

___________________________ Fear me not.

  No, marry, I fear thee!

___________________________ let them begin.

  I will frown as I pass by, and let them take it as they list.

___________________________ if I say "ay"?

  No.

___________________________ bite my thumb, sir.

  Do you quarrel, sir?

___________________________ Well, sir.

Enter Benvolio.

  Say "better"; here comes one of my master's kinsmen.

They fight.

Enter Tybalt.

___________________________ at thee, coward!

They fight.

Enter three or four Citizens, with clubs or partisans

___________________________ all men depart.

Exit.

(Shakespeare, Romeo [Mowat and Werstine],
act 1, scene 1, lines 1–105)

My students are astonished when they see the spare layout of the cue script. They ask such questions as, Why didn't actors receive the whole play? How did actors figure out what was going on in the scene? How did actors build a character out of a cue script?

To address the first question, I discuss the cost and scarcity of paper in early modern England and how impractical it would have been to make dozens of handwritten copies of a playtext. The lack of copyright for intellectual property was also a concern. Theater companies needed to protect the exclusivity of their scripts, which were their most valued possessions. The Lord Chamberlain's Men would have owned one "fair" copy of *Romeo and Juliet*, handwritten by a professional scribe and licensed by the master of the revels, and a transcript of that copy for the prompter, or bookkeeper. I mention the repertory system, as well, and suggest that the demands of learning dozens of parts every season meant that actors would not have had time to read complete plays. Cued parts were economical in both senses of the word.

To explore how actors worked with the cue script, we analyze its details, starting with the cues, which are stacked prominently in the right-hand column. The basic job of the cue is to tell an actor when to speak or when to enter a scene, but what else can be learned from the cues? Knowing that actors memorized their cues suggests that these words not only directed them but were in some ways "about" their characters. It seems logical to assume that the first few cues orient the actor regarding context and give him his first few character notes. Since the cues are drawn from another character's part, we can also ask, How do cues connect two characters? The first cue between Gregory and Sampson—"not carry coals"—suggests an emotional atmosphere of insult, disdain, and bravado. Students are quick to notice that this cue is followed by a sequence that escalates in aggression and provocation, from "we'll draw" and "being moved" to the repetition of the name *Montague*, to "maids to the wall" and "cut off their heads." The actor given Gregory's part would have to consider in what sense to take the violent language in his cues—is Sampson joking, half-serious, threatening? The next sequence suggests stage action, with cues such as "will back thee" and "let them begin." Students consider the implication of each cue: Is Gregory being pushed forward into an altercation, then held back?

Next, we read Gregory's lines in relation to his cues. Students immediately notice how the dialogue moves forward through wit and wordplay—"coals," "draw," and "moved" are cues for "colliers," "draw your neck out of collar," and "thou art not quickly moved," respectively. But is Gregory playfully sly or slow in not "getting" his mate? As we study the script, more questions arise: Why does Gregory move from "we" to "you" to "thou" and back to "you"? Is his use of "you" (formal like the French *vous*)—"while you live"—proverbial and therefore delivered in a different tone? Eventually, students are ready to generate a list of elements for cue-script analysis, which I write on the chalkboard: information packed into the cues, wordplay, puns, repetition, key words that give character notes, rhyme, punctuation, implied stage directions, changes in pronoun use and address, short lines, midline switches, and rhythm.

Our next step is to experiment with the cue script in performance. Since cue scripts did not tell actors which scenes they were in, they relied on the "plot," which listed the scenes, character entrances, props, and major stage actions. I hand out a plot for *Romeo and Juliet*, which I have made in advance from a model by Tucker (354), and then cast students by giving each a cue script (multiple students have the same parts, so everyone has a script). Students take a few minutes to familiarize themselves with their parts, particularly their cues. I point out, for example, that the actors playing Sampson might notice their cue from the Chorus, "strive to mend," which signals when to enter the stage but also gives them information of a thematic kind; "mend" is in opposition to Sampson's first line, "Gregory, on my word we'll not carry coals," which conveys a sense of refusal to mend or suffer humiliation. Once students are ready to perform, we move the chairs to the outer rim of the classroom (either creating a circle or stage space). Students volunteer to play parts and then find a workable "offstage" space. I read the Chorus's speech, then the Sampson and Gregory actors enter. They soon discover the rhythm of their opening dialogue, with Sampson's cues serving up words like tennis balls for Gregory, who lands the joke. This dynamic proceeds until Gregory says, "Draw thy tool," which shifts attention to a palpable threat (and the need for a prop, which a student will brandish in the form of a pencil or water bottle). The spirit of wordplay persists with a chain of sexual innuendos, which causes general laughter—"pretty piece of flesh," "Draw thy tool," and "My naked weapon is out."

Actors enter the scene in waves, with fighting men and shouting Citizens, rival patriarchs and their ladies, all striving to be heard. Students become aware that they need to listen attentively for cues, survey the group quickly for the actor they are meant to address, and navigate the space nimbly or roughly, as the crowd grows. The instructor's role as prompter is important for helping with missed cues and keeping the scene moving. As one of my students commented, "It's frankly astonishing anything works at all in this cut-up format, but it does, and it works well." After the Prince's speech halts the action and the actors "exit," I pose questions for discussion: Which cues and lines gave you direction in the performance? Where did you make unexpected choices, and what prompted them? Which words and dramatic interactions revealed qualities of your character? What themes from the tragedy came to light in this performance?

After our heady first experiment, I ask students to choose a major character whose part they will study and perform. Given the length of some parts, our aim is to make cue scripts for select scenes while reading the rest of a character's part in a modern edition. In preparation for our next class, I have students make a cue script for their character's first major scene and then analyze their cues and lines. To make their cue script, they consult a modern edition or online source. Once their cue scripts are done, students set aside the modern edition for the time being. In class, we explore how these early cues and speeches establish character. Students work together in character groups (e.g., all students with Romeo's part come together) to share their discoveries, which they present to the class. We then choose a few cued parts that work together for performance (for example, Lady Capulet, the Nurse, and Juliet in scene 3) so students can try out their new ideas about individual characters in the context of unrehearsed dialogue.

At the end of the character workshop, I hand out cue scripts for a scene we will perform during the next class—the Capulet ball (1.5.19–160), which contains five major parts (Romeo, Juliet, Lord Capulet, Tybalt, and the Nurse) and three small parts (including Benvolio). I ask students to memorize their parts, cues and all. When they return to class, we choose a first string of actors from each character group (if time permits, a second string can perform, as well), and then the actors gather around the plot, or platt, which I have taped to the chalkboard. They discover that Mercutio, Paris, Lady Capulet, and Maskers are onstage as nonspeaking characters, and they also notice that music is needed (which a resourceful student usually finds on their phone). Students quickly adjust to the demands of the scene, and five or six students from the audience step in to play the unscripted characters.

Having prepared their parts well, students approach this next performance with curiosity and excitement, wanting to know how their parts fit into the scene as a whole. Because they have not read a modern edition of the play (at least not in its entirety), they bring open, investigative minds to the experience. They quickly discover authentic actions and reactions based on what other actors give them. Not knowing other characters' lines, much less how they will be delivered or who will deliver them, adds genuine surprise and spontaneous inventiveness to their delivery of lines. Students are kept slightly off-balance, yet the cues keep calling them to attention. Some cues fit neatly with lines. For example, witness the following excerpt from Lord Capulet's script, which contains a cue from Tybalt:

> __________________________ not endure him.
>
>   He shall be endured.
>   What, goodman boy? I say he shall. Go to.
>   (Shakespeare, *Romeo* [Mowat
>   and Werstine] 1.5.85–86)

Other cues have an oblique relationship with the lines they cue, as in this example from Romeo's cue script (again with a cue from Tybalt):

> __________________________ to bitt'rest gall.
>
>   If I profane with my unworthiest hand
>   This holy shrine, the gentle sin is this:
>   My lips, two blushing pilgrims, ready stand
>   To smooth that rough touch with a tender kiss.
>   (1.5.103–7)

The antithesis of "bitt'rest" and "tender" is evident in the language, but what strikes students in performance is the collision of opposite energies—Tybalt's bitter hate and Romeo's tender love are expressed in the same moment. This discovery, made available through close reading and performing with cue scripts, leads them to notice other figurative expressions and oxymoronic moments in the play.

The rhythm of lines also becomes expressive of character when heard in performance. The Lord Capulet actor, for example, discovers idiosyncratic rhythms, pauses, and abrupt midline switches when he speaks lines such as the following: "Well said, my hearts.—You are a princox, go. / Be quiet, or—More light, more light!—for shame, / I'll make you quiet.—What, cheerly, my hearts!" (1.5.97–99). Each short phrase requires a shift in tone, a transition in role-playing, and a quick scan for an addressee. One of my students who played Capulet found him inherently "performative," as he "juggles his roles in quick succession," responding to cues that keep "shifting the energy." One Romeo actor declared how surprised he was by the "long break" between Romeo's first speech about Juliet's beauty and their actual meeting. In his private study of Romeo's part, he envisioned an "intimate" scene with himself as the "hero" of his own story, not a wildly populated "ballroom." Performance dynamics altered this student's view, yet not entirely, for he gained awareness of Romeo as a self-absorbed lover who must navigate a robust social scene. After the performance, discussions revolve around these surprising disjunctions and revelations.

We prepare and perform three more scenes with cue scripts in the remaining class sessions: the fight scene (3.1, including "Gallop apace" in 3.2), the dawn scene, including Juliet's encounter with her mother (3.5.1–130), and the tomb scene (5.3.1–175). Students organize themselves into groups, each taking charge of one scene. They create a plot or platt, assign parts, prepare their cue scripts (doubling where needed), and find props. Each scene is given a full class period for a quick rehearsal, a performance, and a discussion. Some of the key discoveries students make involve repeated actions, oxymorons coming to life, and intensification of emotion through surprise. The fight scene in act 3, for example, repeats and intensifies the dynamic of the opening scene, where wordplay leads to violent conflict. The Prince appears again to close the scene; his final phrase, "those that kill," is Juliet's cue for her "Gallop apace" speech, which reveals a tragic connecting point between scenes. When Juliet enters on cue, the body of Tybalt is still being carried away by the Capulet men. In this moment of performance, students experience directly the collision between the opposing forces of love and hate, and life and death. The dawn scene, then, extends and deepens Romeo and Juliet's poetic exchange from the Capulet ball, with ominous cues for Juliet, such as "stay and die," "not day," "dark our woes," and "I'll descend." The cues in the tomb scene intensify the sense of immediacy, surprise, and desperation in pressurized moments where fate and agency are impossible to distinguish. By the time we come to our final discussion after the performance of the tomb scene, students feel they own their parts and address one another by their characters' names. We focus on a plethora of discoveries they have made, and to focus their analysis, I ask each student to talk about a cue and a key line or speech that revealed an essential quality or decisive moment for their character.

To help my students reflect further, I ask them to write three short essays, one based entirely on the cue script as a text, and the other two focused on performance. For the essay about the text, they must prepare one last cue script—their character's final scene—and draw conclusions about their character from what they have learned about how to analyze cue scripts. I ask, What do the initial and final cues and lines say about your character? Where do you see changes and moments of discovery reflected in your character's rhythms of speech, perceptions, and language (images, metaphors, thematic words), and what accounts for these changes? Their essays document a genuine, sometimes ardent commitment to investigating character; almost any cue or line seems open to investigation. For the other two essays, students reflect first on moving from cue script to performance in the Capulet ball scene (written immediately after the classroom experience) and then on discoveries made in performing a later scene. As their accounts reveal, the more deeply immersed in an individual character's desires, passions, and conflicts they became, the greater their surprise in performance at the collective tragedy of all "violent delights" meeting "violent ends." Like Shakespeare's earliest actors, my students experience firsthand through study and performance with cue scripts how the macrocosm of the tragedy is distilled in the rich microcosm of the part.

NOTE

In addition to the examples in Palfrey and Stern, *Shakespeare in Parts*, and in Tucker, instructors can also find Shakespeare cue scripts on Patrick Tucker and Christine Ozanne's *Friendly Folio* website.

Scene Variations: *Romeo and Juliet* in the High School Classroom

Abbey Bachmann

The mention of Shakespeare's name in the secondary classroom is often met with groans and apprehension from students. My students often associate Shakespeare with confusion and frustration, so before beginning our annual unit on *Romeo and Juliet*, I try to dismantle these negative connotations and help my students approach the tragedy with an open mind. Many of my students struggle with Shakespeare because they can't connect the words they see on the page to the image those words were originally intended to create. To remedy this, I use film adaptations of *Romeo and Juliet* as a supplement to the text. By exploring this additional medium, my students have become more adept at understanding Shakespeare's language while also learning to appreciate Shakespeare's work as it was originally experienced—as a live theatrical performance. Paired with close reading, this approach allows students to develop and refine their critical thinking skills and to practice supporting claims with evidence.

Preparing for the Unit of Study

The five sections of ninth-grade English I teach fall into two levels: above grade level and on grade level. The above-level sections tend to have a larger number of students and are majority female; the on-level sections are majority male. All sections focus on novels in the fall semester, and the on-level courses receive more-advanced scaffolded literacy instruction. At my campus, all sections complete a unit on *Romeo and Juliet*, usually in late April (after state standardized testing has occurred). By this point, my students are more comfortable with their reading comprehension, fluency, analysis skills, and discussion since they've spent all year practicing these skills and receiving feedback from me and their peers. Because I have had all school year to build relationships and trust in my classroom, my students are more willing to take risks and challenge themselves.

Placing *Romeo and Juliet* near the end of the course also allows me to introduce themes and motifs earlier in the year that students can then recall when reading the play. For students to be engaged readers of a text, allowing them to access their prior knowledge involves them in the process of reading as an active rather than passive participant (Thompson and Turchi 24). Before the *Romeo and Juliet* unit, we explore themes such as young love, individuality, fate, violence, and revenge in the fall semester. All of my sections have completed literature units with book choices that shared the common themes of individuality and fate. Additionally, with my above-level English classes I explore themes of violence, racism, revenge, and coming of age through Harper Lee's *To Kill a Mockingbird*; my on-grade-level students read and discuss themes of fate, revenge, karma, and family with *Ghost*, by Jason Reynolds. Students' interests are piqued at the potential for drama and excitement when themes for *Romeo and Juliet* are introduced. As I mentioned young love, individuality, and fate, students are often reminded of the dystopian young adult novels they read as part of their previous literature units. Some students connect these themes to Reynolds's *Ghost*. Both versions of the fall literature unit were some of students' favorite shared reading experiences during the academic year, and these positive associations set the stage for their interest when preparing for *Romeo and Juliet*.

In addition, I spend time introducing my students to the play's plot, characters, and language before we start reading the actual text so that they are not an obstacle. A few key Shakespearean terms—such as *thou, hath, doth, wherefore,* and *ay*—are worth defining beforehand because of their frequency in the play. Using a *PowerPoint* presentation, we read through the terms as a class, emphasizing their pronunciation and reading them in sample sentences. I also give students a laminated bookmark with the terms to use as a reference. We then spend the rest of the unit reading all of Shakespeare's text. For each class, I have students take cards to determine which characters they will read on that day. I keep one card for myself—most often, the character with the most lines that day, to give more fluency to our reading and to model pronunciation and cadence. We read one to two scenes per class period, and students select a new role each day. Occasionally, I vary this approach by having students listen to a professional reading of a scene, which gives them the opportunity to hear the text in a different, expressive manner. Over time, students feel more confident reading lines themselves.

Close Reading

While students read the entire text, I choose a few sections in which we dive deeper. Earlier in the school year, we discuss the importance of understanding plot, story elements, and the author's purpose, but we also practice taking a closer look at an author's craft through close reading practices with various lenses. I explain to students that when we close read, we think more deeply and critically about the decisions that an author makes in a specific section of text, what those decisions mean, and what implications they have for us as readers. For example, when students read *To Kill a Mockingbird*, we close read passages to examine the role of race in the story, asking such questions as, Whose voices are heard here? Whose are not? This type of close reading helps my students develop critical thinking skills.

For *Romeo and Juliet*, the first section we close read is the balcony scene in act 2, scene 2. As we read this scene, I ask my students to focus on Romeo's and Juliet's emotions and the language they use to convey those emotions to each other. For example, when reading Romeo's soliloquy at the beginning of 2.2, I might stop at Romeo's lines—"Oh, that I were a glove upon that hand, / That I might touch that cheek!" (2.2.66–67)—and ask my students to tell me how Romeo is feeling at this point in the play. When students respond with answers such as "in love" and "infatuated," I ask them to tell me what words Romeo says that lead them to these inferences. We then highlight or mark these words or phrases in the text. After close reading the scene, I ask students to consider further the evolution of Romeo and Juliet's relationship in the episode, possible stagings of the scene, and the expectations that the scene creates for us as readers and audience members. I often do this via a group activity, in which each group of three to four students discusses among themselves the following questions:

> Does Romeo change from the beginning of the scene to the end? What evidence do you have?
>
> Does Juliet change from the beginning of the scene to the end? What evidence do you have?
>
> What do you imagine this scene to look like as you read? Does Shakespeare give you any clues to figure this out?
>
> What plans do Romeo and Juliet make in this scene? What do these plans say about them as characters?
>
> What predictions can you make about what may happen later in the play? What details in the text create these expectations for you?

The second close reading section is the scene of Mercutio's and Tybalt's death in 3.1. At this point, students have had at least one round of close reading practice with the play, and we follow the same process for close reading as with the balcony scene. Because the students are now familiar with this process, I give them a little more freedom to work with partners or in small groups to analyze some of the sections of text without my direction. For example, instead of reading to the end of the scene, I may stop after Mercutio's death and ask the groups to finish close reading the scene on their own. They follow the same close reading process we did as a class, considering how language reveals character emotions and tracing the characters' development in the scene. This close reading approach to *Romeo and Juliet* prompts students to think critically about the text and to practice the important skills of being able to support their statements with evidence from the text.

Use of Film

I have found that using film and performance can help my students navigate a complex text, enabling them to closely examine the meaning behind the characters, language, and literary devices. Once students can visualize possibilities of the play in performance, they can bring these schemata back to the text. In my class, students complete the film activities described below after close reading the scene the day before. The schedule for close reading and film analysis is as follows: during one class period, students complete the close reading of act 2, scene 2. The next day, students watch two film versions of 2.2 and complete the film-comparison activity. A few days pass before we repeat the process. These in-between days are used to finish reading, discussing, and completing activities over the remainder of act 2. Once we are ready to begin act 3, the process starts over. One day we complete the close reading of 3.1 as previously described, and the following day students watch the two film versions of 3.1 and complete the film-comparison chart. The two film versions I ask my students to compare are Franco Zeffirelli's *Romeo and Juliet* and Baz Luhrmann's *William Shakespeare's Romeo + Juliet*. I use these two adaptations because of the contrast between them. Zeffirelli's more traditional version is a good place for my students to start, since it often gives them what they expected and imagined while reading the text. In contrast, Luhrmann gives a more modern, contemporary vibe to the setting, reminiscent of a California beach, and the characters, who use guns instead of swords and daggers. These two adaptations, used to supplement students' reading of the text, allow them to compare a traditional version of a particular scene with a modernizing version (Flachmann 644).

For this activity, students were asked to notice and note the differences in characters, setting, mood, and overall impression between the versions of each scene. Students were given an organizer with the following elements and questions as rows in a chart to help them document their observations about the scene by filling out the prompt for each of the two films:

> *Characters.* How would you describe the characters during this scene in this representation? (Include all characters.)
>
> *Setting.* How is the setting created in this scene?
>
> *Mood.* What mood does each director create in this scene?
>
> *Overall impression.* Which director do you personally feel did a better job of portraying the scene, considering all the factors above?
>
> *Bonus.* Think about the distinct choices that each director makes (e.g., the use of water in the Luhrmann version and the different background music in each version). Choose one element you noticed and

explain what you think the director's reason was for this decision. What effect does it have on the scene?

The last column in the chart prompted students to connect the adaptations back to Shakespeare's text, asking, Which of the two films do you feel better captured the characters, setting, and mood as you envisioned them while reading? Why? Students used the same organizer for both the balcony scene and Mercutio's death scene.

Zeffirelli's balcony scene is a traditional, lusty approach to Romeo and Juliet's professions of love for each other. The period-style dress and expansive, ivy-covered balcony are often what students imagine when reading Shakespeare's text. Leonard Whiting (Romeo) and Olivia Hussey (Juliet) attempt to capture the young lovers' lust for one another with many rushed embraces, kisses, and stares. By contrast, Luhrmann places the Capulet balcony in a Spanish-style mansion with a pool at the bottom, where the dialogue between the two lovers takes place. Leonardo DiCaprio (Romeo) and Claire Danes (Juliet) share a much-slower-paced exchange of love vows, and the kissing is much slower and more passionate.

Overall, students preferred the setting of Zeffirelli's film. Many picked up on the traditional aspect of this version and expressed the connection they felt to the text when watching it. One student said that the film "truly showed the same moods and same description of settings, and relatedness to the book's description of how the characters acted during this scene." Students also mentioned that the castle, hidden among ivy, trees, and dense foliage, better captured the play's indicated setting of the Capulet orchard. As one student noted, "In my opinion the 1968 version had the better setting. It was what I imagined, and I like keeping it to the original plot and what I have already envisioned seeing the big balcony and Romeo climbing through the trees to get to his Juliet." Additionally, many students noted that they preferred the traditional costumes used by Zeffirelli as compared to the modern costumes that DiCaprio and Danes don for the Capulet costume party. According to one student, "Zeffirelli better captured the balcony scene because it's how I would imagine it being performed in Shakespeare's time. Even though both movies used the lines from Romeo and Juliet, Zeffirelli also uses the setting and costumes to show that perspective."

Despite the preferences for these two aspects of Zeffirelli's balcony scene, students preferred the acting of DiCaprio and Danes to that of Hussey and Whiting. Students said the love between Luhrmann's Romeo and Juliet seems accurate to how teenagers in love would act. As one student commented, "I think the characters did better in the 1996 version. The characters involved almost make you forget that they're acting, which is an aspect that I really like." This also contributed to students' preference for the overall mood that Luhrmann created in his balcony scene portrayal. A romantic mood was more evident in Luhrmann's scene as compared to the rushed love that Zeffirelli captured. One student noted that "the 1996 version gave a better mood because the acting was a lot better and they portrayed their roles very well to give off this mood of feeling witty and whimsical. The actors allowed us to see their love for each other."

When examining student responses to the two film versions of the balcony scene, some interesting differences emerge. Students seemed to prefer a more Renaissance-style portrayal of the scene settings and ambiance while expressing a fondness for romance they deemed to be more realistic. Noting this difference in student preferences between setting and mood can lend itself to a class discussion of what students' conceptions of romance are. Some questions to ask students include, What words would you use to describe an authentic romance? What about a forced or inauthentic love? Why was the romance between Romeo and Juliet in Luhrmann's version of the film preferable to Zeffirelli's version of the romance between the characters? These questions can be the beginning of a larger activity or discussion on the idea of love and romance and how ideas of true love have changed over time.

The difference between Zeffirelli's and Luhrmann's portrayals of the deaths of Mercutio and Tybalt is also quite stark. Zeffirelli's adaptation employs Michael York (Tybalt) and John McEnery (Mercutio) in a swordfight in a playful manner until Mercutio is stabbed by Tybalt when Romeo attempts to intervene. Romeo then is fueled by rage when he avenges Mercutio's death by tracking down, fighting, and eventually killing Tybalt. In contrast, the mood that Luhrmann creates at the beginning of act 3 is built on tension and suspense that carries through the entire scene. The fight between John Leguizamo (Tybalt) and Harold Perrineau (Mercutio) never seems playful but is entirely driven by increasing tension and dislike between the characters.

Students overwhelmingly preferred Luhrmann's adaptation of 3.1. While many students noted that Zeffirelli's version aligned well with Shakespeare's text, the liberties that Luhrmann took with casting, music, and other artistic elements made the scene come to life with a deeper level of emotion and sincerity than Zeffirelli's version. One student said, "The way I envisioned this scene was violent and ruthless. Each character went after each other for something the other one did, and I think that [the Luhrmann] version portrayed this perfectly." I asked students to focus on the same elements as they did for the balcony scene (characters, setting, mood, and overall impression), yet many students went a step further and noted Luhrmann's use of music and the weather changes during the scene. As one student noted, "The use of a thunderstorm helps portray the intensity and violence of the fights that happen. As the thunderstorm gets worse the background music also intensifies from Mercutio's death until Romeo and Tybalt's car wreck. The music stops and ends up silent when Romeo kills Tybalt. This element helps the scene become violent and intense because you become suspenseful of the actions each one takes." Examining this detail of the thunderstorm can really help students analyze and question the director's choice of details to include in the film. There are no thunderstorms or music at this point in the text, but what about the text may have led Luhrmann to make these decisions? Asking students to revisit the text to look for evidence to support these decisions can help students understand directors' decisions while critically examining Shakespeare's text more closely.

There were a couple elements in this scene that students felt Zeffirelli captured better. Students noted the action of this scene was likely watched by a variety of townspeople. While Luhrmann's version does capture some passersby, Zeffirelli made the crowd more of a focus. As one student observed, "The 1968 version also had a crowd cheering on the fight while in the 1996 version the crowd was fearing the event taking place." This difference noticed by students could lend itself well to an additional close read of the text for this scene. When revisiting the text, ask students to notice and note what evidence they find to indicate that the fight took place with people in the city of Verona observing as bystanders. What evidence can students find to indicate that the townspeople encourage or fear the fight that's taking place?

Additionally, a few students noted that Zeffirelli was better able to capture the playful personality of Mercutio when using an Italian town square as the setting, having him dip in the town's fountain to cool off. "Zeffirelli's version draws out the scene in more detail and uses the setting to draw out the difference in each character's personality." Another student elaborated on this idea by noting that "the '68 version was originally what I had pictured Tybalt and Mercutio to be in this scene, and the way Tybalt reacted to realizing Mercutio got stabbed instead of Romeo and the reaction on [Tybalt's] face, it was what I pictured him to be as well as Mercutio and how playful he is." Again, this a great moment where students can revisit Shakespeare's text for more close reading. The fact that students took note of Mercutio's playfulness in Zeffirelli's adaptation can be a gateway into asking students to find textual evidence that emphasizes Mercutio's character traits. What does Mercutio do throughout the play that leads you to characterize him as playful? Is it just in this scene? Or where would you go back to for evidence that Shakespeare creates him as such? An additional day of close reading and revisiting the text based on students' responses to their film observations can help students look more closely at what evidence in the text exists to support various interpreted performances of *Romeo and Juliet* while sharpening their critical thinking skills.

Remote Learning Considerations and Final Thoughts

Due to the COVID-19 pandemic, I had half of my students online via *Zoom* and the other half face-to-face in my classroom. I needed a solution for reading the play out loud that would allow both sets of students to hear the lines being read. For this reason, I alternated between reading lines myself, playing the Folger Shakespeare Library audio, and occasionally having one student at a time read selected lines. While not an ideal method for an oral reading of the play, it was the best possible solution to ensure all students, in person and online, had access to hearing the lines read fluently.

Not only did I feel as though my students were better able to grasp the close reading scenes in more depth after the film analysis, but it allowed students to have a frame of reference for future readings of the text. For example, when watching the film adaptations of the balcony scenes, many students noticed and commented on Luhrmann's choice of including the pool as opposed to Zeffirelli's more traditional approach to the setting. Once I see what students focus on while watching the films, I can plan lessons that allow students to examine these aspects more closely. The inclusion of the pool in Luhrmann's balcony scene can connect to a discussion on the use of light in the film and how it connects to the text. Shakespeare has Romeo use the motif of light and dark to emphasize Juliet's innocence and purity. Asking students how they think Luhrmann made the jump from Shakespeare's lines to the pool in the Spanish villa makes for a great class discussion and in-depth examination into an author's craft and a director's adaption.

Another idea for expanding the film-comparison activity can be to further examine students' overall interpretation of 3.1 and the portrayal of Mercutio's death. The two films create different moods during the scene. Once I notice that students have picked up on these differences, we work backward to figure out how each director may have gotten there. What clues did Shakespeare give them to help lead them to these decisions? Students can engage in a scavenger hunt of the text to find clues. Which director had the most clues to pull from to support their representation?

The approach of close reading the text, viewing and comparing film adaptations, and revisiting the text for further examination represents a process that is extremely important not just for exploring Shakespeare's work but for literary analysis overall. We never catch all the details of a text the first time we read, and using film helps opens students' eyes to what they may have missed the first time around.

So You Already "Know" *Romeo and Juliet*? How to Capitalize on Students' Familiarity with the Play

Mary T. Christel

Romeo and Juliet typically serves as a high school student's introduction to Shakespeare. When textbook selection dictated secondary-level English language arts (ELA) curricula, publishers usually included the play in a ninth-grade survey of literary genres and placed it toward the end of the textbook to serve as the capstone experience. The prevailing belief that students can best relate to *Romeo and Juliet*'s adolescent protagonists also bolstered its status as the "gateway" Shakespearean tragedy. Lately, however, the star-crossed lovers have worn out their welcome in some secondary syllabi, in part due to the tragedy's ubiquity in contemporary popular culture.

Despite students' familiarity with a broad plot outline of *Romeo and Juliet*, they may not want to dig deeper into Shakespeare's "version." Whether directly or indirectly, they also may have absorbed the "monumental[izing]" of Shakespeare, which "entombs and mystifies the object of study" and "can . . . weaken the resolve of the learner" (Stredder 8). To counter this reticence, I recommend embracing and capitalizing on the ubiquity of *Romeo and Juliet* in popular culture to assess what students already know from extratextual interactions and to examine why Shakespeare's play, despite its origins as popular entertainment, has maintained its status in highbrow literary culture. This approach opens up the issue of authoritative authorship and raises the question, If there are so many versions of a narrative, what makes one superior to another? This crucial question places Shakespeare in a pool and on par with other creative artists who have shaped and adapted the tale to make it relevant to their distinct cultural communities. Additionally, the tropes of Shakespeare's tragedy connect to even earlier versions found in classical mythology and popular literature, so Shakespeare himself is an adapter, and one of great virtuosity.

During my thirty-three years as a high school English teacher, I actually did not teach *Romeo and Juliet* all that often. It was a staple of ninth-grade English in my department, but I quickly moved on to teaching Shakespeare to eleventh- and twelfth-grade students, which allowed me to select other tragedies, comedies, histories, or romances based on students' interests, reading levels, and confidence with making sense of the Bard. When attending conventions of the National Council of Teachers of English and workshops at Chicago Shakespeare Theater over the years, I encountered teachers who lamented a need for a fresh approach to *Romeo and Juliet* to engage their less-than-eager students, so I often returned to considering what made the star-crossed lovers' tragedy truly a good fit for novice readers of Shakespeare. My decision to contribute this piece emerged from a conversation with a former student who is now an English teacher. She had been asked to join a department committee to revise the ninth-grade curriculum; while she was happy to be part of that team, she was unhappy to discover *Romeo and Juliet* would not be exiting the syllabus as part of the proposed revision process. Though retired from the classroom, I am still active in ELA professional development and now find myself mentoring and supporting early- and mid-career teachers looking to refresh their approaches to challenging texts; *Romeo and Juliet* has been at the center of most of those pedagogical conversations.

While collaborating with teachers seeking new approaches to the play, I quickly discovered most of them begin their units by front-loading information about Shakespeare himself, the time period, and Elizabethan theatrical practices before students open their texts to the first scene. If *Romeo and Juliet* is not being taught in a course whose focus is the history of British literature, I simply ask, Why do students need to know this information before they begin reading the text? How does that information tap into what they already know about *Romeo and Juliet*? How does that information demonstrate the play's relevance to modern readers? And finally, how does this approach stimulate students' curiosity to read Romeo and Juliet's tragedy as Shakespeare wrote it? The historical context of when, where, why, and how the play was written can illuminate a student's understanding of the text, but it probably is not the best previewing strategy, especially with novice readers. For me, the best way to start is to determine what relationship students already have with *Romeo and Juliet* before reading it. In order for students to fully engage in reading and interpreting a challenging text, they need to make meaningful connections based on their prior reading experiences, cultural literacy knowledge, and personal, lived experiences. Learning to make such connections is an essential outcome of successful engagement. Most students do not think to access the prior knowledge and the lived experience they possess if they depend on their teachers to excavate those connections.

The quickest way to determine what students know about the tragedy's characters and storyline involves querying them for a summary of the plot—though one student inevitably dominates that endeavor. To make this task more interactive for the entire class, a teacher collaborator and I created an activity that involves piecing together the essential elements of the narrative. We developed in advance the following thirteen statements that summarize the plot, organized in chronological order:

> Members of the Montague and Capulet families trade insults in the streets of Verona.
> Romeo Montague and his friends crash a party hosted by the Capulets.
> Romeo approaches Juliet not knowing she is a Capulet.
> Juliet's cousin Tybalt confronts Romeo about kissing Juliet.
> Romeo and Juliet meet in secret to declare their love for each other.
> Romeo and Juliet marry in secret.

Romeo kills Juliet's cousin Tybalt.
Romeo must leave Verona without Juliet.
Juliet's parents hastily arrange for her marriage to Paris.
Juliet takes a sleeping potion so she will appear to be dead.
Romeo fails to receive a crucial message about Juliet.
Romeo returns to Verona intending to commit suicide.
The Montagues and Capulets discover Romeo and Juliet dead in the
Capulet tomb.

We put these statements onto individual sheets, scramble their order, and distribute them among thirteen students. Then it is time for students to assemble those details collaboratively into a coherent narrative.

This activity is based on an improvisation game called "string of pearls," which requires participating students to build a story by orally adding one detail at a time (McKnight and Scruggs 94). Select students, usually volunteers, form a small group, and each member receives one plot point on a slip of paper, constituting a narrative "pearl." Remaining classmates serve as observers and monitor the assembly, or stringing together, of those narrative pearls. Students in the small group share their plot points by reading them aloud. Once the entire set of plot points is read, those students must physically place themselves in line at the front of the classroom, stringing those details together in a narratively coherent order. As students join the narrative lineup one by one, some details will have to shift, and students then will need to assume new positions on the line. Once participants string together their version of the thirteen plot points, observing classmates offer feedback and rearrange the details as needed. Students who are already well versed in the story will emerge as opinion leaders, but not to the same degree as if the students had been asked to summarize the plot at the beginning.

Once the class has created their summary of *Romeo and Juliet*, they in turn compare their version to an "authoritative" summary, for which there are several online options. The websites of the Royal Shakespeare Company, Shakespeare's Globe, and the Folger Shakespeare Library all have concise plot summaries. Another option is the *Romeo and Juliet* episode in the *Shakespeare: The Animated Tales* series, a half-hour version with accomplished British actors providing the voices for an expertly animated episode ("Romeo" [Gamburg]). A more irreverent yet still authoritative summary is available in the *Thug Notes* series presented by Sparky Sweets, PhD (played by Greg Edwards; "Romeo" [Bauer]). After reading or viewing one or more of these summaries, students consider how their version compares, considering especially which of the thirteen details were harder to fit into the narrative arc than others.

After students grasp the broad outline of *Romeo and Juliet*'s plot, they can then compare it to Shakespeare's own summary in the play's prologue:

Two households, both alike in dignity,
In fair Verona, where we lay our scene,

> From ancient grudge break to new mutiny,
> Where civil blood makes civil hands unclean.
> From forth the fatal loins of these two foes,
> A pair of star-crossed lovers take their life,
> Whose misadventured piteous overthrows
> Doth with their death bury their parents' strife.
> The fearful passage of their death-marked love
> And the continuance of their parents' rage—
> Which, but their children's end, naught could remove—
> Is now the two hours' traffic of our stage;
> The which, if you with patient ears attend,
> What here shall miss, our toil shall strive to mend.
>
> (lines 1–14)

As students read the speech, they underline words and phrases that establish crucial plot elements and circle possible thematic ideas. Once they examine how Shakespeare creates a previewing device for his audience in the play's opening speech, they address the following questions: Why does Shakespeare provide the audience this information? What might he want the audience to consider carefully besides the plot's tragic outcome? A teacher can supplement this examination of the prologue's function by sharing with students the fact that Shakespeare's audiences saw many plays based on stories well known to them as the subjects of tales from oral tradition, popular songs, or other plays. Here they are introduced to Shakespeare's version of a story that existed already in one form or another and that he is making his own. Students then can consider the question, What is the advantage for a writer in creating a version of a story well known to many members of the audience?

Most, if not all, students know the star-crossed lovers' sad saga because they have encountered references and remakes in all manner of contemporary culture. Shakespeare's play is one of many versions of a familiar tale that preceded its first performance in early modern London. Current high school students can reach back to the animated film *Gnomeo and Juliet* for an example of Shakespeare's influence on contemporary popular culture. Viewing that film offers a springboard to discuss the ubiquity of the story in other films, fiction, poetry, mythology, fairy tales, music, television shows, animation, advertising, single-panel cartoons, comic strips, visual art, news reporting, and even consumer products. No matter what my students were reading, I always dedicated bulletin board space to posting "fantastic finds" to acknowledge how references to a particular work are vitally present in popular culture or how its themes have been addressed in the news cycle or other media. I would post a few items from my collection to pique students' interest and to provide a few models. Students then were invited to add what they discovered, and it was surprisingly easy to fill that bulletin board space with clippings related to most pieces of literature we studied.

Instead of relying on students to randomly add to the "fantastic finds" bulletin board, one of my collaborating teachers developed a more formalized approach to excavating *Romeo and Juliet*'s ubiquity in popular culture, present and past, by having her students conduct an Internet scavenger hunt. For this activity, students work in small groups to search for examples of the story in several related categories: general fiction and young adult, film and television, popular music and multiple genres, news events and reporting, print and television advertising, mythology and folk tales, single-panel cartoons and comic strips. Prior to setting students off on their search, it is helpful to assess how students perform Internet searches and, if necessary, help them learn advanced search techniques. We found when piloting this activity that students tended to perform easy (i.e., broad) searches rather than using strategic search parameters.

After this minilesson on Internet searches, groups are directed to search for several examples per category, including ones that reflect a "deeper dive." With each discovery, the group needs to articulate how the example references *Romeo and Juliet*: direct quotation from the play, iconic imagery, character names, or otherwise. For some examples, students might not be able to fully explain the connection, but they should be encouraged to archive them for later analysis. After groups gather their examples, they showcase their findings in online slideshows or postings to a classroom gallery wall. When examining what each group discovers, the class tracks whether modern retellings or application of elements from *Romeo and Juliet* are presented as dramatic, comedic, satiric—or simply as a quick punch line in a visual or verbal joke. Since students have not read the play, they will need to return to their finds periodically over the course of the unit to evaluate the effectiveness of the references to *Romeo and Juliet* in the examples they discovered. Students should cultivate an awareness of how their understanding of a text is emerging incrementally over the course of a reading experience. Activities to check for expanded understanding threaded throughout the unit might take the form of an oral show-and-tell presentation or written reflections on those previously gathered examples that illustrate students' further discoveries and growing understanding. This approach also offers an opportunity to introduce, define, and explore the concept of intertextuality as well as what constitutes an allusion, a parody, or pastiche when one work is called out or incorporated into another.

For some students, understanding the basic elements of plot will not be the most compelling engagement strategy. If these students already know the plot, they can be engaged by thinking about the play's themes as subjects for debate. When I collaborated with teaching artists from a Chicago-based theater on their classroom residencies, we developed a tool called the "human barometer" (Hart et al. 88). This activity adapts an opinionnaire prereading instrument commonly used in inquiry-based learning approaches. An opinionnaire asks students to react to a series of statements related to the themes, conflicts, and social issues explored in a play. Students place each statement on a continuum expressing how strongly they agree or disagree with it. Typically when using this tool, students score their opinions on their own and bring their opinions to share in a class discussion. Since the teaching artists use active drama approaches throughout their residency, they decided to make the activity more embodied. When students reacted to a statement, instead of jotting their response on a piece of paper, they took their place on a physical continuum by lining up across the front of the classroom. Immediately, the class was able to read the "opinion pressure" in the room and see which statements created the most agreement or controversy. Generally, discussion starts even before students take their seats. Often students revise their opinions by adjusting their physical position on the continuum when they compare their initial reaction with their peers. Some students tend to choose a safer response when they first place themselves on the continuum and only adjust their position when they realize their opinion is indeed supported by others.

To adapt this activity to *Romeo and Juliet*, a teacher needs to consider where the play fits into the aims and themes of a specific unit as well as the broader curriculum. One teacher focuses on how the play portrays the tragic consequences of impetuous romantic love, so she presented the following statements to her students:

> Teenagers don't really experience true love.
> Love at first sight can be proved by modern science.
> We are most attracted to situations we are forbidden to explore.
> Parents tend to know what is best for their children.
> Love at first sight cannot last.
> Parental disapproval usually pushes a person to act recklessly.
> We can easily mistake a crush for being in love.
> Trusted adults outside the family are the best advisers for a young
>   person when their family is in conflict.

When considering these statements, students have to decide whether they "strongly agree," "agree," "disagree," "strongly disagree," or take the neutral middle ground. For another teacher, exploring the various romantic, familial, and civic relationships suited the unit's theme; consequently, those opinionnaire statements focused more on the nature of allegiances, alliances, and prejudices people acquire by birth, choice, or necessity. No matter the approach, these statements can easily be extended and used in an ongoing class discussion or as blog topics.

For many students, the characters and conflicts presented by Shakespeare don't initially seem to speak to their lived experiences, and those readers have a difficult time seeing enough of themselves in *Romeo and Juliet* to accept the challenge of reading and understanding early modern texts. The 2015 documentary *Romeo Is Bleeding* (not the same as the Jet Li film *Romeo Must Die*) provides a vivid portrait of a spoken-word poet from Richmond, California,

Donté Clark, who creates an urban version of *Romeo and Juliet* to address the long-standing gang grievances stretching back generations in his community. The film traces Clark's evolution from a potential gang member to a spoken-word performer, to an instructor at a community arts center, and ultimately to a playwright who adapts the Bard. Richmond's troubled history with gun violence fueled by gang turf wars provides the catalyst for Clark creating the play *Te's Harmony*, which he hoped would generate meaningful dialogue and promote emotional healing when it was performed for the community by nonprofessional actors from the community. Clark ends his adaptation of Shakespeare's tragedy on a different note, with a celebration of life rather than with a cause for grief. Units that begin with this documentary prompt many students to wonder why, with all the resources at Clark's disposal in the arts center library, a Shakespearean tragedy spoke to him, an urban poet who had little experience with the Bard. Examining Clark's inspiration for writing *Te's Harmony* easily sets the stage for discussing ownership and authorship of a text like *Romeo and Juliet* since versions were created prior to and long after Shakespeare wrote his play. If there is not enough classroom time to screen the entire documentary, which runs ninety-three minutes, it is just as effective to share excerpts that focus on the process of adapting, rehearsing, and performing *Romeo and Juliet*. A variety of teaching materials for this film can be accessed online, notably from Blueshift Education's *Re-mixing Shakespeare: Curriculum for Documentary Film* Romeo Is Bleeding at filmplatform.net.

Romeo Is Bleeding represents just one means to open a unit with an introduction to the play via film or television. The PBS series *Shakespeare Uncovered* features a fifty-four-minute episode focusing on *Romeo and Juliet* hosted by Joseph Fiennes, who played the Bard in *Shakespeare in Love* ("*Romeo and Juliet* with Joseph Fiennes"). The episode begins and ends with sound bites from television news stories that reference Romeo and Juliet in reports of tragic events involving modern-day star-crossed lovers. Fiennes initially explores why this play is so often performed onstage and adapted in other artistic forms: ballet, Broadway musicals, contemporary film. The episode then considers Shakespeare's play as a "version" of another writer's work—in fact an adaptation of an adaptation. Shakespeare would have been familiar with Arthur Brooke's *Tragical History of Romeus and Juliet*, an English translation and adaptation of a popular Italian poem. Interviewed scholars, actors, and students provide some challenging and provocative commentary that would complement the "human barometer" activity. For example, the playwright Bonnie Greer calls *Romeo and Juliet* "a dangerous piece of work" for young women reading the play today when one considers the characterization of Juliet as choosing death over life. Fiennes also visits two classrooms to observe and to participate in active drama approaches, which could easily transfer to any classroom interested in either unpacking the shared sonnet spoken by Romeo and Juliet at the ball or composing original lines for Mercutio that combine contemporary vernacular with iambic pentameter. This episode can be screened in full or excerpted; the PBS series website offers further ideas for teaching lessons (pbs.org/wnet/shakespeare-uncovered/).

To help students understand that the social, familial, and romantic conflicts at the heart of *Romeo and Juliet* are still part of lived human experience, the prereading process can include screening a feature film that retains key character relationships and iconic narrative tropes yet translates Shakespeare's poetry into contemporary language and contexts. Director Carey Williams's *R#J* tracks the social media engagement between Romeo, Juliet, their friends, and their families that sets the tragedy in motion. The speed at which information travels in this web of interconnected social media platforms tantalizingly changes the stakes of the lovers' decisions and miscalculations. In addition to reimagining how the plot unfolds on social media, the film explains the reasons behind the Montague-Capulet feud, a significant departure from Shakespeare's approach to the families' conflict. How this adaptation clarifies the long-standing grudge encourages discussion of *why* Shakespeare leaves the grudge's origins undefined. Since this film is not a wholly successful or satisfying adaptation for many viewers or critics familiar with Shakespeare, it offers opportunities throughout the reading process to address what works and what doesn't. Writing a review of this, or any, film adaptation can serve as an ideal summative writing activity to assess students' understanding of the Bard's intentions for his characters and development of the play's themes as well as his dramatic and poetic artistry.

The success of these prereading strategies can be measured by circling back to the activities at various relevant points in the unit. Students who assessed what they knew about the plot of *Romeo and Juliet* can return to those thirteen plot points and revise that set to reflect what they feel are truly the most essential elements of the tragedy. As an extension of that plot review, students can plan and shoot a movie trailer to create their own visual preview. One last scavenger hunt can be conducted to uncover something students missed, dismissed, or didn't fully understand based on a lack of the specific knowledge or context that reading the entire play provides. The human-barometer tool also can be revisited to determine how students' attitudes have changed after reading the play, either by having the class line up once again to literally see where everyone stands or by allowing students to select a statement as the topic for a blog or essay. Any video text screened as a prereading activity can be revisited with a closer analysis to explore either the questions it raises about the play or how it adapts Shakespeare's work into a new version of a familiar and often-retold story. Thus, the prereading work provides rich experiences for both formative and summative assessments.

The activities presented here reflect a range of approaches for teaching *Romeo and Juliet* based on meeting students where their interests and experiences stand at the moment of engagement and instruction. My experience teaching the breadth of world literature, including *The Epic of Gilgamesh* and Dante's *Inferno* along with a variety of Shakespeare's plays, has shown me that seemingly remote and archaic texts don't remain so once they are put in conversation and in context with works students find relevant to their current academic or lived experiences. It has always been important to me to place works like *Romeo and Juliet* in dialogue with a variety of other texts to address those essential questions: Why hasn't the tragedy of *Romeo and Juliet* ever left the cultural conversation? What makes it a narrative for our time, every time?

Romeo and Juliet in a Course on Shakespeare and Race

Maya Mathur

Leonardo DiCaprio. Bella Swan. Taylor Swift. These well-known incarnations of *Romeo and Juliet* inform my students' initial responses to the play, which range from the delight of those who like a good love story to complaints from those who would prefer to tackle "serious" plays like *Hamlet*. While I have historically had greater sympathy for the cynics than the romantics, teaching *Romeo and Juliet* in the undergraduate courses Shakespeare and Race and Shakespeare and Popular Culture has helped me reframe the play in ways that challenge both groups. The students who take these courses at my predominantly white liberal arts university range from advanced English majors interested in early British literature to first-year students fulfilling a general education requirement. Both groups are well versed in methods of textual analysis, but they have less experience examining representations of race and gender in literature. In this essay, I suggest that focusing on representations of race and gender in *Romeo and Juliet* can heighten students' awareness of the constructed nature of these categories, enhance their ability to assess adaptations and citations of the play, and provide them with the tools to generate culturally aware responses to the text.

The cultural filters through which the students interpret *Romeo and Juliet* are visible when they share their first impressions of the text in class. They typically respond by mentioning Juliet's youth, Romeo's impulsive approach to love, and the recklessness of adolescent desire. Since women are in the majority in my courses, their focus on Juliet's age and critique of Romeo's behavior is unsurprising, and their interest in the play's gender dynamics can be used to initiate conversations about its treatment of race. Ambereen Dadabhoy writes that these conversations are especially important in the Shakespeare classroom, where generations of critics have perpetuated the myth that "the Renaissance and early modern England were raceless or race unconscious" (230). Like Dadabhoy, Katherine Gillen and Lisa Jennings draw attention to this erasure and write that educators can address it by centering intersectional readings of the text; assigning works by artists and critics who are Black, Indigenous, or people of color; and providing students with opportunities to speak back to the text.

I follow the framework Gillen and Jennings outline and prepare students to discuss race and gender in *Romeo and Juliet* by projecting images from six well-known films on a slide deck for our first session on the play. The first slide features adaptations with predominantly white casts by Franco Zeffirelli, Baz Luhrmann, and Carlo Carlei, all of which retain fidelity to the text. I pair these images with a screening of Taylor Swift's "Love Story" and invite students to unpack the images of femininity, masculinity, and heterosexual desire in the video. Taken together, the slides and video illustrate how images of whiteness dominate interpretations of the play in American popular culture. I then display images of adaptations of the play such as the 1961 musical *West Side Story*, the martial arts film *Romeo Must Die*, and the queer love story *Private Romeo*. These adaptations often feature nonwhite actors and repurpose the feud between the Montagues and the Capulets to address contemporary conflicts about race, gender, and sexuality. While my students are often more familiar with the first set of films than the second, seeing them together demonstrates how *Romeo and Juliet* can be used to reinforce or challenge the dominant culture and its ideology.

Gender, Race, and Romeo and Juliet

I initiate conversations about race and gender in the play by assigning three blog posts by Farah Karim-Cooper—"Anti-Racist Shakespeare," "*Romeo and Juliet*: A Tale of Heaven to Hell," and "Pilgrims' Hands Do Touch"—and an excerpt from Richard Dyer's *White: Essays on Race and Culture* (14–30) along with the play. The Karim-Cooper posts explain how paired words such as *white/black*, *light/dark*, and *day/night* acquire a religious and moral valence in Shakespeare so that the first term in each pair has positive connotations and the second has negative ones. Karim-Cooper's writing works well with Dyer's essay, which argues that images of ideal white masculinity and femininity in Western literature and film derive from the religious iconography around Christ and Mary (16–17). Dyer holds that Christ acts as the model for male characters, who are measured by their ability to control their desires, whereas Mary becomes the model for female characters, who are valued on the basis of their purity, passivity, and receptivity (27–28).

The works by Karim-Cooper and Dyer serve as the basis for class discussion, written responses, and group activities on *Romeo and Juliet*. Students use the readings to examine the gendered and racialized performances of several characters in the play, including Romeo, Mercutio, Tybalt, Benvolio, Juliet, and the

Nurse. In order to ensure that the students can make these connections, I use the passage of the lovers' first meeting (act 1, scene 5, lines 104–17) to foster group discussion, after which I divide the class into smaller units of three or four students to consider individual passages from the play, including ones that describe Rosaline (1.1.89–100), Juliet (1.5.51–60), Paris (1.3.85–105), and Romeo (1.5.74–83). Students read the passages out loud, underlining words and phrases that describe religion, race, and gender as they do so, and they consider the following questions once they have finished annotating the text: First, how do religious and racial imagery intersect in the portrayals of masculine and feminine characters? Second, what connections do these passages make between a character's appearance and their moral and spiritual qualities? And finally, which characters represent the ideal, and which ones depart from it? Students respond to these prompts by connecting the women's fair complexions to their association with the divine and the men's virtuous behavior with their temperance. We end the session with a conversation on the extent to which Rosaline, Juliet, Romeo, and Paris subscribe to these ideals and an exploration of those characters who deviate from them.

The students demonstrate their engagement with these conversations by completing a short writing assignment in which they pair a quotation from one of the secondary readings with a character and analyze the character's performance of gender and race. The exercise encourages students to display their close reading skills by aligning the depictions of femininity and masculinity they noticed in the play with images of whiteness. For example, in a recent course some students responded to this prompt by focusing on the rhetoric of whiteness that is used to accentuate Rosaline's and Juliet's femininity. Others responded by connecting the battles between Sampson, Gregory, and Abraham (1.1.25–33) and Tybalt and Mercutio (3.1) with poor impulse control, sexual violence, and hegemonic white masculinity. One student examined Benvolio's attempt to keep the peace between these factions as a sign of idealized white masculinity. The students' responses demonstrated that the female characters were praised for their fair complexions and passive behavior while the male characters were framed by their lack of moderation and restraint. The assignment heightened students' awareness of race and gender in the play and prepared them to investigate adaptations that locate the play's defining conflict in racial, ethnic, or sexual intolerance.

Gender, Race, and West Side Story

No film illustrates this pattern better than the musical *West Side Story*, which transforms the feud between the Montagues and the Capulets into a battle between two New York City gangs, the Sharks, who are Puerto Rican, and the Jets, who are white. The 1961 film version illustrates the hostility that immigrants faced in mid-twentieth-century America, but it also perpetuates damaging stereotypes about Puerto Ricans in the process. Frances Negrón-Muntaner notes that *West Side Story* is a "foundational narrative" of US–Puerto Rican relations that depicts its Puerto Rican characters as "inherently musical and performative subjects, ready to wear their sexualized identities for a white audience" (85). Carla Della Gatta also argues that the film's Latinx stereotypes initiate what she terms the "*West Side Story* Effect," or "the reinscribing of Shakespearean differences of various kinds—class, locale, familial—as a cultural-linguistic difference" ("From *West Side Story*" 152). *West Side Story* provided a model for subsequent adaptations centered on intercultural conflict, yet, as Della Gatta notes, this strategy can end up perpetuating stereotypes about marginalized communities as often as dispelling them.

When I assign *West Side Story*, I do so in tandem with essays by Della Gatta and Negrón-Muntaner so that students are aware of the film's damaging stereotypes. When taught with *Romeo and Juliet*, the film illustrates how constructions of gender and race change when they are associated with Latinx characters as opposed to white ones. In order to create awareness of these shifts, I ask students to record their impressions of the changes the film makes to plot and character on index cards after their initial viewing. These "adaptation cards" become the foundation for our opening conversation on the film. The students' initial notes on *West Side Story*, like their reading of *Romeo and Juliet*, center on the agency that its female characters, Maria and Anita, the film's counterparts to Juliet and the Nurse, display. Their comments become a valuable starting point from which to compare white femininity in the play with Puerto Rican femininity in the film. In class, the students chronicle the changes through a scene analysis in which they list the major changes that are made between Shakespeare's play and the film and examine how these deviations might function as stereotypes. In their discussion, students note that Maria transforms from a passive character dressed in white at the beginning of the film to an active one dressed in red who demands a cessation of hostilities between the Sharks and the Jets at the end of the film. They likewise remark that Anita shifts from wearing festive purple to celebrate the material goods that she can enjoy in America to dressing in black and critiquing the possibility of peace among rival ethnic groups after the death of her fiancé, Bernardo (an amalgam of Tybalt and Lord Capulet). They also draw attention to elements of brownface, accentism, and tropes of the "spicy Latina" in their characterization.

The opening conversations about Maria and Anita enable additional investigation of how Latina femininity is tied to appearance, costume, and agency. Students navigate this topic by working in small groups to examine Maria's and Anita's portrayal in three songs, "I Feel Pretty," "America," and "A Boy like That." In the prompt that accompanies the activity, I ask students to meditate on the following questions: First, how are the characters dressed, and what do their costumes reveal about them? Second, what gender stereotypes do their clothing, voice, and appearance produce? And finally, do specific words and phrases in these songs reinforce, complicate, or resist the stereotypes that frame them? Once the groups have reported on their findings, we have a broader conversation about the differences between the white femininities that Rosaline, Juliet, and the Nurse embody and the forms of Latina femininity that Maria and Anita convey. These discussions illustrate that the directors of *West Side Story* not only endow women with more agency but also mark their deviation from white femininity in doing so. These images of femininity also work against the heterosexual ideal, leaving Maria and Anita without male partners at the end of the film.

An adaptation centered on Latinx characters and communities can also be used to open up conversations about Shakespeare's role in the social and political life of the nation. Indeed, Shakespeare's name—and the cultural capital associated with it—has been invoked repeatedly in debates about the place of minorities in the United States. As James Shapiro explains, early-twentieth-century politicians invoked Shakespeare's name to privilege admission for Americans with Anglo-Saxon origins and restrict immigration from southern Europe (145). But Shakespeare's plays could be instruments for assimilation as well. Alden T. Vaughan and Virginia Vaughan note that theaters like the African Grove in New York City gave Black audiences access to Shakespeare, while performances of the plays in Yiddish, German, and Italian gave non-English-speaking immigrants access to his work throughout the nineteenth and twentieth centuries (111–13). Thus, Shakespeare was used to advocate for the exclusion of immigrants at the same time as marginalized communities asserted their right to engage with his work. Alexa Alice Joubin addresses these conflicting uses of Shakespeare by noting, "Acts of appropriation turn Shakespeare into a signifier that can be seized and re-deployed against his will, as it were. However, appropriation can also be therapeutic and politically reparative. The political agency that comes with appropriation can lead to ethical and political advocacy" (31–32). Debates about Shakespeare's place in the nation persist today, as conservatives present his work as embodiments of universal human values while liberals call for greater critical assessment of racist, sexist, and ableist tropes in his plays.

To connect these debates to the portrayal of immigration in *West Side Story*, I pair the film in class with a writing assignment on "The Stranger's Case," the speech attributed to Shakespeare from the sixteenth-century play *Sir Thomas More*. In the speech, Thomas More pacifies anti-immigrant rioters by asking them to place themselves in the position of the marginalized communities that they are attacking. Students read "The Strangers' Case," watch film performances of the speech by Shakespeare's Globe ("Strangers' Case: Shakespeare's Rallying Cry") and the University of Warwick ("Strangers' Case" [Trifunovic]), and read Ruben Espinosa's essay "Your Mountainish Inhumanity" before writing about the image of Shakespeare that these texts convey. The videos were both released on World Refugee Day, 20 June 2018, and use a multiethnic cast to highlight the plight of immigrants and refugees who have been displaced from their homes. The Globe video features a diverse cast of professional actors who recite the speech alongside refugees from Syria, Sierra Leone, and South Sudan, while the University of Warwick film casts the nonwhite actor Ibrahim Knight as Sir Thomas More, whose performance of the speech in an English pub wins over a hostile white audience. Espinosa's essay encourages a more critical reading of these appeals for empathy by inviting readers to examine the racist rhetoric that provokes More's speech. In their responses to this prompt, students discuss the emotional appeal and inclusive casting that the directors of the videos use in order to invite empathy from the audience. They also note that Shakespeare was aligned with those who lacked authority in all three texts. The students' responses illustrate the ways in which individuals and institutions use Shakespeare to articulate moral and social codes.

I use this assignment as a springboard for discussing the solutions to the racial hostility that the Puerto Ricans in *West Side Story* face. The film closes by denying the possibility of an interracial union as Tony, the film's Romeo, dies, facilitating Maria's demand for peace between the Sharks and the Jets. Since Maria and Anita have a hand in bringing about the end of the hostilities between the groups and are the only women to appear in the conclusion, I close discussion of the film by asking students to consider the significance of Maria and Anita to the final scene. Does their presence emphasize their assimilation or resistance to white cultural codes? Do they reinforce or complicate stereotypes about Latina femininity in the film? And how do their calls for peace act as a rejoinder to Lord Montague and Lord Capulet's calls for an end to the feud in *Romeo and Juliet*? While there are no absolute answers to these questions, asking them encourages students to compare the portrayals of gender and race in *Romeo and Juliet* with those in *West Side Story*.

Gender, Race, and Appropriation

Studying *Romeo and Juliet* and *West Side Story* in terms of race and gender prepares students to examine adaptations of the play that treat race, gender, or sexuality as the source of the tragic conflict. In courses on race and popular culture, I ask students to give a presentation on a film, television, or web production that reorients *Romeo and Juliet* in terms of gender, sexuality, race, or disability. Laura Turchi and Ann Christensen chronicle the advantages and drawbacks of studying films rooted in difference and recommend that students "explore how productions use stereotypes or other shorthand to present difference. When we teach productions that make those kinds of casting and performance choices, we can help students recognize that cultural conflict is both historical and current, but not inevitable" (111). Turchi and Christensen's suggestion informs the guidelines for the presentation assignment, which ask students to focus on the following elements in the films they investigate: setting, or the cultural context within which the film occurs; theme, or how race, gender, sexuality, and ability are treated in the film; and genre, whether setting and theme enable a tragic or comic ending. Students can choose to examine films like *Romeo Must Die* and television shows like *Noughts + Crosses* that focus on racial and ethnic rivalries; those like *Private Romeo, Romeu and Romeu, Romil and Jugal,* and *Rome and Juliet* that explore queer desire; or those like *Warm Bodies* that are set in alternate worlds. The assignment encourages students to display their analytical skills and to share their perspective on how different filmmakers engage with Shakespeare's work. The presentations also invite students to consider whether the adaptations they study reinforce prejudices rooted in sexism, racism, and ableism or offer an inclusive message that complicates, or even challenges, the portrayal of white masculinity and femininity in *Romeo and Juliet.*

The presentations expose students to multiple interpretations of the play and set them up for their final project, which is a creative response to *Romeo and Juliet.* Students work individually or in groups to rewrite scenes from the play, produce visual art based on the text, or create a *Spotify* playlist, *Instagram* post, or *TikTok* video about its major characters. The projects that students submitted in two recent courses parody the terms of white masculinity and femininity in the play. In one project, a group of students followed the model of clickbait videos, which use sensational headlines to generate clicks or views on *YouTube,* to feature the Nurse's confession that she killed Juliet by accident. Another video recreated the "Best Friends Challenge," a game popularized on *The Tonight Show Starring Jimmy Fallon* in which contestants demonstrate their affinity with their friends or partners by answering a series of questions about them. The video used responses from Romeo and Mercutio to indicate their compatibility and invited a queer reading of the play. Students also created a *TikTok* video in which they used the vocal stylings of Lady Gaga in "Bad Romance" to illustrate the lovers' emotional excesses. The student videos described above drew attention to a marginal female character, interrogated the play's representation of aristocratic white masculinity, and parodied its heteronormative framework. Such creative projects illustrated the students' desire to reimagine *Romeo and Juliet*'s portrayal of gender, sexuality, and race.

Romeo and Juliet constructs images of white masculinity and femininity that continue to circulate widely in popular culture. Focusing on gender and race can expose students to the constructed nature of these categories in the play and adaptations based on it. Teaching the play in concert with *West Side Story* can also enhance students' knowledge of Shakespeare's place in ongoing conversations about race, migration, and immigration in the United States. Expanding the film's sphere of influence to include the study of global adaptations can generate awareness of how writers and directors around the world have reimagined *Romeo and Juliet* to address local prejudices about race, gender, sexuality, and disability. Creative projects can turn students' gaze inward and give them an outlet through which to share their investment in the text. As the students in my courses discover, the play can help unpack conversations about queer desire, the undead, and even Taylor Swift.

Dancing with the Queen of Sheba: *Romeo and Juliet*, Ballet, and Race Studies

Jehbreal Muhammad Jackson and Julia Reinhard Lupton

> The origin of ballet, contrary to most ballet history books,
> has its rise in Persian, Indian and Islamic cultures. The
> term *arabesque*, the pavane—which predated the waltz—
> all speak of other origins. . . . Viewing the present as the
> peak of civilization that has emerged from an inferior past
> is a misconception which future historians . . . will
> discard.
>
> —the choreographer Alonzo King

> How beautiful are thy goings with shoes, O prince's
> daughter!
>
> —Song of Songs 7.1

Romeo falls in love with Juliet while watching her dance, and the sonnet they compose together flows into its own choreography of speech and movement.[1] Likely, the guests at the Capulet ball are engaged in one of the many courtly social dances that would lend their steps to ballet. During one of these dances, Romeo sees Juliet moving hand in hand with Paris:

> ROMEO. What lady's that which doth enrich the hand
> Of yonder knight?
> SERVINGMAN. I know not, sir.
> ROMEO. Oh, she doth teach the torches to burn bright!
> It seems she hangs upon the cheek of night
> As a rich jewel in an Ethiop's ear:
> Beauty too rich for use, for earth too dear.
>
> (act 1, scene 4, lines 153–58)

Renaissance dance historians have used this passage to infer a specific dance being performed, such as the torch or candlestick branle, befitting Romeo's office as torchbearer, or a processional pavane, allowing for Juliet's simple, stately display to the assembly.[2] The music scholar Albert Cohen lists the pavane and other dances like the sarabande as Spanish dances that were adopted wholesale from Spanish performers by the foundational, Italian-born French composer and choreographer Jean-Baptiste Lully (2987). Scholars are revealing that, like the French tradition, Shakespeare and the English theater also drew significantly from the Spanish theater (see Fuchs; Carnegie and Taylor; Chartier).

But what about the passage's racialized imagery? Kyle Grady comments that Shakespeare's disparaging reference to an African "emphasizes Juliet's value through juxtaposition with African difference" (92). The focus on the body's skin tone as a racial marker, linked with the evocation of commodified value of trade objects, points to the sixteenth-century English vogue for wearing textiles and dyed animal skins to depict the dark skin tones of Afro-diasporic communities, whose captured bodies were being bought, sold, and traded as commodities at the same time as practices of racial impersonation were being utilized in the theater, for court spectacles and royal celebrations (see I. Smith, "Textile Black Body"). The image also reinforces the inherent "whiteness" of courtly dance and later of ballet assumed by standard histories of the form. Yet some scholars of dance, including Jehbreal Muhammad Jackson, the coauthor of this essay, are recovering the multicultural and multiethnic origins of ballet (see Jackson, "Ballet"). Jackson and this essay's other coauthor, Julia Reinhard Lupton, met when Jackson joined the MFA program in dance at the University of California, Irvine, in 2018; instant soulmates, we began collaborating on research, teaching, and public programming about Shakespeare and dance. The first fruit of our collaboration was an essay on love, trust, and wisdom in John Neumeier's *Romeo and Juliet* ballet (Jackson and Lupton). During 2020, as arts organizations and scholarly projects around the world took stock of their racial histories, Lupton realized that incorporating race into the study and teaching of Shakespeare and ballet was an urgent obligation. Lupton invited Jackson to create a lecture and lead a class session on Juliet and ballet's Black[3] history for an online Shakespeare course hosted at UC Irvine.

In the pages that follow, we briefly inquire into the danced identity of Romeo's nameless "Ethiop" and then share how we teach *Romeo and Juliet* with ballet and race studies. This approach introduces students to dance history, to the cultural debates around the origins of ballet, and to the broader racial and geopolitical horizons of Shakespearean drama and European court culture.[4]

Ethiopian Rhapsody

In *The Book Named The Governour,* a Tudor educational manual for noblemen that Shakespeare most likely knew, Sir Thomas Elyot defends the nobility of dance by lauding its antiquity and global origins. In addition to Proteus, Orpheus, and Museus, he praises the dances of India, "where the people honoureth the sun," and reminds his readers that David danced before the ark. Elyot then turns to "the old inhabitants of Ethiopia," who danced before battle; arranging their darts about their heads "like to rays or beams of the sun," they would only shoot those darts while dancing (72–74).[5] The most famous "Ethiop" of Shakespeare's age was the Queen of Sheba, who visits the court of Solomon bearing precious gifts of gold and perfume in 1 Kings 10. Sheba arrives in search of wisdom, emblematizing the international character of the feminine-friendly knowledge projects associated with Solomon's encyclopedic learning. Citing Josephus, the Geneva Bible identifies her as the queen of Ethiopia (*Geneva*

Bible, 1 Kings 10.1n), and both the Ethiopian Christians and the Ethiopian Jews claim Sheba and Solomon as their progenitors (Bruder 98). In the Quran, Sheba converts to Islam (sura 27).[6] Elizabeth I identified with the wisdom and hospitality of both Solomon and Sheba, and the story of Solomon and Sheba was the subject of a courtly masque that may have inspired Shakespeare's *Antony and Cleopatra* (Tate; Andrea 99–123). Across the Atlantic, in a fascinating piece performed by Afro-Latin American women in Mexico City in 1640, dancers acted out the story of Sheba for the new viceroy, likely drawing on artistic traditions from Africa and North America (Valerio).

Sheba was associated with the beautiful beloved in the Song of Songs, understood by Jerome and Thomas Aquinas to depict the love between the Israelite king and his African consort. In the Song of Songs, the beloved declares, "I am black, O daughters of Jerusalem" (*Geneva Bible*, Song of Sg. 1.4), rendered in the Bishop's Bible as "I am blacke (O ye daughters of Hierusalem) but yet fayre and well fauoured" (qtd. in Caporicci 361). In these Protestant texts, the word "but" translates the Hebrew letter *vav*, which can mean either "but" or "and" (Lowry), asserting a contrast between blackness and beauty. The Septuagint, or Greek Old Testament, commissioned for the Greek-speaking Jews of Alexandria, chose the more affirmative, additive meaning. The Septuagint rendering speaks to the different relationship to race that European and Middle Eastern writers of antiquity had with people from the African continent (Derbew 1–28) and underscores the formations of racial thinking that developed from the Middle Ages into early modernity and that establish our current racial understanding (Ndiaye 30). Whereas in *Romeo and Juliet*, Shakespeare tends to contrast blackness and beauty, in his later, more Alexandrian play, *Antony and Cleopatra*, Shakespeare's approach to his heroine renews the spirit of the Septuagint. Reading *Romeo and Juliet* with the Queen of Sheba and the Song of Songs supplements the play's racializing language with a rich counterhistory of diverse knowledges communicated through music and movement. The Song of Songs is a duet, a song for two voices that stages the kind of co-compositional reciprocity that Romeo and Juliet share in their sonnet scene. Romeo's hymn to the dancing, glancing Juliet remixes the riches of the Bible's Ethiopian queen, predicting the play's global adaptations as well as Shakespeare's own revisions of *Romeo and Juliet* in his iconic African romances, *Othello* and *Antony and Cleopatra*, both resplendent with echoes of Sheba and rife with opportunities for dance. A staging of *Antony and Cleopatra* created by Jean-Georges Noverre in 1765 may have been the first story ballet based on Shakespeare, a piece that choreographed a whole kingdom of ancient wisdom, female sovereignty, and imperial exchange for Romeo's Ethiop (Campana 164).

Teaching Ballet's Black History

These and other associations between Juliet, Blackness, and the multicultural history of ballet informed our decision to create a unit on this topic for an online general education Shakespeare course at UC Irvine.[7] In spring 2021, Jackson, now a PhD student in Columbia University's theater studies program, created a twenty-minute illustrated virtual lecture entitled "Juliet and Ballet's Black History" (J. Jackson, "Juliet"). The lecture begins with an account of the Moors in Spain and the impact of Islamic geometry on European courtly dances, which would later be adapted into the rudiments of ballet (Mattingly et al.). While most accounts of ballet history present the court and theatrical dances from this period as exclusively white and Anglo-European, Jackson reveals instead a direct but largely disavowed lineage from North African, West African, and Indigenous American cultures. A foundational part of this story is al-Andalus, the rule of Iberia by Islamic Moors from the eighth through the fifteenth century. Under the Moors, Jews, Christians, and Muslims built the great syntheses between Abrahamic and Greek wisdom traditions that would culminate in scholasticism (Dodds et al.). The Reconquista of Spain by the Christians in 1492 led to the expulsion of both Jews and Muslims from the Iberian Peninsula. Subsequently, the Islamic art forms, philosophies, and sciences of the Moors, composed in dialogue with Persian, Indian, Egyptian, and Greek wisdom traditions, were absorbed by Europe and birthed many of the court dances foundational to ballet technique. Jackson used patterns such as the Islamic *girih* (knot) and the *shabaka* (grid), rendered in European languages as *arabesque*, to introduce basic ballet principles in an expanded cultural frame (figs. 1 and 2; "Juliet").[8]

An image of a dark-skinned morisca or morris dancer is included in the historical section of the lecture. The morisca may commemorate the Reconquista

Figure 1. *Muqarnas* vaulting *shabaka* (grid) pattern, from the Hall of the Two Sisters in the Palace of the Lions of the Alhambra, Granada, Spain. Drawing by Raheem Tutein.

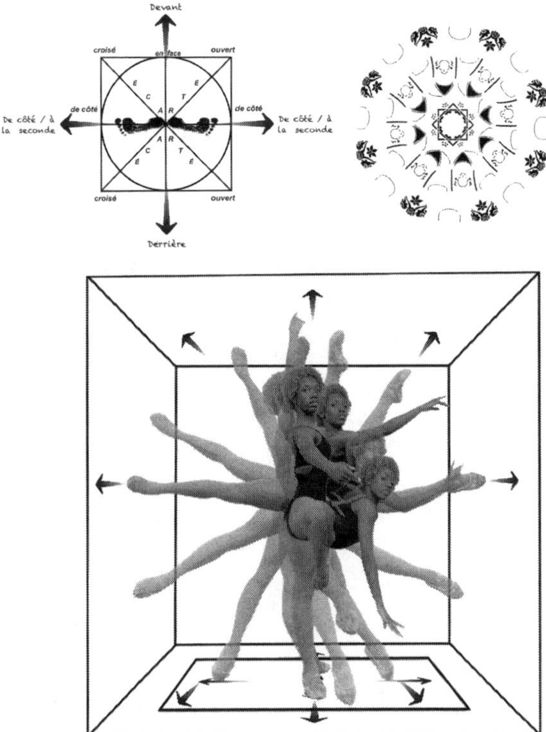

Figure 2. *Shabaka* patterns in classical ballet, with the dancer Marja'
Miller. Artwork by Raheem Tutein.

of Spain from the Moors but likely draws on non-Christian forms; the morisca,
or morris dance, is the ancestor of courtly masques, many of which incorporate
"exotic" narrative types that were often depicted with cosmetically blackened
faces (such as Ben Jonson's *Masque of Blackness*; Dewulf; see also Nevile 31;
Ndiaye). Though it may not have originated with the Moors, the morisca
appears to be one of many references to their presence in Europe as well as that
of other Afro-diasporic groups (Terry). Jackson also introduced students to the
zarabanda, or sarabande, a popular dance featuring the dramatic turnout or
rotation of the legs and feet that would become definitive of ballet as an art
form but was initially perceived as unseemly and grotesque, a "bowlegged" dis-
tortion of what is often considered the body's natural posture.[9] The dance is
associated with Granada as well as with Mexico and may reflect both Indigenous American and Moorish traditions.[10] The sarabande's explosion in popularity at the end of the sixteenth through the seventeenth century coincides with a
shift in European dancing manuals prescribing turned-out legs instead of parallel legs and, therefore, seems to have inspired the introduction and codifica-
tion of turnout in Europe's court dances. This orthogonal ordering of the legs

harmonized with botanically curved and extended arms, the two combined in the classical arabesque and Islamic design, has remained a signature of Western classical dance (fig. 2; J. Jackson, "Ballet"; see also Fairfax). In the historical segment of their lecture, Jackson showed students how the influence of the Moors on European arts, sciences, and court dances diversifies and globalizes the history of ballet. In the process, our students reencountered the apparently elitist and overwhelmingly white institutions of ballet in a very different set of sociohistorical and aesthetic frames, decentering Eurocentric pedagogies while also introducing our largely working-class and nonwhite students to a form of "high art" that had been unfamiliar to many of them.

Since the presentation for UC Irvine, Jackson's research has come to include a possible lineage to the diasporic Bukôngo religion of West and Central Africa that entered Spain's port cities, like Seville, via the transatlantic slave trade through Afro-Cuban retentions (Jones). The Palo Monte Mayombe tradition, a Cuban iteration of Bukôngo, contains dances and cosmological symbols (cosmograms) that facilitate communication with the spirit world, such as the N'kisi Sarabanda (fig. 3), which has been found across the Americas (Bettelheim; Gundaker).[11] The formal qualities of the image have clear resonances with the basic floor and spatial pathways of ballet and Islamic art as well as shared principles, philosophies, and aesthetics in their construction (J. Jackson, "Ballet"). This dance was performed on early modern Spanish stages by Afro-diasporic and non-Afro-descended performers alike to depict Moors, sub-Saharan Africans, and other racialized groups, often wearing "black-up" (Ndiaye 3). Those who were not of African descent desired to portray convincing Africans for the Afro-diasporic audience members of cities like Seville and learned this and other dances from Afro-diasporic dancers (Jones). In addition to precolonial relationships between Islamic and Bukôngo traditions, there are accounts of Moors, Moriscos, and sub-Saharan Africans dancing in the city squares for enjoyment; therefore, it is likely that further synthesis occurred between the groups within this dance, speaking to its uncertain origin and irresistible appeal (K. Goldberg).

In the second half of their lecture, Jackson turned to *Romeo and Juliet* and the case of Misty Copeland, the first African American woman to be promoted to principal dancer in the history of the American Ballet Theatre. The author of a memoir, a children's book, and other works, Copeland

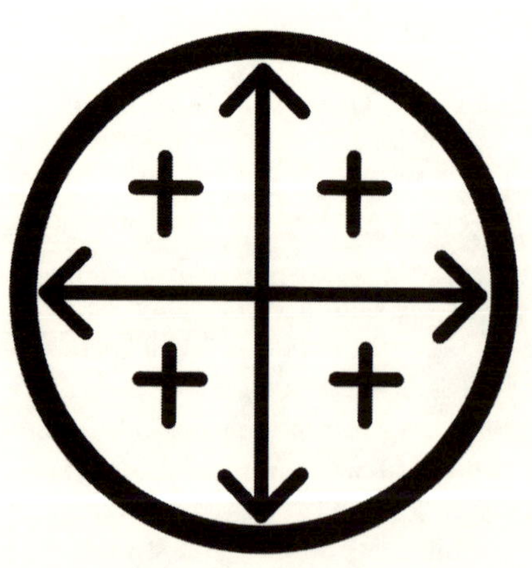

Figure 3. N'kisi Sarabanda symbol. Drawing by Raheem Tutein.

is a powerful advocate for equitable representation in the arts. Copeland also engaged in a debate with the Bolshoi Ballet about its recent productions of *La Bayadère* that used techniques of blackening the skin to approximate Middle Eastern and African identities (Marshall).[12] In three short clips of Copeland's performance of *Romeo and Juliet*, culled from the sonnet scene (*Romeo e Giulietta* 43:02–46:32), the balcony scene (52:55–1:01:05), and the crypt scene (2:26:40–2:36:20), the lecture presents the music of Sergei Prokofiev, who used leitmotif and contrasting moods to weave together the themes of the ballet (Bennett 314). These clips demonstrate the artistry of Copeland's partnering with Roberto Bolle, dancing at La Scala in Milan, and thus bringing the Romeo and Juliet story home to Italy with an international cast. In a voice-over commentary, Jackson explains the formal conventions and expressive possibilities of the pas de deux, a duet traditionally performed by a male and a female dancer. A grand pas features an extended sequence of solo and partner dances shared by the ballet's lead couple. In their commentary, Jackson also points out affectively revealing details, such as how the open chest and extended neck of Copeland's Juliet communicates vulnerability and trust. Developing this theme, they also note that every lift in a pas de deux requires trust on the part of the two dancers and can also express the trust between characters in the ballet narrative, as it does in these scenes between the lovers. At the end of the ballet, Romeo tries to enact the earlier trust pas de deux, but Juliet's limp body no longer allows it—a feat that requires even greater trust on the part of the dancers as they work with the dead weights, unsupported falls, and interrupted energies of their bodies. Through this lecture, we were thus able to expose students to an idea that we discuss at greater length in our collaborative writing—namely, that trust is a fundamental feature of complex performances such as ballet and theater, which engage bodies, souls, scores, settings, and art forms in dynamic feedback loops of attentive response (Jackson and Lupton). The students witnessed the performers donate their trust to each other and the audience, whose receipt of these offerings has the power to build communities inside and outside the world of the play.

In addition to sharing this prerecorded lecture with UC Irvine students, Jackson also led a synchronous remote section meeting from their home in New York City. They shared their dance background and journey with undergraduates, and they introduced another Shakespearean dance piece, "His Romeo," a pas de deux featuring two male dancers, Roberto Vega Ortiz and Joshua Stayton. "His Romeo" was produced by Ballet22, a company that commissions original works starring male and nonbinary dancers on pointe, a technique associated overwhelmingly with female ballerinas.[13] This moving piece, produced during the COVID-19 pandemic and dramatizing the deep longing for touch between two men during quarantine, greatly expanded students' understanding of what a pas de deux can symbolize in the twenty-first century.

"His Romeo" was shown through a special arrangement with Ballet22, but a trailer is available that communicates the concept and artistry of the piece ("'His Romeo' Trailer"). In addition, there are several Shakespeare-inspired dance works available for comparison with Copeland's classical performance. For example, the Mexican American choreographer José Limón's 1949 work *The Moor's Pavane* uses a Renaissance social dance for two couples to recreate the story of *Othello* in a twenty-minute composition, initially starring Limón himself as the Moor (*Moor's Pavane*). Since the pavane is one candidate for the dance at the Capulet ball, this piece makes a rich tie-in with *Romeo and Juliet*, especially in a syllabus that includes *Othello*, as ours does. *The Suit*, choreographed by Cathy Marston for Ballet Black, adapts an *Othello*-like short story by the South African writer Can Themba into a contemporary ballet set in working-class Johannesburg and featuring Black and Asian dancers. The choreographer Alonzo King explicitly incorporates the Sephardic and Islamic history of Baroque dance and music into new compositions that renew ballet from within its own "resinous" resources, as captured in the governing metaphor of his piece *Resin* and explored in other works. In these and works such as *Scheherazade* and *The Moroccan Project*, King composes dance as history—an expanded, decolonized history enriched by the multiple wisdom traditions swirling in the open porches of the Ethiop's listening, yearning ear.

Our course culminated in an opportunity for students to analyze and evaluate Lar Lubovitch's 1997 balletic adaptation of *Othello*, a task for which these earlier exposures to ballet's Black history had prepared them. One student, Alexander Canellos, noted that Lubovitch's ballet "fails to capture many of the deeper aspects of race commentary" presented by Shakespeare; we were pleased to see this student using the tools introduced across the course to integrate questions around adaptation with racial histories.[14] In these and other written responses, students exercised their new understanding of how dancers use the vocabulary of ballet to respond to Shakespeare in an expanded cultural space that includes diverse bodies and global bodies of knowledge. Dancers who want to "bestride the gossamers" (*Romeo and Juliet* 2.6.18) in the exultant heights of a pas de deux require great trust in each other as well as years of training. Those trusting tactics become wisdom when kinetic ideas are affirmed and enlivened by free acts of transmission and reception, whether between ballet master and student, between dancer and dancer, between ensemble and audience, or between distinctive performance cultures whose confluences often go unrecognized. In ballet, this greater wisdom encompasses Muslim, Sephardic, Ethiopian, Egyptian, West African, and North American teachings alongside Hellenistic and Christian ones. So, too, is our coauthoring and coteaching itself a pas de deux that enacts a palmers' kiss between literary and dance studies in search of magnanimous new syntheses.

NOTES

    1. See Shaw; Campana 165–67.

    2. Brissenden argues for the torch dance, and Shaw concurs. On the pavane, see Winerock; McJannet.

3. We adopt the orthographic practices of Noémie Ndiaye when distinguishing between premodern and modern contexts of racial thinking. When referring to the empowering, modern politico-cultural category of self-identification, we capitalize the *B* in *Black* and *Blackness*. When referring to early modern processes of racializing people of African descent, we utilize a lowercase *b* (28–29).

4. For more about those racial and geopolitical horizons, see Chapman and Wainwright; Ndiaye and Markey.

5. On Elyot's defense of dancing and *Romeo and Juliet*, see McGuire.

6. On Jewish and Islamic folklore about Sheba, see Nissan; Bechmann. See also Bowersox.

7. The course, E9 Shakespeare, was developed with a grant from the Innovative Learning Technology Initiative of the University of California in 2019 and is available to students across the UC system. It is a designed-online, team-taught course directed by Julia Lupton with participation from colleagues in English, dance, and drama under the guidance of instructional designer Janet DiVincenzo.

8. On *girih*, see Rogers 224. On *shabaka* (grid, net, web, lattice), see Tabbaa 183. The *shabaka* in figure 1 shows the geometric elements (numbered 1–4, 6, 7, and 9 in the legend) and botanical elements (numbered 5 and 12) that are staples of Islamic art and cosmologies. These elements are also foundational to classical ballet technique and share contact zones across Spain, Italy, and France.

9. See, for example, act 2 of Vega's *Las ferias de Madrid*. In the play, a character describes the *zarabanda* as requiring "zambo" feet, which refers to ethnic lineages to Africa and Indigenous Americans, as well as "bowed/bandied" legs ("Sambo"). This action of the legs likely refers to the outward leg rotation with bent knees that constitutes a *plié* in classical ballet.

10. Juan Carvajal explores the potential journey of the *zarabanda* genre from precolonial encounters with Islamic and Bukôngo traditions tracing back at least to the tenth century and follows its diasporic diffusion in a parallel fashion. One branch travels northward into the Mediterranean. The other travels south of the Sahara, through the Americas, and returns to meet the other branch in Spain during the transatlantic slave trade (224). See K. Goldberg; Locke 101–36; and Reynolds 231 on the *zarabanda*'s diasporic, Moorish, and Morisco associations.

11. The N'kisi Sarabanda signature forms a cross-like pattern representing the four winds of creation, the spiral galaxy, death, and the intersection of the material and spiritual worlds that meet and communicate at its center (on the cosmogram's Afro-diasporic history, see "Nkisi Sarabanda").

12. For examples of organizations that seek to examine and correct the history of the racialization of African and Asian diasporic groups while also recovering and promoting unacknowledged artists from these communities, see the websites *MOBBallet: Curating the Memoirs of Blacks in Ballet* and *Final Bow for Yellowface*.

13. "The creation of Ballet22 was inspired by a lack of representation and opportunities in the ballet field for men, mxn, transgender, and non binary artists to perform professionally 'en pointe'" (Ballet22).

14. Alexander Canellos, paper written for E9 Shakespeare, taught by Jehbreal Muhammad Jackson and Julia Reinhard Lupton, UC Irvine, spring 2021.

Not-So-Ancient Grudges:
Grounding *Romeo and Juliet* in
the Histories of the US-Mexico Borderlands

Kathryn Vomero Santos

Students often wonder about the origins of the "ancient grudge" that the Chorus introduces in the first four lines of *Romeo and Juliet*:

> Two households, both alike in dignity
> In fair Verona, where we lay our scene,
> From ancient grudge break to new mutiny,
> Where civil blood makes civil hands unclean.
> (prologue, lines 1–4)

In many ways, the details of how the Montagues and Capulets came to be locked in mutual hatred are beside the point. As the Chorus goes on to note, the long-standing animosity is so powerful that it takes the suicide of two young people to bring about the possibility of peace in Verona. But for many artists who have adapted or appropriated Shakespeare's tragedy, the ambiguity surrounding the interfamilial feud has presented an opportunity for critical engagement with the histories of strife and imbalances of power that shape their identities and communities. In this essay, I focus on the teaching possibilities opened up by two afterlives of *Romeo and Juliet* that use the gap in the play's backstory to interrogate the colonial past and present of what is now known as the US-Mexico Borderlands. By examining Taos Pueblo playwright James Lujan's *Kino and Teresa* alongside Mexican American author Guadalupe García McCall's young adult novel *Shame the Stars*, I show how *Romeo and Juliet*—a mainstay in many high school curricula—might become a vehicle for conversations about histories that have largely been absent from classrooms. Such a decolonial and antiracist approach to the play not only grounds its central conflict in specific events and contexts that are relevant to modern audiences but also reveals the ways in which these understudied "grudges" are not so ancient after all.

Lujan's play and García McCall's novel are examples of a growing trend in Shakespearean appropriation that Katherine Gillen, Adrianna M. Santos, and I term Borderlands Shakespeare: critical and creative re-visions of the plays that mobilize Shakespeare's cultural capital to examine forms of colonization, racialized violence, linguistic discrimination, police brutality, economic inequality, and environmental injustice that continue to affect inhabitants of the region surrounding the current international boundary between the US states of Texas, New Mexico, Arizona, and California and the Mexican states of Tamaulipas, Nuevo León, Coahuila, Chihuahua, Sonora, and Baja California. This region is home to dozens of Indigenous tribes and nations, many of whom are divided by the present border that was established by the Treaty of Guadalupe Hidalgo in 1848 and the Gadsden Purchase in 1853–54. As Gillen, Santos, and I argue in the introduction to our open-access anthology *The Bard in the Borderlands*, appropriations of Shakespeare that engage with the cultural complexities of the Borderlands "do not simply reproduce Shakespeare in new contexts but rather use his work in innovative ways to negotiate colonial power, to reframe Borderlands histories, and to envision socially just futures" (Gillen et al. xvi). Pairing *Romeo and Juliet* with the work of Indigenous and Chicanx authors who have adapted it to the contested territories of the Borderlands can create the conditions for starting critical and nuanced conversations with our students about these issues while shifting the focus of Shakespeare pedagogy itself. "Because of its complex negotiation of—and resistance to—coloniality," Gillen contends elsewhere, "Borderlands Shakespeare offers generative approaches from which we might learn as we seek to make English literary studies less colonial" (382). Approaching *Romeo and Juliet* with these goals in mind enables us as instructors to develop culturally responsive and sustaining pedagogies that empower our students to think about how not-so-ancient histories intersect with their own identities and lived experiences.

"We See the Ground whereon These Woes Do Lie"

Set in seventeenth-century Santa Fe in the aftermath of the 1680 Pueblo Revolt and 1692 Reconquista, James Lujan's re-vision of Shakespeare's tragedy recasts Romeo as Kino, a Pueblo Indian from Pecos Pueblo, and Juliet as Teresa, a Spaniard living in the settlement. Lujan thus situates the central conflict of *Kino and Teresa* within the colonial history of New Mexico, highlighting the ways in which Spanish colonizers exploited Indigenous Peoples, stole their land, and attempted to eradicate their languages and cultural practices. While some of Lujan's characters believe Kino and Teresa's love has the power to bring about peace, others believe it will only accelerate ongoing cultural genocide.

Here, Shakespeare's famous tragedy—which was first printed in London just one year before Juan de Oñate established the province of Santa Fe de Nuevo México in 1598—becomes a platform for examining understudied Native histories and addressing the harm caused by ongoing colonization in the region. While I typically introduce the edition of Lujan's play that is available in *The Bard in the Borderlands* after students have read *Romeo and Juliet* in its entirety for my seminar on Shakespeare and race, the details I discuss below demonstrate the potential value of pairing parallel scenes from each play in a range of pedagogical contexts.[1]

With some exceptions, the plotline of Shakespeare's *Romeo and Juliet* remains much the same in *Kino and Teresa*, and the play includes quotations or versions of several familiar Shakespearean lines that many readers and audiences will undoubtedly recognize. What students have found most intriguing about *Kino and Teresa* in my teaching experiences, however, are the historical and cultural details that establish its colonial New Mexican setting and further develop its characters in ways that Shakespeare's play does not. The role of the Chorus, for instance, is assumed by a Pueblo medicine man, whose deep spiritual knowledge allows him to situate the story within a long history of human tragedy:

> The future can only be seen in the realm of the spirit world where the souls of the departed return to where they started. In this land of Indians and Spanish, hope for the future does not bode well for these two peoples, both alike in dignity, but whose ancient feuds will mark the end for a pair of star-crossed lovers, children of old enemies, who as in so many tragedies must pay for their fathers' sins. It is the lessons of such sacrifice that will decide the fate of fair Santa Fe, where we lay our scene.   (Lujan 147)

My students also observe that this same Medicine Man character fittingly takes on the role of Shakespeare's Apothecary in the second half of Lujan's play. His poverty, brought about by colonial labor practices that left many Pueblo people hungry even as they tended to Spanish fields, is the only reason he "consents" to go against his function as a healer and to sell poisonous herbs to Kino (209). By merging the two roles of Chorus and Apothecary in this Indigenous character, Lujan heightens his play's larger commentary on the structural and material violence of Spanish colonial rule.

Indeed, it is the devastating effects of the exploitative labor system known as the repartimiento that fuel the deep-seated anger of Kino's mother, Anieri—wife of the historical Don Felipe de Chistoe—as she confronts the play's Prince figure, the historical gobernador Don Diego de Vargas:[2]

> You lied to my husband, Governor. When you first sought the protection of my tribe, you promised my husband that our people would be treated with dignity and respect. You promised the repartimiento would come to an end, but our people are still toiling in the Spanish cornfields while the

farmland of our own families is drying up, untended. I demand that you share your food supplies with our sick and elderly, and treat us with the simple courtesy that is our due.   (150)

Whereas Shakespeare's Prince is a relatively neutral arbiter of justice and the law, Gobernador Vargas clearly acts in the interest of the Spanish colonizers, and it is his son Juan who becomes the rival suitor to Teresa. Thus, as my students and I have noted in our discussions, Lujan's re-vision of Shakespeare's play is not just about intercultural conflict between two warring families but about the racialized hierarchies of power that colonialism creates and perpetuates.

Lujan's characterization of Anieri as a strong voice of Indigenous resistance also reflects the structural aspect of his play that many students find most compelling: the larger presence of the parental figures and the clear stakes of the conflict between the two families. While Gobernador Vargas wishes for peaceful coexistence in the aftermath of the Revolt and Reconquista, Anieri believes that peace will only come with the return of the land to the Pueblo Peoples. Her son's possible marriage to a Spaniard, moreover, represents the acceleration of Pueblo erasure and ongoing genocide. "She'll destroy you," Anieri warns Kino. "And mixing with the likes of her will destroy us all. Don't you understand? One day, our great, great grandchildren won't be Indians anymore. They'll be Spaniards" (188). Because Lujan gives Anieri many more lines than the three that Shakespeare gives to Lady Montague, students are able to see that Anieri's aversion to a marriage between the young lovers is not rooted in irrational interracial hatred but in a legitimate fear for the future of her people and their occupied land.

Crucially, *Kino and Teresa* does not end with peace after the death of its title characters. Whereas Chistoe wishes to bury the strife between the Spaniards and the Pecos People along with his son, Anieri vows to avenge Kino's death in anticolonial terms, proposing that they combine forces with other Pueblos and Indigenous Peoples of the region to "kill the Spaniards and finally take back our land" (216). This alternative ending affirms many students' sense that the supposed reconciliation at the conclusion of *Romeo and Juliet* rings somewhat hollow, and it prompts us to confront the reality that the continued colonization of this land by Spain and later annexation by the United States were not historical inevitabilities. Students come away from our discussions of *Kino and Teresa* with a renewed sense of responsibility for learning about the wrongs of the past and present as well as an understanding that while we cannot change what has already occurred, we can commit to seeking a more complete and complex knowledge of colonial history in order to imagine decolonial futures.

"But the True Ground of all These Piteous Woes"

The desire to seek out and tell a more honest history of the US-Mexico Borderlands is precisely what motivated Mexican American author Guadalupe García McCall to write *Shame the Stars*, a young adult novel that reimagines the plot of Shakespeare's *Romeo and Juliet* as a narrative about two young people named Joaquín del Toro and Dulceña Villa and their community. Set in the fictional Texas border town of Montesco around the year 1915, *Shame the Stars* situates Shakespeare's play during a time of unrest caused by the Mexican Revolution and a period of intense anti-Mexican violence perpetrated by the Texas Rangers and Anglo settlers. Although initially divided in their approaches to self-protection and resistance in the face of such state-sanctioned racial violence, the two families at the center of the novel learn to follow the lead of Joaquín and Dulceña and eventually unite in the name of truth, justice, and survival. As in the case of Lujan's play, I have assigned García McCall's novel in its entirety for my seminar on Shakespeare and race, but key scenes could be used to demonstrate García McCall's unique and deeply personal approach to adapting Shakespeare's play for this particular historical and geographical context.

García McCall recalls hearing about the horrific acts of anti-Mexican terror that she depicts in *Shame the Stars* through her father's storytelling when she was a child, but it was not until her own son was taking a college history class that she came to understand how little she had learned about "what happened to our people" in school (García McCall, Author's Note). After educating herself about this incredibly painful history alongside her son, García McCall wanted to use her fiction-writing skills to share her newfound knowledge with young readers whose textbooks were unlikely to include such information:

> History books being published and printed for American schools today still make no mention of this part of our history. . . . I've included in this book a small ofrenda, a different point of view—a rebellious, contentious voice—along with a small sampling of source materials, both fiction and nonfiction, so that American students might be able to cull through them and better educate themselves. May this book open up important and truthful conversations with teachers, family, and friends.
>
> (García McCall, Author's Note)

García McCall's use of writing as an instrument of truth is reflected in the plot and formal composition of *Shame the Stars*, which centers two teenagers who not only exchange letters with one another but are also invested in the power of the written word to document and resist injustice in their community. Joaquín—the novel's narrator—maintains a journal, in which he frequently writes poetry in response to the harm caused by the Texas Rangers. Dulceña works in the print shop of her family's newspaper, *El Sureño*, which serves as an important venue for reporting on events that would otherwise not be covered fairly or at all by mainstream papers run by Anglos. Throughout the narrative of *Shame the Stars*, García McCall interweaves the fictional documents generated by these young writers with actual newspaper clippings and headlines that she found in the Library of Congress archives. As R. Joseph Rodríguez has noted, this "blending of history, romance, creative works, and historical documents gives the novel an expanded and realistic rendering of the violent histories and prejudices in Texas" (163). For students, it also offers an occasion for thinking about the relationship between historical fact and fictional storytelling as well as a model for using writing in all of its forms as a means of pursuing and expressing the truth.

Although written for a young adult readership, *Shame the Stars* does not shy away from the facts of the violence enacted upon ethnic Mexicans by the Texas Rangers and other Anglo settlers in the region—facts which have been documented and studied by historians such as Benjamin Heber Johnson, Nicholas Villanueva, and Monica Muñoz Martinez. As the ethnic Mexican characters in García McCall's novel discuss with great fear and dismay, it was not just men who were lynched and women who were sexually assaulted. Mexican and Mexican American boys and girls were also victims of this devastating violence. As difficult as it may be for young people to discuss such realities, García McCall believes that telling these stories with care—and in ways that resonate with young readers—can begin to facilitate healing. Referring to Toni Morrison's 1988 lecture on "Speaking the Unspeakable," García McCall notes that "[i]t is only by shedding light on the 'unspeakable' that we can begin to dialogue, to heal those old wounds" (qtd. in Rodríguez 175). Such healing conversations certainly can—and should—happen without the assistance of a canonical white male author, but García McCall has demonstrated the power of using Shakespeare's cultural and curricular prominence to illuminate the obscured histories of her people and the land on which they continue to live.

"We Cannot without Circumstance Descry"

I began this essay with a meditation on the prologue to *Romeo and Juliet* as a means of introducing two modern appropriations that ground the play's infamously unexplained "ancient grudge" in specific histories of the US-Mexico Borderlands. I have titled the essay's three main sections, however, after a set of lines spoken by the Chief Watchman in *Romeo and Juliet*'s final scene that take on a powerful new set of meanings in light of these adaptations. Soon after seeing that "the ground is bloody," the Chief Watchman discovers the source of that blood when he comes upon Juliet's lifeless body (5.3.172). As he directs the other watchmen to summon the Prince and to bring the Montagues and Capulets together, he proclaims, "We see the ground whereon these woes do lie, / But the true ground of all these piteous woes / We cannot without circumstance descry" (5.3.179–81). When I invite my students to return to these lines and consider them anew after reading *Kino and Teresa* and/or *Shame the Stars*, they are quick to observe that the Chief Watchman's play on the word "ground"—meaning both the surface of the earth and a reason or cause—raises a crucial question about the relationship between the land and the truth about what transpired on it.

What does he mean when he modifies his third use of the word "ground" with the adjective "true"? Who has a claim to the truth? Whose truths get recorded and told? Students often emphasize the importance of the Chief Watchman's final line, which insists on gathering facts or "circumstance" in order to arrive at the truth—or, in the case of my classes, to reconsider the so-called truths that we have been taught as well as the truths that have been suppressed.

What this concluding exercise shows is that, in addition to helping students to gain knowledge of obscured histories, texts such as *Kino and Teresa* and *Shame the Stars* also encourage them to arrive at a more complex, cross-historical understanding of Shakespeare's play as an early modern text and an ongoing cultural phenomenon that shifts and refracts when placed in different lights and read from fresh perspectives. By studying how contemporary authors have reinterpreted *Romeo and Juliet* or addressed its gaps, my students come away with a clearer appreciation for the features and mechanics of playwriting; a vocabulary for discussing forms of adaptation and appropriation; and a set of models for their own creative expressions that may draw on their own cultural and personal histories or connect Shakespeare's play to current and past events. As I hope to have demonstrated in this essay, my investment is less in teaching *Romeo and Juliet* than it is in using *Romeo and Juliet* and its status as a curricular stronghold as an opportunity to equip students with the historical knowledge and critical skills required to work toward more just futures. Such an approach is all the more urgent during a moment when teaching the truth about the not-so-ancient past is increasingly considered to be a radical act.

NOTES

1. A critical scholarly edition of *Kino and Teresa* is available in Gillen et al., an open-access anthology. Quotations in this essay are from Lujan.

2. The repartimiento, meaning "partition" or "distribution," was a Spanish colonial system in which Indigenous persons were distributed among Spanish settlers and forced to labor on their behalf. Diego de Vargas was a Spanish governor of New Mexico from 1691 to 1697 and again from 1703 to 1704. He is best known for leading the Reconquista, or reconquest, of the territory in 1692 after twelve years of Pueblo control following the Pueblo Revolt in 1680.

Erasing for Inclusion: *Romeo and Juliet* at Hispanic-Serving Institutions

Jonathan Burton

In her short story "Shakespeare, New Mexico," the MacArthur Fellow and American Book Award winner Valeria Luiselli depicts a Latinx family that moves from Chicago to take up jobs as historical reenactors in the American Southwest. "Tired of dancing huapangos and jarabes" with the Ballet Folklórico Mexicano de Chicago, the father argues that "for [the] children's sake, we had to assimilate better into the United States" (212). The mother is less enthusiastic, although not because she identifies more with the *folklórico* dancing, which she finds worryingly antiquated. Instead, it is the prospect of acting that she finds daunting, given her painful memory of auditioning for the role of Macbeth as a middle school student. The drama teacher, she recalls,

> congratulated me on my good memory and fine diction, but afterwards suggested I take the role of a tree. . . . In that production, the trees would actually be seen advancing from Birnam Wood to Dunsinane during the traitor's last hours. But the trees didn't speak a single line and that bothered me. Gathering up my dignity, I'd refused the offer, and never again trod the boards as an actor. Instead, I'd spent my whole life playing the traditional parts of China Poblana, Jarocha, Indian Woman, and even an Adelita in folkloric Mexican dances. (Luiselli 213)

A similarly demoralizing experience occurs in the Southwest, when the family is denied the lead roles of "Billy the Kid, Wyatt Earp, Big Nose Kate, and Doc Holliday" and cast instead as degrading Mexican stereotypes. The indignity is only sharpened by the fact that they are assigned to the ghost town of Shakespeare, New Mexico, instead of the more prominent Tombstone, Arizona. The family accepts these roles and the subsistence wages they are offered, even as their white coworkers in the marquee roles bristle at the paltry remuneration and make plans to move on to roles at Disneyland. There is more to say about this story of brown people criminalized, sexualized, and rendered victims of a casual and institutional violence that draws the applause of white tourists. I find it more productive, however, to consider why the students I teach at Whittier College, a Hispanic-serving institution in Los Angeles County with a student body that is seventy percent students of color, find this story validating and ultimately rousing as they approach Shakespeare's *Romeo and Juliet.*

In what follows, I draw upon some of the research on Latinx educational experiences to consider why my students see themselves in Luiselli's text and how the story can stir them to acts of creative and intellectual daring in their approaches to *Romeo and Juliet.* My class reads Luiselli's story before

Shakespeare's play. Preempting Shakespeare's voice with the voice of a celebrated Latina author is one of several pedagogical moves I discuss here, each designed to encourage Latinx students to recognize their own experience as a valuable perspective from which to read *Romeo and Juliet*. Luiselli's story alone is not enough to validate students and unleash their creativity, but the surprising reversal in its conclusion (to which I will return) helps to inspire an exercise in creative appropriation that dislodges Shakespeare from a seemingly inaccessible past and a realm of incomparable genius by treating the so-called Bard as one in a line of adapters that continues into our own classroom.

Using a literary genre known as erasure, the unit culminates with students transforming a single page of *Romeo and Juliet* into something new, surprising, and locally engaged. The project appeals to students interested in poetics, visual studies, textual history, and appropriation while providing them with opportunities to demonstrate their engagement with the play and its criticism through multiple modes of expression. Beginning from an understanding that Shakespeare's works "should not be segregated and quarantined from identity politics" (Thompson and Turchi, "Active Shakespeare" 58), this two-week project offers Latinx students (as well as their diverse group of classmates) an opportunity to leverage their own linguistic and cultural dexterities, treating them as valuable collaborative elements no less interesting or valuable than Shakespeare's characters and language.

The term *erasure* refers to a genre of altered literature that is created by selectively erasing, redacting, illustrating over, annotating around, cutting out, or collaging onto or behind an existing text. My assignment asks students to select and alter a single page of *Romeo and Juliet* in order to draw out or emphasize an idea relevant to their own lives. This concept of erasure, which can be traced to Robert Rauschenberg's 1953 *Erased de Kooning Drawing*, has a retaliatory appeal for students who see their own lives erased from majority culture or who recognize in erasure a kind of activist art akin to sampling or graffiti. I introduce the genre, before students begin reading Shakespeare's play, with a series of examples, many of which can be found online. Some are simple, such as Jen Bervin's *Nets*, where Shakespeare's sonnets are grayed out except for key terms or phrases—resulting in a text that condenses, interrogates, or reframes the original. For example, Bervin's version of Sonnet 136, one of the "Will" sonnets, fades all but the words "hold me . . . to . . . my name." Others are more ambitious, such as Tom Phillips's dazzling *A Humument*, where painting, collage, and cut-up techniques radically transform each page of W. H. Mallock's 1892 triple-decker novel, *A Human Monument*. Students also gain clarity and inspiration from related work done in other media, including Shimon Attie's *The Writing on the Wall*, projecting photographs of Jewish street life in pre–World War II Berlin onto the same locations or nearby where the photos were originally taken, or Krzysztof Wodiczko's *Abraham Lincoln: War Veteran*, where a New York City statue of Abraham Lincoln is animated through projections of American veterans of the Iraq and Afghanistan wars and their testimonies of war.[1] The palimpsestic qualities of these works offer students examples of artists reclaiming monumental figures and structures in ways that insist upon their shifting meaning in emerging cultural contexts.

Venerating Shakespeare

Transforming monumental works does not come easily for many students. Latinx students, in particular, often approach canonical narratives as Luiselli's narrator does, with reverence and trepidation. Core family values of *respeto* (respect) and *consejos* (advice from elders) predispose Latinx students to defer to established authority and perceived wisdom (Hershberg; Calzada et al.), and these values are impactful in the educational experiences of Latinx students (López and Vázquez; Elenes et al.). Yet both in and beyond the classroom, Latinx students are accustomed to being ushered, like Luiselli's narrator, into the ethnic margins or, worse, having their allegiances or citizenship questioned. When it comes to studying Shakespeare, then, veneration functions as a kind of shibboleth for students "forced to negotiate perceptions of their linguistic and cultural inferiority in the United States" (Espinosa, "Chicano Shakespeare" 77). These perceptions are heightened in middle and high schools where, as Ruben Espinosa demonstrates, Latinx students are taught by implication that people who look or speak like them don't fit in Shakespeare's plays ("Stranger Shakespeare"). The single play that nearly all study in high school is *Romeo and Juliet*, and the film versions they invariably watch in their classes feature either an all-white cast or one with a single Latino actor cast as a menacing, homicidal Tybalt.

Intimidation and veneration are common responses to Shakespeare among first-generation students, and, with the exception of Native Americans, Latinx students are more likely to be first-generation college students than any other ethnic group in the United States. In a recent issue of *Early Modern Culture* on the unique problems posed by Shakespeare for first-generation college students, scholars propose strategies to foster inclusion and build students' confidence in their authority as interpreters of Shakespeare's works (Olson and Pietros). Stephanie Pietros describes a class built around "problem plays," pointing out that "the use of 'problem' as a kind of hermeneutic is one that invites students to reflect explicitly on Shakespeare's cultural status and ultimately engage more critically with his work" (90). For Cassie Miura, "one way to better serve first-generation students is to make visible the process of canon formation alongside our teaching of canonical works" (46). Others discuss strategies involving performance, Shakespeare's biography, and less canonical plays like *Titus Andronicus*: such strategies mitigate the "uneven distribution of prior knowledge about Shakespeare that can disproportionately negatively affect first generation students, working class students, and students of color" (Thompson, "Response" 184). Some show that an exercise in textual editing can empower first-generation students because it "places them in an authoritative position as both editors and as critical readers, destabilizing the authority of both Shakespeare and of editorial apparatuses, and, in turn, cultivating their own interpretative authority" (W. Taylor 135).

None of the essays in this issue of *Early Modern Culture* attend to the particular intersectionality of first-generation Latinx students, who are often reluctant to question Shakespeare's authority in a political climate that consistently urges people of Mexican and Central American heritage to either assimilate or "go back where they came from." On my own campus, fifty-six percent of the Hispanic and Latino students are first-generation college students (as opposed to twenty-seven percent of Black, twenty-one percent of white, and nineteen percent of Asian students). A high percentage of these commute between home and campus, experiencing a particularly powerful form of what Gloria Anzaldúa has described as *un choque*, or cultural collision, between individualistic college norms such as "realizing your potential" and community values that focus on "giving back" and serving one's family (Rendon et al.). These students' sense of belonging and inclusion is therefore doubly tenuous, further diminishing their confidence when it comes to questioning authorities, making meaning, and, in the context of the Shakespeare class, enlisting four-hundred-year-old language and characters in their own individual development. As a result, even when Latinx students are invited to claim Shakespeare for themselves, they are often more reverential toward Shakespeare than their white peers are. In other words, efforts to promote student appropriations of Shakespeare can easily miscarry and yield instead the very reifications of Shakespeare's universal authority that exclude students of color. How, then, do we transform our Shakespeare pedagogy from an accidental prop for hegemony into a deliberate invitation to creation, self-discovery, and systematic inclusion?

Destabilizing and Appropriating Shakespeare

To prepare my students for the erasure project, it is crucial to deconsecrate *Romeo and Juliet* and show students how it has always been altered to suit the needs of a particular time, place, or individual. I point out that Shakespeare's play is itself an altered text, based upon Arthur Brooke's 1562 poem *The Tragicall Historye of Romeus and Juliet*, itself translated from Pierre Boaistuau's 1559 *Histoires tragiques*, which had previously borrowed the story from Matteo Bandello's 1554 *Novelle*. Students are often familiar with modern adaptations of Shakespeare's play, but this history encourages them to locate Shakespeare in the middle of a longer chain of adaptations continuing through novels, movies, Broadway musicals, animated television episodes, and (finally) into our classroom.

To further destabilize Shakespeare's text, I invite students to work with a nineteenth-century edition on *Google Books*, or alternatively one of several twentieth-century high school editions that maintain Victorian bowdlerization in letter or spirit. Crucial suppressions in these texts appear as early as the play's opening exchange, where Sampson boasts about his capacity to commit rape, promising to "push Montague's men from the wall, and thrust his maids to the wall."[2] Many high school editions tend to omit this line or minimize its violence in strained notes focused on the desire to be nearest the wall and away from the gutter. When students are alert to the "ongoing history of (mis)use" (Grier 249) and editorial whitewashing of moments like these, they begin to recognize that others before them have not felt constrained by reverence. Indeed, students are often inspired to expose and counter-edit those places where an editor may have expurgated or excused via footnote features of the text that unsettle claims for the play's beauty or universality.

These elements of the unit may help to demote *Romeo and Juliet* from its iconic status, but many Latinx students are still unlikely to see themselves as fully entitled to the liberties taken by earlier authors and editors. They are stirred, however, by the conclusion of Luiselli's story to which we return upon completing our reading of the play. This is the moment when Luiselli's narrator rejects her marginal role and grabs the power by jerking Shakespeare's language into her own madcap, violent, and creative act of resistance. In a moment when, we are told, "Shakespeare was silent" (233), Luiselli's protagonist binds and strips the actor playing Billy the Kid before displaying him naked before an audience of octogenarian tourists and reciting Macbeth's "Out, out brief candle!" speech. Macbeth's nihilistic picture of life as "a tale / Told by an idiot, full of sound and fury, / Signifying nothing" (act 5, scene 5, lines 26–28)—the very speech denied the woman as an aspiring adolescent—is here decontextualized and repurposed in an assertion of her worth and refusal to thoughtlessly accept a life of silence and marginality. Billy's confused final words, allegedly the same as his historical original, take on an entirely new meaning in this context. "¿Quién es, quién es?" he implores (Luiselli 233).

"¿Quién es?" Who are you? This is the question that Adhar Noor Desai asks us to put first in his urgent call for a pedagogy "de-contextualizing Shakespeare's plays and instead emphasizing the context of students' own lives" (29). With Desai's question in mind, we can hear in Billy's question a confession that he has underestimated the woman and failed to attend to her life, identity, and capacity for creative appropriation. Although still nameless, the narrator emerges from stereotype here, demonstrating her command of English even as Billy is left to make sense of the world in a second language. As she stands over Billy, a kind of iconoclasm occurs: a cherished symbol is stripped down to a bare, forked animal, upheld only by generations of unquestioned reverence. At the same time, it is the Latina woman who draws applause and commands the attention of the crowd as she seizes Shakespeare's words and surgically transplants them into the circumstances of her own life.

Valorizing Culture and Context

To answer Desai's call and help my students to seize and transplant Shakespeare's language, I ask them to train their intellectual powers on their own lives at the same time that they are working on Shakespeare's text. Here I am attempting to practice what Django Paris terms "culturally sustaining pedagogy," an approach to teaching and learning that "seeks to explore, honor, extend, and, at times, problematize [students'] cultural practices and investments" (Paris and Alim 3). The goal of this work is not to lure students of color into performing white, middle-class norms but rather "to perpetuate and foster—to sustain—linguistic, literate, and cultural pluralism as part of the democratic project of schooling" (Paris 93).

Because students' ability to claim Shakespeare for themselves depends upon first seeing their own lives as complex and worthy, I ask my students to select and read alongside Shakespeare's play an article that addresses their own community or one they wish to know and understand more fully. They are encouraged to explore topics that provide thematic intersections between elements of local identity formation and aspects of Shakespeare's play. Thus, for example, recent articles used by my students addressed toxic masculinity at college, closeted homosexuality in Latinx and Filipino communities of Los Angeles, and—in the cases presented in this chapter—mother-adolescent communication about sex in Latinx families.

The topics and articles selected for this project can and should change to reflect the shifting demographics and cultural politics of the region in which the class is taught. Student participation in identifying relevant topics minimizes the risk of teachers imposing "static, unidirectional notions of culture and race that center only longstanding cultural practices of communities without also attending to continual shifts and reworkings" (Paris and Alim 12). In my own classes, student participation in this process has generated discussions emphasizing my students' ethnic consciousness; peer networks and familial obligations; their *ganas*, or determination; their spiritual strength; their ability to navigate multiple, diverse worlds; and in some cases their linguistic dexterity. As C. Alejandra Elenes, Francisca E. González, Dolores Delgado Bernal, and Sofia Villenas have argued in their work on Chicana-Mexicana feminist pedagogies, the teaching and learning of subject matter rooted in homes and communities allows Latinx college students "to draw from their own culture to resist multiple axes of domination" (Elenes et al. 597). Only when this material is given the same time and care that we devote to *Romeo and Juliet* will students understand that they can draw upon it to highlight, resist, or reframe something in Shakespeare's play, thereby claiming the work for themselves or to advance the dignity, legitimacy, and social equity of people in their lives.

Practicing Erasure and Illumination

I include here three examples of student erasures that illustrate the ways in which Latinx students reread Shakespeare's play in response to an article entitled "The Content and Process of Mother–Adolescent Communication about Sex in Latino Families" (Guilamo-Ramos et al.). Discussions among these students began with anecdotes about communication about sex in their own families and later turned to Juliet's divergent interactions with her mother and nurse. They confirmed the article's findings that "Latina mothers, because of a cultural focus on *marianismo* and *machismo*, may use a double standard when conveying information about sex to their sons and daughters" (Guilamo-Ramos et al. 178). This meant that whereas their male siblings and cousins were spoken with about sex, the young women in their families experienced silence and embarrassment: One student explained that the "erasure became a tool for me to fictionalize the conversation I never had in my own life and with my own mother." Although the silhouettes in her piece (fig. 1) express a fear that "instead of defending her daughter's virginity as her own to give," her mother might "die" in shame, she agreed with the article's assertion that "most adolescents [are] receptive to discussing sex-specific topics with their parents, provided such messages [are] presented in an open and nonjudgmental way" (Guilamo-Ramos et al. 178). Another student argued that "Latinas are encouraged to find shame in their desires, and . . . ofttimes are at a higher risk [of unwanted pregnancy] than they might've been with communication." For this student (fig. 2), reclaiming "an icon like Juliet as strong and owning her sexuality" put forward an affirming counternarrative to Lady Capulet's advice to her daughter to submit to being the mere "cover" to Paris's more substantive and "precious book of love" (1.4.91–2). A similar motive inspired another student (fig. 3) to set the stage for Juliet's "Gallop apace" speech in 3.2 by culling phrases across thirty-five lines of

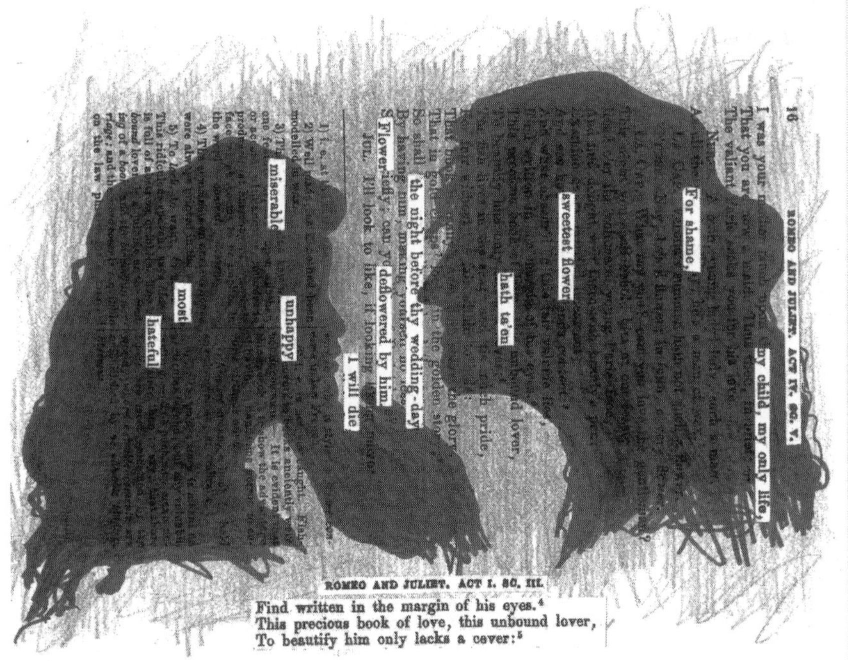

Figure 1. Student erasure example, by Kelsey S. Jimenez.

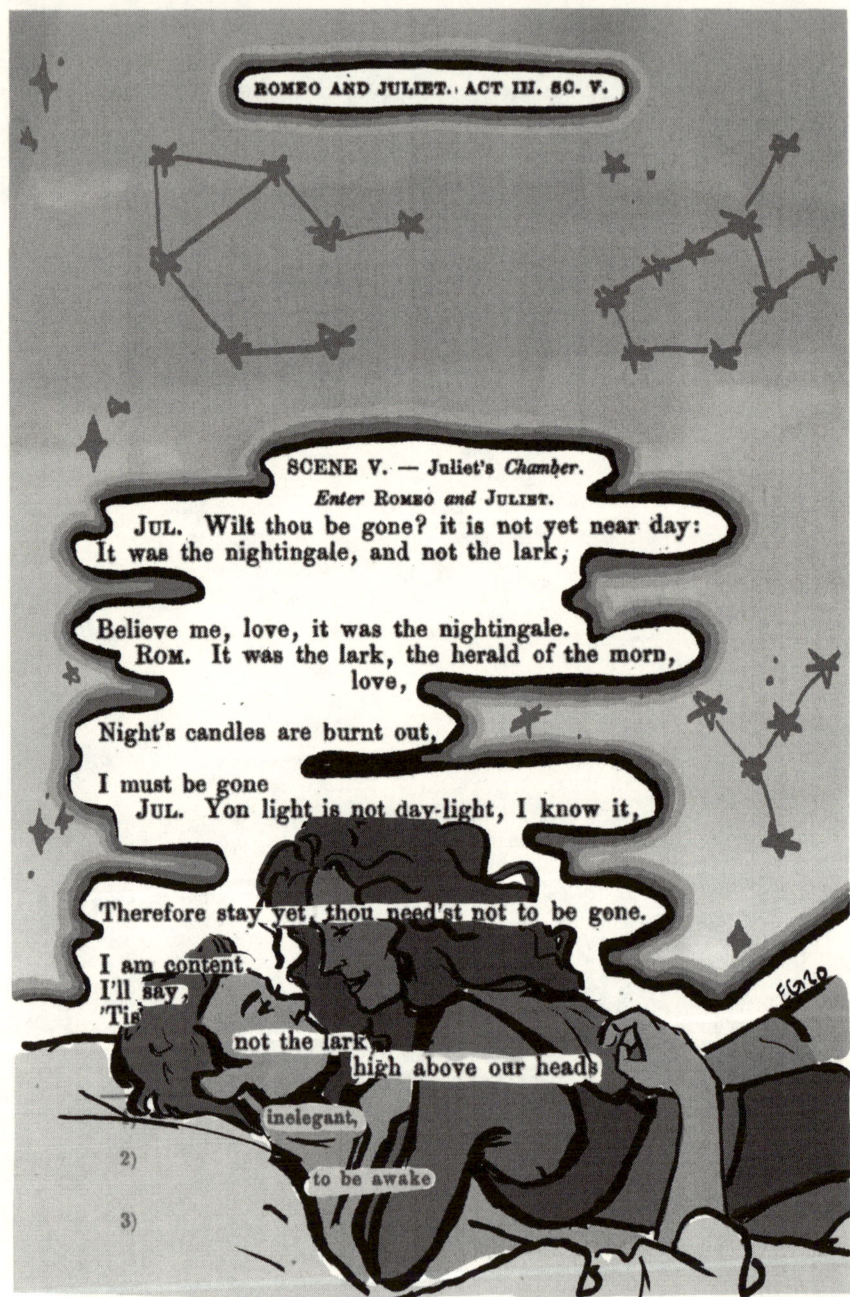

Figure 2. Student erasure example, by Emily Gage.

2.2 to reframe Juliet's more regretful "I should have been more strange" into a desire to "give again . . . and again" so that her own desire is "boundless as the sea" and no less inhibited than Romeo's.

On the final day of the unit, we hang the projects around the room and conduct a "gallery walk," where each student is expected to speak about their work

Figure 3. Student erasure example, by Brianna Martinez.

for two to three minutes and be prepared to answer questions. In addition, they submit short essays explaining precisely what their erasure seeks to illuminate in Shakespeare's text or their own life as well as how the project draws on or responds to ideas in the article they chose to read. The sequence of skills that students are asked to employ in this project begins with close reading and ends in an expository essay, but along the way students consider the history of textual editing, engage with secondary criticism, link seemingly disparate texts and experiences, test out modes of visual expression, and present their ideas orally. This multimodal range also means that students of various talents, backgrounds, and visions all have opportunities to leverage their command of the text. More than that, though, they join the ranks of Luiselli's narrator and other enactors of creative vandalism, transforming *The Tragedy of Romeo and Juliet* into THE [t]RAGE[dy] OF [ro]ME[o] AND [j]U[liet].

NOTES

1. I am grateful to my colleague Danny Jauregui for introducing me to the work of Attie and Wodiczko.

2. For an example of a nineteenth-century edition, see the edition edited by Forbes-Robertson (Shakespeare, *Romeo* [Forbes-Robertson]). A list of twentieth-century editions that contain these suppressions is cataloged by Zweig.

Diversifying Fair Verona:
Shakespeare in Multilingual Classrooms

Robin Alfriend Kello and Rhonda Sharrah

More than any other dramatist of the English-speaking world, Shakespeare bears the simultaneous curse and blessing of a towering reputation that inevitably precedes him, and no play exemplifies his monumental presence in the twenty-first century better than *Romeo and Juliet*. Prior to entering the classroom, students at the high school or undergraduate level will surely have formed some idea about the play—if not from reading or watching the text, then via near-constant reference to and adaptation of it in popular culture. Teachers must therefore decide not only how to present the Shakespearean text with all its linguistic and dramatic intricacies but also how to work with and around Shakespeare as a concept, a historical figure, and a constant presence in the classroom. How might we as teachers guide our students toward new encounters with a text as familiar as *Romeo and Juliet*? How might we, furthermore, bring Shakespeare down from his pedestal and into an ongoing conversation that crosses borders, languages, and eras?

We offer answers to both of those questions through an introduction to the Diversifying the Classics project at the University of California, Los Angeles, and its mission to promote Hispanic classical theater—an art form that was thriving at the same time Shakespeare's plays were on London stages. This rich dramatic corpus can be used to contextualize Shakespeare and the theatrical canon. Such contextualization will help teachers break away from restrictive Anglocentric narratives of literary heritage in the United States, which create a misleading fantasy of English exceptionalism throughout history and marginalize students from other linguistic and cultural traditions.

This essay discusses ways literature and theater teachers can engage with Hispanic classical theater and multilingual pedagogical strategies in order to undo cultural hierarchies that cast non-English works as essentially foreign and supplementary to our national heritage. This approach aims to create more inclusive spaces for students from Latinx cultures, which, despite their long history and importance all over the United States, are rarely reflected in the standard curriculum outside of language-learning classrooms. Comparative and translation-based approaches to drama also encourage students of all backgrounds to critically reflect on important topics such as the history of texts, the formation of the canon, the dramatic and poetic techniques used by playwrights in different traditions, and much more. Putting Spanish-language classics into conversation with Shakespeare can help teachers highlight the diversity of theater past and present and empower all students to "talk back" to Shakespeare.

Introducing Diversifying the Classics and the Comedia

Diversifying the Classics—a collaborative working group that includes scholars, students, and creative artists—was founded at UCLA in 2014 with the animating question, "What lies beyond Shakespeare?" The Spanish Golden Age and the careers of its finest playwrights overlapped with the time period in which Shakespeare was writing in England, yet, while Shakespeare's works are indisputably considered classics in the United States today, thousands of extant early modern Hispanic plays remain largely unknown. These plays, called *comedias*, were written in both Spain and the Americas for audiences from all levels of society; their plots explore a wide variety of complex topics that still resonate with modern audiences: gender, sexuality, class, urban life. Furthermore, while actresses were banned in Shakespeare's England, they were allowed in *comedias* and were often the stars of the show as well as successful producers and playwrights. For these reasons and more, Diversifying the Classics argues that in the theatrical canon of the United States—a nation with millions of Spanish speakers and historical connections to the transatlantic Hispanic world—the *comedia* deserves a place alongside Shakespeare as an integral part of the cultural heritage. To further this goal, we have developed a series of initiatives and a collection of online resources for teachers and anyone interested in learning more about the *comedia*.

The website *Diversifying the Classics* houses a variety of useful materials for teachers looking to include the *comedia* in their classes. The centerpiece of the site is a library of *comedias* in English, all translated by a working group that meets biweekly to translate one new play each year. The plays in the growing database are available as open-access, downloadable pdf files or for purchase in print as part of our publication series. Each translation comes with an informative introduction that explains the *comedia* performance tradition and gives an overview of the play and its author. Many of these translated *comedias* have intriguing resonances with Shakespearean drama, including Ana Caro's *The Courage to Right a Woman's Wrongs*, a cross-dressing comedy of erotic desire and mistaken identities. This play would generate lively classroom discussion around gender and performance when paired with *Twelfth Night* or *As You Like It*, touching on the *comedia*'s use of actresses versus the English theater's use of boy actors. Another play by a female author, Sor Juana Inés de la Cruz's *Love Is the Greater Labyrinth*, presents a very different Theseus from *A Midsummer Night's Dream* or *The Two Noble Kinsmen*, but it similarly explores classical mythology and the clash of love and duty.

Elsewhere in the Diversifying the Classics website, under Resources, we have handouts that can help teachers get started with the *comedia* by illuminating topics such as historical staging conditions in the Spanish Golden Age, common themes in *comedia*, and stock character types. We will soon be expanding this section with additional pedagogical materials—sample lesson plans, study guides, multimedia clips, and more. Most relevant to this chapter, the Classics in the Classroom section contains excerpts and information about a *comedia* that is based on the *Romeo and Juliet* story but has a shockingly different outcome, Lope de Vega's *Castelvines y Monteses*.

Lope de Vega's The Capulets and the Montagues

Although Lope de Vega's *Castelvines y Monteses* was written around 1610, about a decade later than Shakespeare's version, it is not an adaptation of Shakespeare (as some today may assume). Rather, Lope de Vega's play is an independent work based on an earlier Romeo and Juliet prose story contained in Matteo Bandello's 1554 *Novelle*, a popular Italian tale collection that was also the source for several of Shakespeare's other plays. The *Novelle* was one of many such collections that were circulating throughout Europe in multiple languages during the sixteenth and seventeenth centuries. The nearly simultaneous appearance of the two plays reveals the border- and culture-crossing networks of literary exchange that were active at that time—networks that included Shakespeare, Lope de Vega, Bandello, and many other intermediaries and adapters. Bringing Lope de Vega's play into a unit on *Romeo and Juliet* makes clear to students that Shakespeare was not alone in his genius. He was part of a larger artistic conversation across early modern Europe during an era of literary invention—a conversation whose influence flowed in multiple directions.

When the two texts are compared, students soon notice that Lope de Vega and Shakespeare have very different approaches to the material. This is particularly apparent in Dakin Matthews's accessible verse translation of Lope de Vega's play, *The Capulets and the Montagues* (Vega, *Capulets*). Whereas Shakespeare's Elizabethan language may be somewhat alienating and difficult for students today, necessitating frequent pauses to look at footnotes or glosses, Matthews's translation of Lope de Vega opts for the idiomatic flavor of modern English rather than "Shakespearese." This lets Lope de Vega's distinctly humorous take on the story shine through as it would have when it was first written. Lope de Vega's play is in fact considered more of a tragicomedy than Shakespeare's and Bandello's tragedies are. This is partly due to some common features of the *comedia* tradition: the inclusion of a *gracioso* (a comic sidekick) as well as a female lead character with great agency and wit—a convention that stems from the *comedia*'s focus on giving famous actresses meaty roles to play. Moreover, students who are familiar with the Shakespeare version will be surprised to discover that *The Capulets and the Montagues* has a happy ending (spoiler alert: the young lovers *live!*). This twist surely provides a catalyst for a lively classroom discussion.

While lacking the tragic heights of Shakespeare's *Romeo and Juliet*, Lope de Vega's version has much to offer as a well-rounded source of entertainment. Lope de Vega was, after all, complimented as the "Phoenix of Wits" ("*Fénix de los Ingenios"*) during his long and prolific career in Spanish theater, and he literally wrote the book on what makes a successful *comedia*—a 1609 treatise called *El arte nuevo de hacer comedias en este tiempo* (*The New Art of Making Plays in This Time*),[1] in which he argues for the value of the tragicomic form that he employs in *The Capulets and the Montagues*. Close engagement with the play through textual analysis or performance quickly reveals Lope de Vega's consummate skill at plotting, knack for humor, inventive staging, and ear for genuinely touching romance. Lope de Vega is a giant in Hispanic classical theater just as Shakespeare is on the English side, and comparison in the classroom can foster an appreciation of each of their strengths as well as the hallmarks and affordances of each unique performance tradition.

Teaching Multilingually

Lope de Vega's play in translation offers many good scenes to choose from for performance exercises or close reading, both for their own qualities and for their notable contrast with analogous scenes in Shakespeare. Consider the party at the Capulet residence. In Shakespeare's telling, Juliet's affection for her new suitor is suffused with melancholy and tragic foreboding:

> My only love sprung from my only hate!
> Too early seen unknown, and known too late!
> Prodigious birth of love it is to me
> That I must love a loathèd enemy.
> (act 1, scene 4, lines 249–52)

In this portrait of romantic attraction so intertwined with death, these two young lovers never stand a chance. On the other hand, in *The Capulets and the Montagues* Romeo's first meeting with Juliet at the party runs into the obstacle of another suitor, Juliet's cousin Octavio. While Juliet faces Octavio and pretends to have a conversation with him, she arranges a scheme to have a simultaneous conversation with Romeo, who is sitting on her other side, unbeknownst to Octavio. Juliet speaks vows of love that Romeo knows are really meant for him and she even suggests a clandestine meeting in the garden, right under Octavio's nose. Romeo sums it up in an aside: "Her cleverness is / a gift from God, a heavenly art" (lines 460–61). Throughout this meeting scene, and in the relationship that follows (which takes place over several months, rather than just a few nights), Juliet drives the action far more than in Shakespeare's version, trading fatalism for ingenuity as she outwits her male relatives and forthrightly pursues her desires.

Meanwhile, the main love plot between Lope de Vega's protagonists finds a comic counterpoint in the ongoing courtship of their servants Marín and Celia, who parodically ape their masters' hyperbolic vows and sighs of love (lines

1570–700). This offers a mild class critique of the pretensions of the nobles who insist on making problems for themselves, a perspective absent in Shakespeare's version. The crypt scene is also transformed from tragic climax to slapstick comedy, as Romeo and Marín stumble around in the dark and scare themselves nearly to death when they literally run into a Juliet who is very much alive (2579–655). After a lifetime of Romeo and Juliet as a familiar cliché, Lope de Vega's fresh take on the material helps students see both plays with new eyes and illuminates important dramatic concepts through comparison.

For students who have knowledge of Spanish, Lope de Vega's version in the original language can be used alongside Matthews's translation to further explore the relationship between story, language, and performance. Through translation exercises on short passages, the students will gain an appreciation for the ways that each word choice affects tone and characterization as well as firsthand experience connecting them to the labors of the translators who came before them.

One example of a classroom exercise for bilingual students: an instructor could juxtapose the first few lines of the opening scene in Lope de Vega's original and Matthews's translation to evaluate Matthews's chosen translation strategy. The play begins with Romeo, Benvolio, and Romeo's servant Marín noticing the festivities at the Capulet home and considering whether or not to risk getting involved; the students already know, of course, that they will. Below is the Matthews translation:

BENVOLIO.	Look, there's a party—a family feast!
	The house is all ablaze with light!
ROMEO.	Some son or daughter was married tonight.
BENVOLIO.	Or got themselves engaged at least!
ROMEO.	Marín, on thy life, come, do what I say!
	Go sneak inside.
MARÍN.	And eat my fill?
	'Cause after dinner they'll hand me a bill
	that only my funeral can pay.
	Is that an order?
ROMEO.	Who'd notice you?
MARÍN.	When a man is up to no good, I've found,
	there's always witnesses around.
	Sir, that's your enemy's house—and who
	is fiercer, crueler, more merciless
	than a clutch of Capulets can be?
ROMEO.	You're a little bit of a chicken, I see.

(Vega, Capulets, lines 1–15)

And here is Lope de Vega's opening in Spanish[2] (Roselo is the counterpart to Romeo and Anselmo is Benvolio in the original text):

ANSELMO.   Árdese la casa toda
            De fiesta y de regocijo.
ROSELO.   ¿Casa alguna hija o hijo?
ANSELMO.   O es el concierto, o la boda.
ROSELO.   Ve por tu vida, Marín,
            y entra al descuido.
MARÍN.   ¡Harto bien!,
            ¿porque in colación me den
            las exequias de me fin
            en casa de tus enemigos
            me mandas entrar a ver?
ROSELO.   ¿Pues quién te ha de conocer?
MARÍN.   Para mal, siempre hay testigos,
            Son gente crüel y fiera
            los del bando Castelvín.
ROSELO.   Tú, lindo gallina, en fin.
                    (Vega, *Castelvines*
            [*Biblioteca Virtual*], lines 1–15)

When reading aloud, students will recognize in Matthews's English rendering a translation strategy that is a bit loose with exact wording but prioritizes sticking very close to the verse structure of Lope de Vega's lines (repeated patterns of *abba* rhyme, called redondillas).[3] While it is a comic exchange, the demands of rhyme and meter (more pronounced than most Shakespearean blank verse) make the language highly formalized and distinct from twenty-first-century idiomatic expression in either language. Students could then do their own English translations of the Spanish original in prose—an easier task—and compare theirs with Matthews's verse, allowing them to evaluate what is gained or lost between the two translation styles.

In addition, students could adapt a scene into conversational Spanish or English, or mix the two into a Spanglish version, and then perform it for the class in their preferred language. Group discussion would analyze how language choices affect their responses as performers and audience members, even when the literal meaning remains ostensibly the same. How does a love scene feel different when it is formal rhyme versus more casual pickup lines? How might a verse passage resemble the chorus of a modern pop song? How do you translate jokes or expressions between the two languages so that they achieve the same effect and affect?

These exercises ask students to practice critical thinking and writing skills, sometimes in multiple languages, while becoming active participants in artistic creation instead of merely passive receivers of a sacrosanct canon. They reveal the capaciousness of early modern dramatic traditions and the status of play-texts as a set of possibilities for adaptation and response—Shakespeare's English text being just one of these possibilities. Teaching a limited, Anglocentric view of classical drama does a severe disservice to the past and present, in all their infinite variety. The resources and classroom strategies discussed in this chapter offer a set of pedagogical options for teaching *Romeo and Juliet* that bypass the biases and erasures of traditional approaches to Shakespeare and help teachers celebrate their students' diverse backgrounds and skills. Once shown that the classics need not only speak in English, students will be empowered to "talk back" to Shakespeare, to engage the canon critically, and to see that Hispanic cultures are fully alike in dignity.

NOTES

1. For an English translation of *El arte nuevo*, see Vega, "New Rules."

2. *Biblioteca Digital Artelope* offers an online edition of the original Spanish play that includes the option to have verse forms labeled throughout (Vega, *Castelvines* [*Biblioteca Digital*]).

3. The Matthews edition includes a chart listing all the verse forms throughout the play and a discussion of Matthews's verse choices in appendix 2 (Vega, *Capulets* 134–36).

NOTES ON CONTRIBUTORS

Meghan C. Andrews was an associate professor of English at Lycoming College. Her research focused on the idea that Shakespeare's social networks and institutional affiliations were crucial influences on his plays because they provided the most local literary contexts for his drama. Her published work can be found in *Shakespeare Quarterly*, *Renaissance Drama*, *SEL*, and *Early Theatre*, among other venues.

Abbey Bachmann is currently serving as educational programs associate and assistant professor at McGovern Medical School at the University of Texas Health Science Center, Houston. She has more than eleven years of experience teaching secondary English as well as experience teaching secondary English methods courses.

Ariane M. Balizet is professor of English and associate dean of faculty and diversity, equity, and inclusion at Texas Christian University. Her teaching and research interests include games and colonial competition in the early modern literary Caribbean, Shakespeare in adaptation, and intersectional approaches to teaching Renaissance literature. She is the author of two monographs: *Shakespeare and Girls' Studies* (2020) and *Blood and Home in Early Modern Drama: Domestic Identity on the Renaissance Stage* (2014).

Jonathan Burton is professor of English at Whittier College, where he teaches courses on contemporary and early modern drama, transcultural literature, and the graphic novel. His research interests include Shakespeare pedagogy and the history of race. His recent publications include "Segregated Shakespeare" (2022), in *Shakespeare Quarterly*, and "Teaching Shakespeare and Race: Techniques and Technologies," in the forthcoming *Oxford Handbook of Shakespeare and Race*.

Mary T. Christel currently develops curricula for TimeLine Theatre's Living History, an education outreach initiative, and has contributed to Chicago Shakespeare Theater's teacher handbooks for a variety of productions. She has contributed to *Teaching Shakespeare Today: Practical Approaches and Productive Strategies*, *Teaching Shakespeare into the Twenty-First Century*, and *For All Time? Critical Issues in Teaching Shakespeare*. More recently, she coauthored *Bring on the Bard: Active Drama Approaches for Shakespeare's Diverse Student Readers* (2019).

Natalie K. Eschenbaum is professor of English and dean of the School of Interdisciplinary Arts and Sciences at the University of Washington, Tacoma. Her research focuses on sensation studies and affect theory (specifically the affect of disgust) in early modern literature. She has published articles and chapters on Shakespeare and on Robert Herrick, and she is coeditor (with Barbara Correll) of *Disgust in Early Modern English Literature* (2016).

Peter C. Herman is professor of English literature at San Diego State University. He has published numerous books and articles on Shakespeare, Milton, and the literature of terrorism as well as public-facing opinion pieces in *Salon*, *Inside Higher Ed*, *Times of San Diego*, and *Newsweek*. His most recent book is *Early Modern Others: Resisting Bias in Renaissance Literature* (2023).

Jehbreal Muhammad Jackson is an artist and scholar who writes, choreographs, and directs story ballets for film. Their most recent research focuses on the Andalusian Arabic and Bukôngo influences on ballet, music, literature, and theater, specifically the Afro-Islamic roots of classical ballet. Jackson danced with Dance Theater of Harlem before freelancing in New York, Mexico, and Europe. They are a featured vocalist on Samora Pinderhughes's albums *Transformations Suite* and *Grief.* They have also performed as a featured vocalist with Jon Batiste and Kris Bowers.

Robin Alfriend Kello is now a faculty member in the English Department at Seton Hall University and lecturer in comparative literature at Princeton University. He focuses on Shakespeare, the theater of migration, and early modern literature in English and Spanish. His other interests in teaching, research, and community outreach include bilingual theater, adaptation and appropriation, translation, abolitionist and prison-education initiatives, and Shakespeare and social justice on the stage and in the classroom.

Julia Reinhard Lupton is distinguished professor of English at the University of California, Irvine, where she has taught since 1989. She is the author or coauthor of five books on Shakespeare and has edited and coedited many collections, including *A Critical Guide to* Romeo and Juliet (2016) and Romeo and Juliet: *Adaptation and the Arts* (2022).

Maya Mathur is professor of English at the University of Mary Washington. Her research focuses on the social and political significance of comic characters in early modern drama. Her recent work examines intersectional approaches to teaching Shakespeare. Her scholarship has appeared in the *Journal for Medieval and Early Modern Studies*, the *Journal for Early Modern Cultural Studies*, *Early Theatre*, and *Early Modern Literary Studies*.

Robert Matz is professor of English at George Mason University and dean of George Mason's international campus in Incheon, South Korea. He has written on Shakespeare and on early modern English poetry. His edition *Two Early Modern Marriage Sermons: Henry Smith's A Preparative to Marriage (1591) and William Whately's A Bride-Bush (1623)* was published in 2016.

Sarah Neville is associate professor of English and theater, film, and media arts at Ohio State University, where she runs Lord Denney's Players, an academic theater company that investigates conjunctions of performance and textual history. She is an assistant editor of the *New Oxford Shakespeare* (2016–17), an associate coordinating editor of the *Digital Renaissance Editions*, and the author of *Early Modern Herbals and the Book Trade: English Stationers and the Commodification of Botany* (2022).

Rebecca Olson teaches early modern literature and culture at Oregon State University. She is the author of *Arras Hanging: The Textile That Determined Early Modern Culture* (2013), and she oversaw the production of the student-edited open textbook *Romeo and Juliet* (open.oregonstate.education/romeoandjuliet/). She has published articles in journals including *Pedagogy*, *PMLA*, and *Modern Philology* and coedited, with Stephanie Pietros, the seminar issue *First-Generation Shakespeare*, volume 14 of *Early Modern Culture*.

Joseph M. Ortiz is the Dorrance D. Roderick Professor of English at the University of Texas at El Paso. He is the author of *Broken Harmony: Shakespeare and the Politics of Music* and *Gordon Merrick and the Great Gay American Novel*, as well as the editor of *Shakespeare and the Culture of Romanticism*. Some of his essays have appeared in the journals *Shakespeare, Milton Studies,* and *Early Music* and in *Elizabethan Narrative Poems: The State of Play, Vergil and Elegy,* and *The Oxford Handbook of Shakespeare and Music.* He is currently working on a book on translation in Renaissance epic.

Anthony Guy Patricia is associate professor of English in the Department of Humanities at Concord University in Athens, West Virginia. He is the author of *Queering the Shakespeare Film: Gender Trouble, Gay Spectatorship and Male Homoeroticism.* He has also published a number of essays in edited collections ranging from *Presentism, Gender, and Sexuality in Shakespeare* to, most recently, *The Arden Research Handbook of Contemporary Shakespeare Criticism.*

Stephanie Pietros is associate professor of English and director of the honors program at the College of Mount Saint Vincent. With Rebecca Olson, she coedited the 2019 issue of *Early Modern Culture* entitled *First-Generation Shakespeare,* on teaching Shakespeare to first-generation college students. Her essay "The Willow Song and Comedy in *Othello*" is forthcoming in *SEL,* and her articles and reviews have been published in *Early Modern Women, Shakespeare Bulletin,* and elsewhere.

Joshua Reid is associate professor of early modern studies in English at East Tennessee State University. His publications include articles on the Italian romance epic, Dantean portraiture, early modern translation studies, and *Paradise Lost* illustration. His scholarly edition *The Italian Romance Epic in English, 1590–1600* is forthcoming from the Modern Humanities Research Association. He is general editor of the Manchester Spenser, Manchester University Press's monograph series on the life and works of Edmund Spenser.

Kathryn Vomero Santos is assistant professor of English and codirector of the Humanities Collective at Trinity University. She is completing a book entitled *Shakespeare in Tongues* and coediting a collection entitled *The Ethical Implications of Shakespearean in Performance and Appropriation* with Louise Geddes and Geoffrey Way. With Katherine Gillen and Adrianna M. Santos, she cofounded the Borderlands Shakespeare Colectiva. Together, they are editing *The Bard in the Borderlands: An Anthology of Shakespeare Appropriations en La Frontera.*

Rhonda Sharrah is a PhD candidate in the Department of English at the University of California, Los Angeles. Her research focuses on translation and the transnational book trade in the early modern period. She has also been a practicing dramaturg and translator of Spanish Golden Age drama with UCLA's Diversifying the Classics project since 2018.

Marguerite A. Tassi is professor of Shakespeare and Renaissance literature at the University of Nebraska, Kearney. She is the author of *Women and Revenge in Shakespeare: Gender, Genre, and Ethics* and *The Scandal of Images: Iconoclasm, Eroticism, and Painting in Early Modern English Drama* as well as numerous articles on Shakespeare, early modern English drama, classical mythology, and Mary, Queen of Scots.

SURVEY PARTICIPANTS

Kerri Allen, *Dalton State College*
Meghan C. Andrews, *Lycoming College*
Amanda Atkinson, *Southern Methodist University*
Emma Atwood, *University of Montevallo*
Abbey Bachmann, *Cypress-Fairbanks Independent School District*
Ariane M. Balizet, *Texas Christian University*
Stephen M. Buhler, *University of Nebraska, Lincoln*
Jonathan Burton, *Whittier College*
Ethan Campbell, *King's College, New York City*
Terrilynn Cantlon, *Independent Scholar*
Linda Carroll, *Tulane University*
Rebecca Cepek, *Duquesne University*
Stephanie Chamberlain, *Southeast Missouri State University*
Nina Chordas, *University of Alaska Southeast*
Mary T. Christel, *Stevenson High School*
Rosanne Fleszar Denhard, *Massachusetts College of Liberal Arts*
Paramita Dutta, *Ryerson University*
Julie Empric, *Eckerd College*
Natalie K. Eschenbaum, *University of Washington, Tacoma*
Ruben Espinosa, *Arizona State University*
José Ramón Diaz Fernández, *University of Malaga*
Susan L. Fischer, *Bucknell University*
Barry Gaines, *University of New Mexico*
Susan Paun de Garcia, *Denison University*
Amy Garnai, *Kibbutzim College of Education*
Daniel Gates, *Saginaw Valley State University*
Nicholas Gomez, *Saint Louis University*
Jaime Goodrich, *Wayne State University*
Susan Gorman
Jacenta Green, *Fort Bend Independent School District*
Robin Gunther, *Huntingdon College*
David Hartwig, *Weber State University*
Alvin Henry, *St. Lawrence University*
Peter C. Herman, *San Diego State University*
Esther Hu, *Boston University*
Amanda Hughes, *University of North Texas*
Hirohisa Igarashi, *Toyo University*
Sujata Iyengar, *University of Georgia*
Emily Griffiths Jones, *University of South Florida*
Deborah J. Knuth Klench, *Colgate University*
Katy Krieger, *University of Oklahoma*
Jess Landis, *Franklin Pierce University*
Douglas M. Lanier, *University of New Hampshire*

Jennifer Lodine, *Washington State University, Tri-Cities*
Nelson Lopez, *Bellarmine University*
Julia Reinhard Lupton, *University of California, Irvine*
Maya Mathur, *University of Mary Washington*
Robert Matz, *George Mason University*
Margaret Mauer, *Colgate University*
Carla Mazzio, *University at Buffalo, State University of New York*
Elizabeth Mazzola, *City College of New York*
William Thomas McBride, *Illinois State University*
Andrew D. McCarthy, *University of Tennessee, Chattanooga*
Teresa Michals, *George Mason University*
Emily Miller, *Virginia Military Institute*
Jesus Montaño, *Hope College*
Ann Pleiss Morris, *Ripon College*
Alisia N. Muir, *Northwest Early College High School*
Vin Nardizzi, *University of British Columbia*
Sarah Neville, *Ohio State University*
Rebecca Olson, *Oregon State University*
Stephen Orgel, *Stanford University*
Barbara L. Parker, *New York University*
Caro Pirri, *Rutgers University*
Todd Preston, *Lycoming College*
William Reginald Rampone, Jr., *South Carolina State University*
Joshua Reid, *East Tennessee State University*
Megan Riddle, *Northern Oklahoma College*
Kathryn Vomero Santos, *Trinity University*
David K. Sauer, *Spring Hill College*
Jacqueline Smilack, *Denver Public Schools*
Stephen Spiess, *Babson College*
Abraham Stoll, *Johns Hopkins University*
Marguerite A. Tassi, *University of Nebraska, Kearney*
Miranda Fay Thomas, *Trinity College Dublin*
Emily E. Tucker, *Saint Anselm College*
Deborah Uman, *Weber State University*
Bethany Veith, *Mariner High School*
Daniel Vitkus, *University of California, San Diego*
Katherine Walker, *University of North Carolina, Chapel Hill*
Nadine Weiss, *University of Cambridge*
Jessica Winston, *Idaho State University*

WORKS CITED

Akhimie, Patricia. *Shakespeare and the Cultivation of Difference: Race and Conduct in the Early Modern World*. Routledge, 2018.

Albertson, Alana Quintana. *Ramón and Julieta*. Jove, 2022.

Amar te duele. Directed by Fernando Sariñana, Altavista Films / Videocine, 2002.

Ambrose, Susan A., et al. *How Learning Works: Seven Research-Based Principles for Smart Teaching*. Jossey-Bass, 2010.

Amussen, Susan D., and David E. Underdown. *Gender, Culture and Politics in England, 1560–1640: Turning the World Upside Down*. Bloomsbury Academic, 2017.

Anderegg, Michael. "James Dean Meets the Pirate's Daughter: Passion and Parody in *William Shakespeare's Romeo + Juliet* and *Shakespeare in Love*." *Shakespeare, The Movie, II: Popularizing the Plays on Film, TV, Video, and DVD*, edited by Richard Burt and Lynda E. Boose, Routledge, 2003, pp. 56–71.

Andrea, Bernadette. *The Lives of Girls and Women from the Islamic World in Early Modern British Literature and Culture*. U of Toronto P, 2017.

Appelbaum, Robert. "'Standing to the Wall': The Pressures of Masculinity in *Romeo and Juliet*." *Shakespeare Quarterly*, vol. 48, no. 3, 1997, pp. 251–72.

Arber, Edward, and Thomas Seccombe, editors. *Elizabethan Sonnets*. Archibald Constable, 1904. 2 vols. *Bartleby.com*, 2012, www.bartleby.com/358/.

Attie, Shimon. *The Writing on the Wall*. 1991–93, Berlin, Germany.

Balizet, Ariane M. "Breastfeeding, Grief, and the Fluid Economy of Healthy Children in Shakespeare's Plays." *(Dis)Ability, Health, and Happiness in the Shakespearean Body*, edited by Sujata Iyengar, Routledge, 2014, pp. 223–39.

———. *Shakespeare and Girls' Studies*. Routledge, 2020.

Ballet22. "About." *Ballet22*, www.ballet22.com/company.

Bandello, Matteo. "Novella IX." 1942. *Novelle di Matteo Bandello*, Letteratura italiana Einaudi, pp. 128–42, www.letteraturaitaliana.net/pdf/Volume_4/t77.pdf.

Barry, Jackson G. "Poem or Speech? The Sonnet as Dialogue in *Love's Labor's Lost* and *Romeo and Juliet*." *Papers on Language and Literature*, vol. 19, no. 1, 1983, pp. 13–36.

Bate, Jonathan, and Eric Rasmussen, editors. *The RSC Shakespeare: Complete Works*. 2nd ed., Modern Library, 2022.

Bechmann, Ulrike. "Biblical Figures of Women in the Qur'an." *The Early Middle Ages*, edited by Franca Ela Consolino and Judith Herrin, Society of Biblical Literature Press, 2020, pp. 345–76.

Bennett, Karen. "Star-Cross'd Lovers: Shakespeare and Prokofiev's 'Pas de Deux' in *Romeo and Juliet*." *Cambridge Quarterly*, vol. 32, no. 4, 2003, pp. 311–48.

Bervin, Jen. *Nets*. Ugly Duckling Presse, 2003.

Bettelheim, Judith. "Palo Monte Mayombe and Its Influence on Cuban Contemporary Art." *African Arts*, vol. 34, no. 2, 2001, pp. 36–96.

Bicks, Caroline. *Cognition and Girlhood in Shakespeare's World: Rethinking Female Adolescence.* Cambridge UP, 2021.

———. "Incited Minds: Rethinking Early Modern Girls." *Shakespeare Studies*, vol. 44, 2016, pp. 180–202.

Black, Joseph, and Anne Lake Prescott, editors. *The Broadview Anthology of British Literature: The Renaissance and the Early Seventeenth Century.* 3rd ed., Broadview, 2016.

Blank, Paula. *Shakesplish: How We Read Shakespeare's Language.* Stanford UP, 2018.

Bloom, Harold, editor. *William Shakespeare's* Romeo and Juliet. Infobase, 2009. Bloom's Modern Critical Interpretations.

Bly, Mary. "Bawdy Puns and Lustful Virgins: The Legacy of Juliet's Desire in the Comedies of the Early 1600s." *Shakespeare Survey*, vol. 49, 1996, pp. 97–109.

Bowersox, Jeff. "Blackening the Queen of Sheba (ca. 1402–1405)." *Black Central Europe*, blackcentraleurope.com/sources/1000-1500/blackening-the-queen-of -sheba-before-1405/.

Brenner, Gerry. "Shakespeare's Politically Ambitious Friar." *Shakespeare Studies*, vol. 13, 1980, pp. 47–58.

Brissenden, Alan. *Shakespeare and the Dance.* Humanities Press, 1981.

Brown, Carolyn E. "Juliet's Taming of Romeo." *Studies in English Literature, 1500–1900*, vol. 36, no. 2, 1996, pp. 333–55.

Bruder, Edith. *The Black Jews of Africa: History, Religion, Identity.* Oxford UP, 2008.

Bruster, Douglas. "Teaching the Tragi-comedy of *Romeo and Juliet.*" Hunt, pp. 59–68.

Bullinger, Heinrich. *The Golde[n] Boke of Christen Matrimonye . . . .* London, 1542. *Early English Books Online Text Creation Partnership*, name.umdl.umich.edu/ A17171.0001.001.

Burnett, Mark Thornton. *Shakespeare and World Cinema.* Cambridge UP, 2013.

Calzada, Esther J., et al. "Incorporating the Cultural Value of *Respeto* into a Framework of Latino Parenting." *Cultural Diversity and Ethnic Minority Psychology*, vol. 16, no. 1, 2010, pp. 77–86.

Campana, Joseph. "Dancing Will: The Case of *Romeo and Juliet.*" *Romeo and Juliet: A Critical Reader*, edited by Julia Reinhard Lupton, Bloomsbury, 2016, pp. 153–76.

Caporicci, Camilla. "Black but yet Fair: The *Topos* of the Black Beloved from Song of Songs in Shakespeare's Work." *Shakespeare*, vol. 14, no. 4, 2017, pp. 360–73.

Carnegie, David, and Gary Taylor, editors. *The Quest for Cardenio: Shakespeare, Fletcher, Cervantes, and the Lost Play.* Oxford UP, 2012.

Caro, Ana. *The Courage to Right a Woman's Wrongs.* Translated by the UCLA Working Group on the *Comedia* in Translation and Performance, Juan de la Cuesta Press, 2021.

Caulfield, Keith. "Taylor Swift's Re-Recorded 'Love Story' Sells Ten Thousand in U.S. on First Day." *Billboard*, 13 Feb. 2021, www.billboard.com/articles/business/ chart-beat/9526014/taylor-swift-love-story-re-recording-sales-first-day/.

Chapman, Matthieu, and Anna Wainwright, editors. *Teaching Race in the European Renaissance: A Classroom Guide.* ACMRS Press, 2023.

Chartier, Roger. Cardenio *between Shakespeare and Cervantes.* Polity Press, 2013.

Cho, Sumi, et al. "Toward a Field of Intersectionality Studies: Theory, Applications, and Praxis." *Signs*, vol. 38, no. 4, 2013, pp. 785–810.

Cleaver, Robert. *A Godly Forme of Houshold Gouernment: Carefully to Be Practised of All Christian Housholders*. London, 1598. *Early English Books Online Text Creation Partnership*, name.umdl.umich.edu/A67866.0001.001.

Cohen, Albert. "Spanish National Character in the Court Ballets of J.-B. Lully." *Revista de Musicología*, vol. 16, no. 5, 1993, pp. 2978–87.

"Cotquean, N. (3)." *Oxford English Dictionary*, 2023, www.oed.com/dictionary/cotquean_n?tab=meaning_and_use&tl=true.

Crenshaw, Kimberlé. "Demarginalizing the Intersection of Race and Sex: A Black Feminist Critique of Antidiscrimination Doctrine, Feminist Theory and Antiracist Politics." *The University of Chicago Legal Forum*, vol. 1989, no. 1, 1989, pp. 139–67.

Cruz, Sor Juana Inés de la. *Love Is the Greater Labyrinth*. Translated by the UCLA Working Group on the *Comedia* in Translation and Performance, Juan de la Cuesta Press, 2023.

Dadabhoy, Ambereen. "The Unbearable Whiteness of Being (in) Shakespeare." *Postmedieval*, vol. 11, 2020, pp. 228–35.

Della Gatta, Carla. "From *West Side Story* to *Hamlet, Prince of Cuba*: Shakespeare and Latinidad in the United States." *Shakespeare Studies*, vol. 44, 2016, pp. 151–56.

———. *Latinx Shakespeares: Staging U.S. Intracultural Theater*. U of Michigan P, 2023.

Derbew, Sarah F. *Untangling Blackness in Greek Antiquity*. Cambridge UP, 2022.

Desai, Adhaar Noor. "Topical Shakespeare and the Urgency of Ambiguity." Eklund and Hyman, pp. 27–35.

Desmet, Christy, et al., editors. *The Routledge Handbook of Shakespeare and Global Appropriation*. Routledge, 2020.

Dewulf, Jeroen. "From Moors to Indians: The Mardi Gras Indians and the Three Transformations of St. James." *Louisiana History: The Journal of the Louisiana Historical Association*, vol. 56, no. 1, 2015, pp. 5–41.

Dodds, Jerrilynn, et al. *The Arts of Intimacy: Christians, Jews, and Muslims in the Making of Castilian Culture*. Yale UP, 2009.

Donaldson, Peter S. *Shakespearean Films / Shakespearean Directors*. Routledge, 1990.

Dutton, Richard. *Shakespeare, Court Dramatist*. Oxford UP, 2016.

Dyer, Richard. *White: Essays on Race and Culture*. 2nd ed., Routledge, 2017.

Earl, A. J. "*Romeo and Juliet* and the Elizabethan Sonnets." *English: Journal of the English Association*, vol. 27, no. 128–29, 1978, pp. 99–120.

Edmondson, Paul, and Stanley Wells. *All the Sonnets of Shakespeare*. Cambridge UP, 2020.

———. *Shakespeare's Sonnets*. Oxford UP, 2004.

Eklund, Hillary, and Wendy Beth Hyman, editors. *Teaching Social Justice through Shakespeare: Why Renaissance Literature Matters Now*. Edinburgh UP, 2019.

Elenes, C. Alejandra, et al. "Introduction: Chicana/Mexicana Feminist Pedagogies: *Consejos, Respeto, y Educación* in Everyday Life." *International Journal of Qualitative Studies in Education*, vol. 14, no. 5, 2001, pp. 595–602.

Elias, Norbert. *Power and Civility*. Translated by Edmund Jephcott, Pantheon, 1982.

Elyot, Thomas. *The Book Named The Governor*. Edited by S. E. Lehmberg, Dutton, 1962.

Enterline, Lynn. *The Rhetoric of the Body from Ovid to Shakespeare*. Cambridge UP, 2000.

Erne, Lukas, editor. *The First Quarto of* Romeo and Juliet. Cambridge UP, 2007. The New Cambridge Shakespeare: The Early Quartos.

Espinosa, Ruben. "Chicano Shakespeare: The Bard, the Border, and the Peripheries of Performance." Eklund and Hyman, pp. 76–84.

———. *Shakespeare on the Shades of Racism*. Routledge, 2021. Spotlight on Shakespeare.

———. "Stranger Shakespeare." *Shakespeare Quarterly*, vol. 67, no. 1, 2016, pp. 51–67.

———. "Your Mountainish Inhumanity." *The Sundial*, 16 Aug. 2019, medium.com/the-sundial-acmrs/shakespeare-and-your-mountainish-inhumanity-d255474027de.

Evans, G. Blakemore, editor. *The Riverside Shakespeare*. Houghton Mifflin, 1974.

Evans, Maurice, editor. *Elizabethan Sonnets*. J. M. Dent and Sons, 1992.

"An Excellent and Conceited Tragedy of Romeo and Juliet." *Lord Denney's Players*, www.lorddenneysplayers.com/productions/romeoandjuliet.

Fairfax, Edmund. "Turnout." *Eighteenth-Century Ballet*, eighteenthcenturyballet.com/turnout/.

Farley-Hills, David. "The 'Bad' Quarto of *Romeo and Juliet*." Romeo and Juliet *and Its Afterlife*, edited by Stanley Wells, Cambridge UP, 1996, pp. 27–44. Vol. 49 of *Shakespeare Survey*.

Farmer, Alan B. "Shakespeare as Leading Playwright in Print, 1598–1608/09." *Shakespeare and Textual Studies*, edited by Margaret Jane Kidnie and Sonia Massai, Cambridge UP, 2015, pp. 87–104.

Flachmann, Michael. "Teaching Shakespeare through Parallel Scenes." *Shakespeare Quarterly*, vol. 35, no. 5, 1984, pp. 644–46.

Foakes, R. A. "The 'Part' of Orlando in Robert Greene's Play." *The Henslowe-Alleyn Digitisation Project*, Dulwich MS 1, article 138, folio 8r, henslowe-alleyn.org.uk/essays/the-part-of-orlando-in-robert-greenes-play/.

Freccero, Carla. "Romeo and Juliet Love Death." *Shakesqueer: A Queer Companion to the Complete Works of Shakespeare*, edited by Madhavi Menon, Duke UP, 2011, pp. 302–08.

Fuchs, Barbara. *The Poetics of Piracy: Emulating Spain in English Literature*. U of Pennsylvania P, 2013.

Garber, Marjorie. *Shakespeare after All*. Anchor Books, 2004.

———. *Shakespeare and Modern Culture*. Anchor Books, 2009.

García McCall, Guadalupe. *Shame the Stars*. Tu Books, 2016.

Geneva Bible. 1599. *Bible Gateway*, www.biblegateway.com/versions/1599-Geneva-Bible-GNV/#booklist.

Gillen, Katherine. "The Decolonial Imaginary of Borderlands Shakespeare." *Decolonizing the English Literary Curriculum*, edited by Ato Quayson and Ankhi Mukherjee, Cambridge UP, 2024, pp. 367–85.

Gillen, Katherine, and Lisa Jennings. "Decolonizing Shakespeare? Toward an Antiracist, Culturally Sustaining Praxis." *The Sundial*, 26 Nov. 2019, medium .com/the-sundial-acmrs/decolonizing-shakespeare-toward-an-antiracist -culturally-sustaining-praxis-904cb9ff8a96.

Gillen, Katherine, et al., editors. *The Bard in the Borderlands: An Anthology of Shakespeare Appropriations en La Frontera*. Vol. 1, ACMRS Press, 2023. *ASU*, asu.pressbooks.pub/bard-in-the-borderlands-volume-1.

Gnomeo and Juliet. Directed by Kelly Asbury, Touchstone Pictures / Rocket Pictures / Arc Productions, 2011.

Goldberg, Jonathan. "*Romeo and Juliet*'s Open Rs." *Queering the Renaissance*, edited by Goldberg, Duke UP, 1994, pp. 218–35.

Goldberg, K. Meira. *Sonidos Negros: On the Blackness of Flamenco*. Oxford UP, 2019.

Gong, Chole. *These Violent Delights*. Margaret K. McElderry Books, 2020.

Gouge, William. *Of Domesticall Duties: Eight Treatises*. London, 1622. *Early English Books Online Text Creation Partnership*, name.umdl.umich.edu/A68107 .0001.001.

Gowing, Laura. *Common Bodies: Women, Touch and Power in Seventeenth-Century England*. Yale UP, 2003.

———. *Gender Relations in Early Modern England*. Routledge, 2012.

Grady, Kyle. "'Envy Pale of Hew': Whiteness and Division in 'Fair Verona.'" *White People in Shakespeare: Essays on Race, Culture and the Elite*, edited by Arthur L. Little, Jr., Bloomsbury, 2023, pp. 91–103.

Great Performances: Romeo and Juliet. Directed by Simon Godwin, National Theatre, 2021. *PBS Video* app.

Greenblatt, Stephen, editor. *The Norton Anthology of English Literature: The Sixteenth Century; The Early Seventeenth Century*. Vol. B of *The Norton Anthology of English Literature*, 10th ed., W. W. Norton, 2018.

Greenblatt, Stephen, et al., editors. *The Norton Shakespeare*. 3rd ed., W. W. Norton, 2016.

Grier, Miles. "Are Shakespeare's Plays Racially Progressive? The Answer Is in Our Hands." Thompson, *Cambridge Companion*, pp. 237–53.

Guilamo-Ramos, Vincent, et al. "The Content and Process of Mother–Adolescent Communication about Sex in Latino Families." *Social Work Research*, vol. 30, no. 3, 2006, pp. 169–81.

Gundaker, Grey. *Signs of Diaspora / Diaspora of Signs: Literacies, Creolization, and Vernacular Practice in African America*. Oxford UP, 1998.

Hall, Kim F. *Things of Darkness: Economies of Race and Gender in Early Modern England*. Cornell UP, 1995.

Harrison, Thomas P. "*Romeo and Juliet, A Midsummer Night's Dream*: Companion Plays." *Texas Studies in Language and Literature*, vol. 13, no. 2, 1971, pp. 209–13.

Hart, Juliet, et al. *Acting It Out: Using Drama in the Classroom to Improve Student Engagement, Reading, and Critical Thinking*. Routledge, 2017.

Hartley, Andrew James. "Dialectical Shakespeare: Pedagogy in Performance." *The Oxford Handbook of Shakespeare and Performance*, edited by James C. Bulman, Oxford UP, 2017, pp. 122–37.

Hendricks, Margo. "Gestures of Performance: Rethinking Race in Contemporary Shakespeare." Thompson, *Colorblind Shakespeare*, pp. 187–203.

Herman, Peter C. "Tragedy and the Crisis of Authority in Shakespeare's *Romeo and Juliet.*" *Intertexts*, vol. 12, no. 1, 2008, pp. 89–109.

Hershberg, Rachel M. "Consejos as a Family Process in Transnational and Mixed-Status Mayan Families." *Journal of Marriage and Family*, vol. 80, 2018, pp. 334–48.

Higginbotham, Jennifer. *The Girlhood of Shakespeare's Sisters: Gender, Transgression, Adolescence.* Edinburgh UP, 2013.

"'His Romeo' Trailer." Choreographed by Joshua Stayton, performances by Roberto Vega Ortiz and Stayton, San Francisco. *YouTube*, uploaded by Ballet22, 16 Jan. 2021, www.youtube.com/watch?v=eCo-ygkJfWQ.

Holland, Peter. Introduction to *Romeo and Juliet*. Orgel and Braunmuller, pp. 1251–56.

Holmer, Joan Ozark. "'Draw, If You Be Men': Saviolo's Significance for *Romeo and Juliet.*" *Shakespeare Quarterly*, vol. 45, no. 2, 1994, pp. 163–89.

Hunt, Maurice, editor. *Approaches to Teaching Shakespeare's* Romeo and Juliet. Modern Language Association of America, 2000.

Hunter, Lynette. "Adaptation and/or Revision in Early Quartos of *Romeo and Juliet.*" *Papers of the Bibliographical Society of America*, vol. 101, no. 1, 2007, pp. 5–54.

Ioppolo, Grace. "The 'Platt' (or Plot) of *The Second Part of the Seven Deadly Sins.*" *The Henslowe-Alleyn Digitisation Project*, MS 19, henslowe-alleyn.org.uk/essays/the-platt-or-plot-of-the-second-part-of-the-seven-deadly-sins/.

Jackson, Jehbreal Muhammad. "Ballet as Artistic, Scientific, and Existential Inquiry: Incorporating Ballet's Broader History in a Syllabus and in the Studio." *Antiracism in Ballet Teaching*, edited by Kate Mattingly and Lyun Ashani Harrison, Routledge, 2024, pp. 116–28.

———. "Juliet and Ballet's Black History." Hosted by Julia Lupton, 2021, U of California, Irvine, uci.yuja.com/V/Video?v=2852793&node=9996709&a=173975930. Recording of a lecture.

Jackson, Jehbreal Muhammad, and Julia Reinhard Lupton. "Holy Palmers' Kiss: Love, Trust and Wisdom in John Neumeier's *Romeo and Juliet* Ballet." Romeo and Juliet, *Adaptation and the Arts: "Cut Him Out in Little Stars,"* edited by Ariane Helou and Lupton, Arden Shakespeare, 2022, pp. 59–88.

Jackson, Russell. *Shakespeare Films in the Making: Vision, Production and Reception.* Cambridge UP, 2007.

James, Heather. "The Ovidian Girlhood of Shakespeare's Boy Actors: Q2 Juliet." *Shakespeare and Rome*, edited by Peter Holland, Cambridge UP, 2016, pp. 106–22. Vol. 69 of *Shakespeare Survey*.

James VI and I (king). *Basilicon Doron. Political Writings*, edited by Johann P. Sommerville, Cambridge UP, 1994, pp. 1–61.

Johnson, Benjamin Heber. *Revolution in Texas: How a Forgotten Rebellion and Its Bloody Suppression Turned Mexicans into Americans*. Yale UP, 2005.

Jones, Nicholas R. *Staging* Habla de Negros: *Radical Performances of the African Diaspora in Early Modern Spain*. Penn State UP, 2019.

Joubin, Alexa Alice. "Others Within: Ethics in the Age of Global Shakespeare." Desmet et al., pp. 25–36.

Juan Carvajal, Mara Lioba. *La zarabanda: Pluralidad y controversia de un género musical*. Plaza y Valdez Editores, 2008.

Kahn, Coppélia. "Coming of Age in Verona." *Modern Language Studies*, vol. 8, no. 1, 1977–78, pp. 5–22.

———. *Man's Estate: Masculine Identity in Shakespeare*. U of California P, 1981.

Karim-Cooper, Farah. "Anti-Racist Shakespeare." *Shakespeare's Globe*, 26 May 2020, www.shakespearesglobe.com/discover/blogs-and-features/2020/05/26/anti-racist-shakespeare.

———. "Pilgrims' Hands Do Touch." *Shakespeare's Globe*, 3 May 2018, www.shakespearesglobe.com/discover/blogs-and-features/2018/05/03/pilgrims-hands-do-touch/.

———. "*Romeo and Juliet*: A Tale of Heaven to Hell." *Shakespeare's Globe*, 16 Apr. 2020, www.shakespearesglobe.com/discover/blogs-and-features/2020/04/16/a-tale-of-heaven-to-hell/.

Kebab Connection. Directed by Anno Saul, Lifesize Entertainment, 2005.

Kennedy, William J. *Petrarchism at Work: Contextual Economies in the Age of Shakespeare*. Cornell UP, 2016.

King, Helen. *The Disease of Virgins: Green Sickness, Chlorosis and the Problems of Puberty*. Routledge, 2004.

Kinney, Arthur F. *Shakespeare by Stages: An Historical Introduction*. Blackwell, 2003.

Kirschbaum, Leo. "An Hypothesis concerning the Origin of the Bad Quartos." *PMLA*, vol. 60, no. 3, 1945, pp. 697–715.

Kottman, Paul A. "Defying the Stars: Tragic Love as the Struggle for Freedom in *Romeo and Juliet*." *Shakespeare Quarterly*, vol. 63, no. 1, 2012, pp. 1–38.

Lanier, Douglas. "Shakespearean Rhizomatics: Adaptation, Ethics, Value." *Shakespeare and the Ethics of Appropriation*, edited by Alexa Huang and Elizabeth Rivlin, Palgrave Macmillan, 2014, pp. 21–40.

Lee, Harper. *To Kill a Mockingbird*. Grand Central Publishing, 1960.

Lehmann, Courtney. *Screen Adaptations: Shakespeare's* Romeo and Juliet: *The Relationship between Text and Film*. Bloomsbury Methuen Drama, 2010.

Letters to Juliet. Directed by Gary Winick, Applehead Pictures, 2010.

Levenson, Jill L. "The Definition of Love: Shakespeare's Phrasing in *Romeo and Juliet*." *Shakespeare Studies*, vol. 15, 1982, pp. 21–36.

———. Introduction. Shakespeare, *Romeo and Juliet*, Levenson, pp. 1–126.

Lewis, C. S. *The Allegory of Love: A Study in Medieval Tradition*. Oxford UP, 1958.

Liebler, Naomi Conn. "The Critical Backstory." Romeo and Juliet: *A Critical Reader*, edited by Julia Reinhard Lupton, Bloomsbury, 2016, pp. 19–51. Arden Early Modern Drama Guides.

"Literary Devices: Themes." *SparkNotes*, www.sparknotes.com/shakespeare/ romeojuliet/themes/.

Locke, Ralph P. *Music and the Exotic from the Renaissance to Mozart*. Cambridge UP, 2015.

Lodge, Edmund, editor. *Illustrations of British History, Biography, and Manners in the Reigns of Henry VIII, Edward VI, Elizabeth and James I*. John Chidley, 1838. 2 vols.

López, Gerardo R., and Vanessa A. Vázquez. "Parental Involvement in Latina/Latino-Impacted Schools in the Midwest: Recognizing the Role and Function of Home-Based Knowledge and Practices." *Journal of School Public Relations*, vol. 27, no. 4, 2006, pp. 365–96.

Lowry, Richard. "A Regrettable Translation: Song of Songs 1:15," *Sefaria*, www.sefaria .org/sheets/397573.80.

Luiselli, Valeria. "Shakespeare, New Mexico." Translated by Christina MacSweeney. *Lunatics, Lovers and Poets: Twelves Stories after Cervantes and Shakespeare*, edited by Daniel Hahn and Margarita Valencia, And Other Stories Publishing, 2016, pp. 209–34.

Lujan, James. *Kino and Teresa: A Full-Length Play in Two Acts*. Native Voices, 2005.

MacDonald, Joyce Green. *Shakespearean Adaptation, Race and Memory in the New World*. Palgrave Macmillan, 2020. Palgrave Shakespeare Studies.

Maré, nossa historia de amore. Directed by Lúcia Murat, Taiga Filmes / Limite, 2008.

Marshall, Alex. "Blackface at the Ballet Highlights a Global Divide on Race." *The New York Times*, 23 Dec. 2019.

Martinez, Mónica Muñoz. *The Injustice Never Leaves You: Anti-Mexican Violence in Texas*. Harvard UP, 2018.

"Match Made in Hell." *YouTube*, uploaded by Ryan Reynolds, 2 Dec. 2020, www .youtube.com/watch?v=KABSYzPqTTg&t=3s.

Mattingly, Kate, et al. "Ballet Pedagogy and a 'Hard Re-Set': Perspectives on Equitable and Inclusive Teaching Practices." *Dance Chronicle*, vol. 46, no. 1, 2023, pp. 40–65.

Matz, Robert, editor. *Two Early Modern Marriage Sermons: Henry Smith's* A Preparative to Marriage *(1591) and William Whately's* A Bride-Bush *(1623)*. Routledge, 2016.

McDonald, Russ, and Lena Cowen Orlin, editors. *The Bedford Shakespeare*. Bedford/ St. Martin's, 2015.

McGuire, Philip C. "On the Dancing in *Romeo and Juliet*." *Renaissance and Reformation / Renaissance et Réforme*, vol, 5, no. 2, 1981, pp. 87–97.

McJannet, Linda. "'A Hall, a Hall! Give Room, and Foot It, Girls': Realizing the Dance Scene in *Romeo and Juliet* on Film." *Borrowers and Lenders*, vol. 10, no. 2, 2017.

McKnight, Katherine S., and Mary Scruggs. *The Second City Guide to Improv in the Classroom: Using Improvisation to Teach Skills and Boost Learning*. Jossey-Bass, 2008.

Merritt, Nicole, et al. "Romeo and Juliet: Impressions." *YouTube*, uploaded by Ohio State English, 11 Apr. 2019, www.youtube.com/watch?v=8NSiALEkMkw.

A Midsummer Night's Dream. Directed by Dominic Dromgoole, 2013. *Globe Player*, player.shakespearesglobe.com/productions/a-midsummer-nights-dream-2013/.

A Midsummer Night's Dream. Directed by Michael Hoffman, Regency Enterprises, 1999.

Miura, Cassie M. "Empowering First-Generation Students: Bardolatry and the Shakespeare Survey." Olson and Pietros, pp. 44–56.

The Moor's Pavane. Choreographed by José Limón, 1949. *YouTube*, uploaded by Karl Skellenger, 11 Feb. 2017, www.youtube.com/watch?v=0aGj6pJpzZQ&t=216s.

"*The Moroccan Project* (Excerpt) Alonzo King LINES Ballet." Choreographed by Alonzo King, 2005. *YouTube*, 22 Aug. 2013, www.youtube.com/watch?v=n5NcPI4pvoU.

Mulvey, Laura. "Visual Pleasure and Narrative Cinema." *The Film Theory Reader: Debates and Arguments*, edited by Marc Furstenau, Routledge, 2010, pp. 200–08.

Muravyeva, Marianna G., et al. *Parricide and Violence against Parents: A Cross-Cultural View across Past and Present*. Routledge, 2021.

Ndiaye, Noémie. *Scripts of Blackness: Early Modern Performance Culture and the Making of Race*. U of Pennsylvania P, 2022.

Ndiaye, Noémie, and Lia Markey, editors. *Seeing Race before Race: Visual Culture and the Racial Matrix in the Premodern World*. ACMRS Press, 2023.

Negrón-Muntaner, Frances. "Feeling Pretty: *West Side Story* and Puerto Rican Identity Discourses." *Social Text* 63, vol. 18, no. 2, summer 2000, pp. 83–106.

Nevile, Jennifer, editor. *Dance, Spectacle, and the Body Politick, 1250–1750*. Indiana UP, 2008.

Neville, Sarah, and Natalie Dalea. "Thinking *DEEP*-ly: The *Database of Early English Playbooks* in the Undergraduate Classroom." *Teaching the History of the Book*, edited by Matteo Pangallo and Emily B. Todd, U of Massachusetts P, 2023.

Nissan, Ephraim. "The Importance of Being Hairy: A Few Remarks on the Queen of Sheba, Esau, and the Andromeda Myth." *Erreffe: La ricera folklorica*, vol. 70, 2015, pp. 273–83.

"Nkisi Sarabanda—Signature of the Spirit." *African Burial Ground. National Park Service*, 5 Nov. 2015, www.nps.gov/afbg/learn/historyculture/nkisi-sarabanda.htm.

Norbrook, David, and H. R. Woudhuysen, editors. *The Penguin Book of Renaissance Verse, 1509–1659*. Penguin Books, 1993.

Noughts + Crosses. Written by Toby Whithouse, Mammoth Screen / Participant / Roc Nation, 2000. *BBC One*.

Ocampo-Guzman, Antonio. "My Own Private Shakespeare; or, Am I Deluding Myself?" Thompson, *Colorblind Shakespeare*, pp. 125–36.

O'Dair, Sharon, and Timothy Francisco, editors. *Shakespeare and the 99%: Literary Studies, the Profession, and the Production of Inequity*. Palgrave Macmillan, 2019.

Olson, Rebecca, and Stephanie Pietros, editors. *First-Generation Shakespeare*. Special issue of *Early Modern Culture*, vol. 14, 2019.

Orgel, Stephen, and A. R. Braunmuller, general editors. *The Complete Pelican Shakespeare*. Penguin Books, 2002.

Osenbruck, Andreas. *Diana as an African Woman*. Mid–sixteenth century. *Kunsthistoriches Museum Wien*, www.khm.at/en/objectdb/detail/73922/. Cameo.

Othello. Choreographed by Lar Lubovitch, music by Elliot Goldenthal, Kultur Video, 2003. DVD.

Palfrey, Simon, and Tiffany Stern. *Shakespeare in Parts*. Oxford UP, 2007.

———. "What Does the Cued Part Cue? Parts and Cues in *Romeo and Juliet*." *A Companion to Shakespeare and Performance*, edited by Barbara Hodgdon and W. B. Worthen, Blackwell, 2005, pp. 179–96.

Palliser, D. M. *The Age of Elizabeth: England under the Later Tudors, 1547–1603*. New York: Longman, 1983.

Paris, Django. "Culturally Sustaining Pedagogy: A Needed Change in Stance, Terminology, and Practice." *Educational Researcher*, vol. 41, no. 3, 2012, pp. 93–97.

Paris, Django, and H. Samy Alim, editors. *Culturally Sustaining Pedagogies: Teaching and Learning for Justice in a Changing World*. Teachers College Press, 2017.

Paster, Gail Kern. *The Body Embarrassed: Drama and the Disciplines of Shame in Early Modern England*. Cornell UP, 1993.

Patricia, Anthony Guy. *Queering the Shakespeare Film: Gender Trouble, Gay Spectatorship and Male Homoeroticism*. Bloomsbury, 2017.

———. "Queer Studies." *The Arden Research Handbook of Contemporary Shakespeare Criticism*, edited by Evelyn Gajowski, Bloomsbury, 2021, pp. 173–85.

———. "The (Un)Queering of *Romeo and Juliet* on Film." *Shakespeare on Screen: Romeo and Juliet*, edited by Victoria Bladen et al., Cambridge UP, forthcoming.

Petrarch, Francesco. *Rime Sparse. Petrarch's Lyric Poems: The* Rime Sparse *and Other Lyrics*, translated and edited by Robert M. Durling, Harvard UP, 1976, pp. 35–584.

Phillips, Tom. *A Humument: A Treated Victorian Novel*. 5th ed., Thames and Hudson, 1987.

Pietros, Stephanie. "'If We Shadows Have Offended': Shakespeare's 'Problems' and First-Generation Students." Olson and Pietros, pp. 88–100.

Planinc, Zdravko. "Politics, Religion, and Love's Transgression: The Political Philosophy of *Romeo and Juliet*." *Philosophy and Literature*, vol. 43, no. 1, Apr. 2019, pp. 11–37.

Potter, Ursula. "Navigating the Dangers of Female Puberty in Renaissance Drama." *Studies in English Literature, 1500–1900*, vol. 53, no. 2, 2013, pp. 421–39.

Private Romeo. Directed by Alan Brown, Wolfe Video, 2011.

Prusko, Rachel. "Youth and Privacy in *Romeo and Juliet*." *Early Theatre*, vol. 19, no. 1, 2016, pp. 113–36.

Regan, Stephen. *The Sonnet*. Oxford UP, 2019.

Re-mixing Shakespeare: Curriculum for Documentary Film Romeo Is Bleeding. Blueshift, 2016, www.filmplatform.net/wp-content/uploads/2017/08/RE-MIXING-SHAKESPEARE-Curriculum-1st-Edition.pdf.

Rendón, Laura I., et al. Ventajas/*Assets y* Conocimientos/*Knowledge: Leveraging Latin@ Strengths to Foster Student Success*. Center for Research and Policy in Education, U of Texas at San Antonio, 2014.

"Resources." *Folger Shakespeare Library*, 2023, www.folger.edu/teach/resources/.

Reynolds, Dwight F. *The Musical Heritage of Al-Andalus*. Routledge, 2021.

Reynolds, Jason. *Ghost*. Atheneum / Caitlyn Dlouhy Books, 2016.

Riess, Amy J., and George Walton Williams. "'Tragical Mirth': From *Romeo* to *Dream*." *Critical Essays on Shakespeare's* Romeo and Juliet, edited by Joseph A. Porter, G. K. Hall, 1997, pp. 100–06.

R#J. Directed by Carey Williams, Interface Films, 2021.

"'R#J' Cast on Filming Shakespeare through Social Media." *YouTube*, uploaded by Variety, 2 Feb. 2021, www.youtube.com/watch?v=mPdZ6_-mClo.

Rodríguez, R. Joseph. *Teaching Culturally Sustaining and Inclusive Young Adult Literature: Critical Perspectives and Conversations*. Routledge, 2018.

Rogers, J. M. "The Eleventh Century—A Turning Point in the Architecture of the Mashriq?" *Islamic Civilisation 950–1150*, edited by D. S. Richards, Cassirer, 1973, pp. 211–49. Vol. 3 of *Papers on Islamic History*.

Rome and Juliet. Directed by Connie Macatuno, Cinema One, 2017.

Romeo and Juliet. Directed by Carlo Carlei, screenplay by Julian Fellowes, Echo Lake / Swarovski, 2013.

Romeo and Juliet. Directed by Renato Castellani, Universalcine / Verona Produzione, 1954.

Romeo and Juliet. Directed by George Cukor, Metro-Goldwyn-Meyer, 1936.

Romeo and Juliet. Directed by Don Roy King, BroadwayHD / Fathom Events, 2014.

Romeo and Juliet. Directed by Alvin Rakoff, BBC Television Productions, 1978.

Romeo and Juliet. Directed by Erica Whyman, Royal Shakespeare Company, 2018.

Romeo and Juliet. Directed by Franco Zeffirelli, Paramount Pictures, 1968.

"Romeo and Juliet." *Shakespeare: The Animated Tales*, directed by Efim Gamburg, Ambrose Video, 2004.

"*Romeo and Juliet*." *Thug Notes Summary and Analysis*, season 2, episode 8, created by Jared Bauer, presented by Greg Edwards, Wisecrack, 2014.

"*Romeo and Juliet*: No Fear Translation." *SparkNotes*, www.sparknotes.com/nofear/shakespeare/romeojuliet/. No Fear Shakespeare.

"*Romeo and Juliet* with Joseph Fiennes." *Shakespeare Uncovered*, series 2, episode 4, hosted by Joseph Fiennes, Public Broadcasting Service / Shakespeare's Globe, 2015. www.pbs.org/wnet/shakespeare-uncovered/uncategorized/romeo-juliet-joseph-fiennes-full-episode/.

Romeo e Giulietta: Balletto in tre atti. Choreographed by Kenneth MacMillan, performances by Misty Copeland and Roberto Bolle, Teatro alla Scala, Milan, 2016. *YouTube*, uploaded by May Wang, www.youtube.com/watch?v=7AnpPu7j6Dg.

Roméo et Juliette. Directed by Yves Desgagnés, Cinémaginaire, 2006.

Romeo Is Bleeding. Directed by Jason Zeldes, RoCo Film International, 2015.

Romeo Must Die. Directed by Andrzej Bartkowiak, Warner Brothers, 2000.

Romeu and Romeu. Directed by Jonathan Mendonça, Mistura de Artes / Substrato Filmes, 2016.

Romil and Jugal. Created by Ekta Kapoor, Balaji Telefilms, 2017.

Rozett, Martha Tuck. "The Comic Structures of Tragic Endings: The Suicide Scenes in *Romeo and Juliet* and *Antony and Cleopatra.*" *Shakespeare Quarterly*, vol. 36, no. 2, 1985, pp. 152–64.

Ruiter, David, editor. *The Arden Research Handbook of Shakespeare and Social Justice.* Bloomsbury, 2020.

"Sambo, N. (1)." *Oxford English Dictionary*, Oxford UP, June 2021, www.oed.com/dictionary/sambo_n1?tab=meaning_and_use#24446182.

Sanchez, Melissa E. *Shakespeare and Queer Theory.* Bloomsbury, 2019.

Sanford, Richard. "Review: Lord Denney's Players Charming and Vibrant *Romeo and Juliet.*" *Columbus Underground*, 8 Apr. 2019, www.columbusunderground.com/review-lord-denneys-players-charming-and-vibrant-romeo-and-juliet-rs1.

Schalkwyk, David. *Speech and Performance in Shakespeare's Sonnets and Plays.* Cambridge UP, 2002.

Scott, Lindsey. "'Closed in a Dead Man's Tomb': Juliet, Space, and the Body in Franco Zeffirelli's and Baz Luhrmann's Films of *Romeo and Juliet.*" *Literature/Film Quarterly*, vol. 36, no. 2, 2008, pp. 137–46.

Shakespeare, William. *An Excellent Conceited Tragedie of Romeo and Iuliet.* London, 1597. First quarto (Q1).

———. *A Midsummer Night's Dream.* Greenblatt et al., pp. 1037–96.

———. *The Most Excellent and Lamentable Tragedie of Romeo and Juliet.* London, 1599. Second quarto (Q2).

———. *The Most Lamentable Tragedy of Romeo and Juliet.* Greenblatt et al., pp. 967–1035.

———. *Mr. William Shakespeares Comedies, Histories and Tragedies, Published according to the True Originall Copies.* Edited by John Heminges and Henry Condell. London, 1623. First Folio.

———. *Romeo and Juliet.* Edited by J. A. Bryant, Jr., Penguin Random House, 1998.

———. *Romeo and Juliet.* Edited by Johnston Forbes-Robertson, Nassau Press, 1895.

———. *Romeo and Juliet.* Edited by Peter Holland, Penguin Books, 2016. The Pelican Shakespeare.

———. *Romeo and Juliet.* Edited by Jill L. Levenson, Oxford UP, 2000.

———. *Romeo and Juliet.* Edited by Gordon McMullan, Norton Critical Edition, W. W. Norton, 2016.

———. *Romeo and Juliet.* Updated ed., edited by Barbara A. Mowat and Paul Werstine, Folger Shakespeare Library, 2011.

———. *Romeo and Juliet.* Edited by René Weis, Bloomsbury, 2012. Arden Shakespeare Third Series.

———. Romeo and Juliet: *A Textbook Edition of Shakespeare's Play Created by Students, for Students.* Edited by Rebecca Olson, Oregon State U, 2021, open.oregonstate.education/romeoandjuliet/.

———. Romeo and Juliet: *Texts and Contexts*. Edited by Dympna Callaghan, Bedford/St. Martin's, 2003.

———. *The Winter's Tale*. Greenblatt et al., pp. 3121–204.

Shapiro, James. *Shakespeare in a Divided America: What His Plays Tell Us about Our Past and Future*. Penguin Books, 2020.

Shaw, Brandon. "Shakespeare's Dancing Bodies: The Case of Romeo." *The Oxford Handbook of Shakespeare and Dance*, edited by Lynsey McCulloch and Shaw, Oxford UP, 2019, pp. 173–94.

Smith, Henry. *The Sermons of Mr. Henry Smith* . . . . Edited by Thomas Fuller, W. Tegg, 1866. *HathiTrust Digital Library*, hdl.handle.net/2027/njp.32101066075654.

Smith, Ian. *Race and Rhetoric in the Renaissance: Barbarian Errors*. Palgrave Macmillan, 2009.

———. "The Textile Black Body: Race and 'Shadowed Livery' in *The Merchant of Venice*." *The Oxford Handbook of Shakespeare and Embodiment: Gender, Sexuality, and Race*, edited by Valerie Traub, Oxford UP, 2016, pp. 170–85.

Snyder, Susan. *The Comic Matrix of Shakespeare's Tragedies:* Romeo and Juliet, Hamlet, Othello, *and* King Lear. Princeton UP, 1979.

———. "*Romeo and Juliet*: Comedy into Tragedy." *Essays in Criticism*, vol. 20, no. 4, 1970, pp. 391–402.

Sokol, B. J., and Mary Sokol. *Shakespeare, Law, and Marriage*. Cambridge UP, 2003.

Sparey, Victoria. "Performing Puberty: Fertile Complexions in Shakespeare's Plays." *Shakespeare Bulletin*, vol. 33, no. 3, 2015, pp. 441–67.

Spiller, Michael R. G. *The Development of the Sonnet: An Introduction*. Routledge, 1992.

Stern, Tiffany. *Documents of Performance in Early Modern England*. Cambridge UP, 2009.

———. *Rehearsal from Shakespeare to Sheridan*. Clarendon, 2000.

———. "Sermons, Plays and Note-Takers: *Hamlet* Q1 as a 'Noted' Text." *Working with Shakespeare*, edited by Peter Holland, Cambridge UP, 2013, pp. 1–23. Vol. 66 of *Shakespeare Survey*.

Stone, Lawrence. *The Family, Sex and Marriage in England 1500–1800*. Harper and Row, 1977.

"The Strangers' Case." Directed by Peter Trifunovic, British Black and Asian Shakespeare / U of Warwick. *YouTube*, uploaded by The Strangers' Case, 20 June 2018, www.youtube.com/watch?v=YaeDoTaYK5k.

"The Strangers' Case: Refugee Week." *Shakespeare's Globe*, 20 June 2018, www.shakespearesglobe.com/discover/blogs-and-features/2018/06/20/the-strangers-case-refugee-week/.

"The Strangers' Case: Shakespeare's Rallying Cry for Humanity." International Rescue Committee / Shakespeare's Globe. *YouTube*, uploaded by Shakespeare's Globe, 20 June 2018, www.youtube.com/watch?v=4Bss2or4n74.

Stredder, James. *The North Face of Shakespeare: Activities for Teaching the Plays*. Cambridge UP, 2009.

The Suit. Choreographed by Cathy Marston, Ballet Black, 2018.

Swift, Taylor. "Love Story." *Genius*, 2008, genius.com/Taylor-swift-love-story-lyrics. Transcript of lyrics.

———. "Love Story." *YouTube*, uploaded 16 June 2009 by Swift, www.youtube.com/watch?v=8xg3vE8Ie_E.

Sylvester, Richard S., editor. *English Sixteenth-Century Verse: An Anthology*. W. W. Norton, 1984.

Tabbaa, Yasser. *The Transformation of Islamic Art during the Sunni Revival*. U of Washington P, 2001.

Tate, William. "King James I and the Queen of Sheba." *English Literary Renaissance*, vol. 26, no. 3, 1996, pp. 561–85.

Taylor, Gary, et al., editors. *The New Oxford Shakespeare*. Oxford UP, 2016.

Taylor, Whitney B. "The Pedagogical Possibilities of Editing a Digital Text in the Shakespeare Classroom." Olson and Pietros, pp. 130–45.

"Teaching Resources." *Shakespeare's Globe*, 2023, www.shakespearesglobe.com/learn/teaching-resources.

"Ten Questions for Taylor Swift." *Time*, 23 Apr. 2009, content.time.com/time/subscriber/article/0,33009,1893502,00.html.

Terry, Esther J. "Choreographies of Trans-atlantic Primitivity: Sub-Saharan Isolation in Black Dance Historiography." *Early Modern Black Diaspora Studies: A Critical Anthology*, edited by Cassander L. Smith et al., Palgrave MacMillan, 2018, pp. 65–82.

Thompson, Ayanna, editor. *Colorblind Shakespeare: New Perspectives on Race and Performance*. Routledge, 2006.

———. "Did the Concept of Race Exist for Shakespeare and His Contemporaries? An Introduction." *The Cambridge Companion to Shakespeare and Race*, edited by Thompson, Cambridge UP, 2021, pp. 1–16.

———. "Response: Shakespeare, My Sparring Partner." Olson and Pietros, pp. 183–86.

Thompson, Ayanna, and Laura Turchi. "Active Shakespeare: A Social Justice Framework." Ruiter, pp. 47–59.

———. *Teaching Shakespeare with Purpose: A Student-Centered Approach*. Bloomsbury, 2016.

Tosh, Will. "Was Shakespeare Gay?" *Shakespeare's Globe*, 1 Feb. 2019, www.shakespearesglobe.com/discover/blogs-and-features/2019/02/01/was-shakespeare-gay/.

Tucker, Patrick. *Secrets of Acting Shakespeare: The Original Approach*. 2nd ed., Routledge, 2017.

Turchi, Laura B., and Ann C. Christensen. "When the 'House' (of Montague) Is a Color, Not a Clan." Teaching Shakespeare, *The English Journal*, vol. 108, no. 2, 2018, pp. 111–14.

Urkowitz, Steven. "Good News about 'Bad' Quartos." *"Bad" Shakespeare: Revaluations of the Shakespeare Canon*, edited by Maurice Charney, Farleigh Dickinson UP, 1988, pp. 189–206.

Valerio, Miguel Alejandro. "The Queen Sheba's Manifold Body: Creole Black Women Performing Sexuality, Cultural Identity, and Power in Seventeenth-Century Mexico City." *Afro-Hispanic Review*, vol. 35, no. 2, 2016, pp. 79–98.

Vaughan, Alden T., and Virginia Mason Vaughan. *Shakespeare in America*. Oxford UP, 2012.

Vega, Lope de. *The Capulets and the Montagues*. Translated by Dakin Matthews, Juan de la Cuesta Press, 2021.

———. *Castelvines y Monteses*. Circa 1610. *Biblioteca Digital Artelope*, digital markup by Eva Soler Sasera, artelope.uv.es/biblioteca/textosAL/AL0549_CastelvinesYMonteses.php.

———. *Castelvines y Monteses*. *Biblioteca Virtual Miguel de Cervantes*, 2003, www.cervantesvirtual.com/obra/castelvines-y-monteses--0/.

———. *Las ferias de Madrid*. 1589. Red Ediciones, 2012.

———. "New Rules for Writing Plays at This Time." Translated by Victor Dixon, Emothe Biblioteca Digital, 2009, emothe.uv.es/biblioteca/textosEMOTHE/EMOTHE0116_NewRulesForWritingPlaysAtThisTime.php.

Villanueva, Nicholas, Jr. *The Lynching of Mexicans in the Texas Borderlands*. U of New Mexico P, 2017.

Warm Bodies. Directed by Jonathan Levine, Make Movies / Mandeville Films, 2013.

Weis, René. Introduction. Shakespeare, *Romeo and Juliet*, Weis, pp. 1–116.

Wells, Robin Headlam. "Neo-Petrarchan Kitsch in *Romeo and Juliet*." *The Modern Language Review*, vol. 93, no. 4, 1998, pp. 913–33.

Wells, Stanley, and Gary Taylor, general editors. *William Shakespeare: The Complete Works*. Oxford UP, 1986.

West Side Story. Directed by Steven Spielberg, screenplay by Tony Kushner, Amblin Entertainment / TSG Entertainment, 2021.

West Side Story. Directed by Robert Wise and Jerome Robbins, United Artists, 1961.

Whitley, Sarah E., et al. *First-Generation Student Success: A Landscape Analysis of Programs and Services at Four-Year Institutions*. Center for First-Generation Student Success, 2018, firstgen.naspa.org/2018-landscape-analysis.

Whittier, Gayle. "The Sonnet's Body and the Body Sonnetized in *Romeo and Juliet*." *Shakespeare Quarterly*, vol. 40, no. 1, 1989, pp. 27–41.

Widdicombe, Lizzie. "You Belong with Me: How Taylor Swift Made Teenage Angst into a Business Empire." *The New Yorker*, 10 Oct. 2011, www.newyorker.com/magazine/2011/10/10/you-belong-with-me.

Williams, Deanne. "Shakespeare and Girlhood." Interview by Neva Grant. *Shakespeare Unlimited*, episode 60, Folger Shakespeare Library, 2016, www.folger.edu/shakespeare-unlimited/girlhood.

———. *Shakespeare and the Performance of Girlhood*. Palgrave Macmillan, 2014.

William Shakespeare's Romeo + Juliet. Directed by Baz Luhrmann, 20th Century Studios, 1996.

Winerock, Emily. "'We'll Measure Them a Measure, and Be Gone': Renaissance Dance Practices and Shakespeare's *Romeo and Juliet*." *Borrowers and*

Lenders, vol. 10, no. 2, 2017, borrowers-ojs-azsu.tdl.org/borrowers/article/view/274/545.

Wodiczko, Krzystof. *Abraham Lincoln: War Veteran*. 2012, Union Square, New York.

Yarn, Molly G. "Katherine Lee Bates and Women's Editions of Shakespeare for Students." *Women's Labour and the History of the Book in Early Modern England*, edited by Valerie Wayne, Arden Shakespeare, 2020, pp. 187–204.

Zweig, Janet. *The 336 Lines Currently Expurgated from Shakespeare's* Romeo and Juliet *in Ninth Grade Textbooks*. J. Zweig, 1989.